DIMENSIONS OF SOCIAL WELFARE POLICY

DIMENSIONS OF SOCIAL WELFARE POLICY
Third Edition

Neil Gilbert
Harry Specht
Paul Terrell

University of California at Berkeley

PRENTICE HALL, Englewood Cliffs, New Jersey 07632

Library of Congress Cataloging-in-Publication Data

Gilbert, Neil
   Dimensions of social welfare policy / Neil Gilbert, Harry Specht,
Paul Terrell. — 3rd ed.
     p.   cm.
   Includes index.
   ISBN 0-13-218108-8
   1. Public welfare.   2. Social choice.   3. Public welfare—United
States.   4. United States—Social policy.   I. Specht, Harry.
II. Terrell, Paul.   III. Title.
HV41.G52   1993
362.973—dc20   91-38091
                                   CIP

Editorial/production supervision
and interior design: *Mary Kathryn Bsales*
Acquisitions editor: *Nancy Roberts*
Editorial assistant: *Pat Naturale*
Prepress buyer: *Kelly Behr*
Manufacturing buyer: *Mary Ann Gloriande*
Cover design: *Joe DiDomenico*
Copy editor: *Barbara Conner*

© 1993, 1986, 1974 by Prentice-Hall, Inc.
A Simon & Schuster Company
Englewood Cliffs, New Jersey 07632

ISBN 0-13-218108-8

90000>

Printed in the United States of America
10 9 8 7 6 5 4 3 2

ISBN   0-13-218108-8

9 780132 181082

Prentice-Hall International (UK) Limited, *London*
Prentice-Hall of Australia Pty. Limited, *Sydney*
Prentice-Hall Canada Inc., *Toronto*
Prentice-Hall Hispanoamericana, S.A., *Mexico*
Prentice-Hall of India Private Limited, *New Delhi*
Prentice-Hall of Japan, Inc., *Tokyo*
Simon & Schuster Asia Pte. Ltd., *Singapore*
Editora Prentice-Hall do Brasil, Ltda., *Rio de Janeiro*

CONTENTS

PREFACE

In writing about social welfare policy analysis, authors encounter many opportunities to take sides and to argue their own points of view. There are, too, temptations to slip prescriptions into the analysis because the subject matter deals with compelling issues of human welfare. We recognize that many readers would like a book that provides solutions to the weighty problems of social welfare whether or not they agree with our views; if they agree, they can congratulate their wisdom, and if they disagree, they can reaffirm their own position by dissecting our biases and our faulty logic. In either case, a book that gives firm and sure direction to social welfare policy provides more immediate gratification to some students than one that analyzes the terrain and debates the hazards of the different roads that can be taken.

Nonetheless, we offer few explicit and firm prescriptions for specific social welfare policies. (In the few cases where we do prescribe, it is less by design than from an inability to resist temptation.) Thus readers are forewarned that they will not find many specific answers to questions of social policy in this book. Rather, we attempt in this text to share with the reader the intellectual challenges that are confronted in making social welfare policy choices. "Good" and "righteous" answers to fundamental questions in social welfare policy are not easily come by. Addressed seriously, these questions require a willingness to abide complexity, an ability to tolerate contradictions, and a capacity to appraise empirical evidence and social values critically, which is to say that professionals engaged in the business of making social welfare policy choices require patience, thought, and an intelligent curiosity.

To speak of policy choices implies that plausible alternatives exist. Our second objective in writing this book is to present and illuminate these alternatives. The book is organized around what we consider to be the basic dimensions of choice in social welfare policy. We place these dimensions of choice in a theoretical framework that provides a way of thinking about and analyzing social welfare policies that is applicable to a wide range of specific cases. With this framework, we explore policy alternatives, questions they raise, and values and theories that inform different answers. Ultimately the purpose of this book is to help students come to grips with the complexities of social choice. We hope we will have equipped them to appraise and further develop their own thoughts on social welfare policy.

This book was written over a period of years in which we had many discussions (and sometimes disagreements) with our students. We are pleased with whatever benefit they may have derived from exposure to the developing ideas for the book, and we are grateful for the tolerance and critical comments they offered in response to our ruminations. We thank the editors of *Social Work* and *Welfare in Review* for permission to use material that originally appeared in those journals.

In preparing this third edition of the book, we were impressed by the extent to which the basic concepts of social policy choice-making have held up since the book was first published in 1974. We are equally impressed with the rapidity of change in the structure and content of American social welfare programs to which these concepts are applied. For example, when we were preparing the first edition, social welfare was at the apex of thirty-five years of growth; however, we are finishing this third edition at a time when government is attempting to control and reduce expenditures. Hence, chapter five (The Structure of the Delivery System) has been expanded to include discussion of cut-back management. Similarly, we have integrated material on other new developments such as the enormous growth of federal tax expenditures (chapters one and six) and for-profit programs in social welfare (chapter five).

We owe special appreciation to Wayne Vasey of the School of Social Work, University of Michigan; Wyatt Jones of the Florence Heller School for Advanced Studies in Social Welfare, Brandeis University; Eveline M. Burns of the School of Social Work, Columbia University; and Riva Specht who edited the first edition. Each read the original manuscript and provided us with thoughtful criticisms and constructive suggestions. While their good advice helped us to clarify and improve this work, we must, of course, claim exclusive responsibility for whatever deficiencies remain. We also must thank Lorretta Morales, Ruth Mundy, and Kathleen Vergeer who provided great care and cheerful assistance in typing the manuscript.

It will become quickly evident to our readers that we, like other contemporary students of social welfare policy, have been considerably influenced by the writings of Eveline M. Burns and Richard H. Titmuss. Their impact on this field is of such magnitude as to be pervasive, and footnotes are an inadequate means of recognizing how much they have done to illuminate social welfare policy.

Finally, we must acknowledge our debts to those who bore the brunt of the moments of strain and weariness that all authors inevitably experience. Our wives and children demonstrated remarkable perseverance and good humor in supporting us as we tried to find our way through the dimensions of choice. To Barbara, Evan, and Jesse; Riva, Daniel, and Eliot; and Kathy, Joshua, Benjamin, and Sean, mere thanks are not enough to express the extent of our gratitude and affection.

Neil Gilbert
Harry Specht
Paul Terrell

CREDITS

P. 125: From FRANZ KAFKA: THE COMPLETE STORIES by Franz Kafka. Copyright 1946, 1947, 1948, 1949, 1954 © 1958, 1971 by Schocken Books Inc. Reprinted by permission of Schocken Books, published by Pantheon Books, a division of Random House, Inc. P. 159: The Ideologies of Taxation by Louis Eisenstein. Copyright © 1961 by The Ronald Press Company. Reprinted by Permission of John Wiley & Sons, Inc. "TAXMAN" Words and Music by JOHN LENNON and PAUL McCARTNEY © Copyright 1966 by NORTHERN SONGS. All rights controlled and administered by MCA MUSIC PUBLISHING, A Division of MCA INC., Under license from NORTHERN SONGS. ALL RIGHTS RESERVED. USED BY PERMISSION. P. 215: Friedrich A. Hayek, The Road to Serfdom, with permission of The University of Chicago Press.

Chapter One
THE FIELD OF SOCIAL WELFARE POLICY

"I don't think they play at all fairly," Alice began, in rather a complaining tone, *"and they all quarrel so dreadfully one can't hear oneself speak—and they don't seem to have any rules in particular: at least, if there are, nobody attends to them—and you've no idea how confusing it is all the things being alive: for instance, there's the arch I've got to go through next walking about at the other end of the ground—and I should have croqueted the Queen's hedgehog just now, only it ran away when it saw mine coming!"*

Lewis Carroll
Alice's Adventure in Wonderland

Students entering the field of social welfare policy quickly come to feel somewhat like Alice at the Queen's croquet party. They confront a vast landscape that may be puzzling and complex. The territory it covers has constantly changing internal features and outer boundaries.[1] Its knowledge base is fragmented and less immediately related to the realities of day-to-day social work practice than other subject areas. Yet the study of social welfare policy is central for those who practice in the social services because, to a large extent, it shapes the forms of practice that professionals use and determines the client systems to be served. At least in part, the relative demand for services such as social casework, employment counsel-

1

ing, liaison and advocacy, case management, and community development result from the choices that frame social welfare policies at a given time.

The objectives of this introductory chapter are to provide a general orientation to the field of social welfare policy and to illustrate the interrelatedness of practice and policy analysis. By presenting the subject matter of social welfare in a clearly understandable form, we hope that students will become interested in and comfortable with it and recognize the importance and power of policy studies. The purpose of this book, as the title suggests, is to develop an operational understanding of social welfare policy by identifying the dimensions of choice that the subject matter allows.

First, however, we want to explore four major perspectives that illustrate the field of social welfare policy studies: institutional, theoretical, analytical, and developmental. The focus on institutions defines what social welfare policy is about and delineates some of its boundaries. The focus on theory examines several schools of thought about how and why social welfare has evolved. The focus on analysis indicates different approaches to studying policy and for relating policy knowledge to social work practice. The focus on development describes the process of social policy formulation and implementation, and the associated roles of professionals.

SOCIAL WELFARE FUNCTIONS: AN INSTITUTIONAL PERSPECTIVE

Social welfare policy is an elusive concept, and one could easily exhaust an introductory chapter simply by describing alternative approaches to its definition. We will not do this, nor will we review the ongoing discussion over the relationships among social policy, public policy, and social welfare policy.[2] It is enough to say that no single definition is universally, nor even broadly, accepted. However, some effort must be made to stake the boundaries that form a common realm of discourse among those concerned with this subject. Seeking to skirt the conceptual swamp of social policy, public policy, and social welfare policy distinctions, we will focus instead on trying to delineate, by using an institutional perspective, the broad range of functions that may be influenced by social welfare policies.

In beginning to define the scope of social welfare policy it is helpful to examine the constituent terms, *social welfare* and *policy,* separately. The term *policy* is somewhat easier to formulate. In this text we will examine policy as an explicit course of action. In this sense, policy is akin to what Kahn calls a "standing plan," what Rein describes as the substance of planning choices, and what Mangum explains as "a definite course of action . . . to guide and determine present and future decisions."[3]

Throughout this book our concern will be on the decisions and choices that go into determining the social welfare course of action. What binds and delineates these decisions and choices is that they relate to social welfare in all its various aspects. More specifically, they address the functioning of the major institutions in our society that organize and provide social welfare.

The second term of concern, *social welfare,* can be approached by examining the character and functioning of these fundamental institutions. All human societies organize their essential social functions—child rearing; the production, consumption, and distribution of goods and services; social protection and so forth—into certain enduring patterns of conduct. All societies, for example, maintain institutions with responsibilities and expectations for raising and training the young. In most cases, one primary institution seldom exhausts the patterns a society uses to deal with its essential functions. Whereas the family is the primary institution for socialization, for example, it is by no means the only one. Religious and educational organizations and social service agencies also assume some socialization responsibilities, although socialization is not their primary activity.

There are five fundamental social institutions within which the major activities of community life occur: kinship, religion, economics, mutual assistance, and politics. As indicated in Table 1–1, all of society's basic day-to-day activities are organized in one or more of these spheres. And each of these social institutions, to one degree or another, also carries out important social welfare functions.

TABLE 1–1: Institutions, Organizations, Functions

SOCIAL INSTITUTIONS	KEY ORGANIZATIONAL FORM	PRIMARY FUNCTIONS	SOCIAL WELFARE FUNCTIONS
Kinship	Family	Procreation, socialization, protection, intimacy, and emotional support	Care for dependent members, interfamilial financial support
Religion	Church	Spiritual development	Sectarian welfare, health, education, social services, counseling
Economics	Business, union	Production, distribution, consumption	Employee benefits, delivery of commercially produced social welfare provisions
Mutual assistance	Support group, voluntary agency	Mutual aid, philanthropy	Self-help, volunteering, community social services
Politics	Government	Mobilization and distribution of resources for collective goals	Antipoverty, economic security, health, education, housing services

Kinship. The family has always been society's major institution for procreation, emotional support, and economic well-being. The family is also the key instrument of socialization, helping society to transmit prevailing knowledge, social values, and behavior patterns from one generation to the next. As an instrument of social welfare, the family frequently provides private arrangements for income security through life insurance policies, private savings and other kinds of investments, and gifts.

The full extent to which the family provides financial and in-kind assistance to its members, mostly between generations, is difficult to measure.[4] According to an estimate by Robert Lampman, interfamily transfers of cash, food, and housing amounted to $86 billion in 1978.[5] A more recent calculation, based on a 1985 survey by the Census Bureau, estimates that cash transfers alone totaled $18.9 billion. These figures suggest an average family aid payment of $3,006—children helping aging parents with nursing or medical care expenses, parents helping children to buy homes or deal with financial emergencies, or separated parents paying alimony and child support.[6]

The family is also a welfare-providing institution in that it assists dependent members in noneconomic ways. Elders often rely on adult children for shopping and personal care, and families help disabled relatives of all ages who otherwise might require state-sponsored residential care or in-home assistance. In 1982, for example, 2.2 million Americans provided unpaid help to 1.6 million disabled elderly relatives. Most of these caregivers were women, and most lived with the person needing assistance. A full 80 percent of all caregivers provided care seven days a week, on an average of four hours daily.[7]

Finally, the importance of the family is reflected in the way people seek help when faced with critical problems. Responding to a 1980 Gallup poll asking where they sought "advice, assistance, or encouragement" when problems arose, far and away most respondents said family members. (The second most popular choice was friends, and further down the list were professional helpers like social workers, counselors, and psychiatrists.)[8]

Religion. Religious institutions manifest the spiritual aspect of human society through ceremonies and observances that form systems of worship. Beyond this, churches sponsor elaborate social welfare provisions ranging from informal support and counseling to multi-million-dollar health, education, and social service programs.

The Church of the Latter Day Saints (Mormons), for example, operates over 600 food production projects for the poor, including 20 canneries and numerous meat-packing and dairy operations supplied by church-owned welfare farms. A recent estimate indicates that each year about 200,000 church members receive nearly 32 million pounds of commodities from Mormon storehouses and auxiliaries.[9] The Mormons also run Deseret Industries, which provides work and shelter for the elderly and handicapped; places members in jobs through church-sponsored employment offices; and organizes an extensive program of child welfare, foster care, and adoption services.[10]

Catholic, Jewish, and Protestant welfare organizations similarly have explicit social welfare objectives, implemented both through professionalized agencies such as Catholic Charities and the counseling activities of priests, ministers, and rabbis. The range of church-related services has been broadened even further in recent years by "family ministries" and "family life education" programs focused on married couples and their children, premarrieds and singles, and people facing special problems like alcoholism and divorce.[11]

Economics. Economics involves the production, distribution, and consumption of goods and services. Although the primary economic institution in most democratic industrial societies is the business firm, other organizations—professional bodies, unions, nonprofit entities, and government—also create and distribute goods and services. In this fashion, all these bodies affect how people earn their living and fulfill their needs.

Business organizations often promote the welfare of their members— their work force—by providing job-related goods and services, along with regular paychecks. One's job is the most important single source of support for most Americans—both by providing the income necessary for everyday life and through welfare arrangements attached to the job, generally known as fringe benefits. The word *fringe,* however, seriously understates the importance of these benefits since their average value in 1986 exceeded $10,000 per employee, or about 40 percent of a typical worker's overall compensation.[12] These benefits have become an increasingly important part of an employee's work-related package of compensation. Whereas wage income rose approximately 500 percent between 1965 and 1984, supplemental employer contributions rose by 1,000 percent. Most of this nonwage compensation went into private pension schemes whose assets increased more than sixfold between 1970 and 1984.[13]

Along with pensions, the most important fringe benefit is health insurance. Unlike most Western nations, which provide health benefits through public programs, Americans obtain their health benefits through their employment; in 1989 nearly two-thirds of all Americans under age 65 had employment-related insurance.[14] Many firms also provide benefits like company cars, parental leaves, college tuition for workers' children, gyms, legal and dental services, relocation assistance, and low-cost housing. Unions occasionally provide special benefits to supplement the public system of unemployment insurance. And many human services such as on-site child care and alcohol and drug counseling are provided as part of company-sponsored EAPs, Employee Assistance Programs.

Some would argue that these benefits embody market exchanges—the basic package of compensation that workers frequently bargain for in lieu of wages—rather than social welfare. But even when fringe benefits are seen as an integral feature of the labor-capital exchange, their tax-preferred treatment means that they are to some extent publicly subsidized.[15]

Fringe benefits constitute one critical aspect of marketplace social welfare. A second aspect is the sale of social welfare goods and services as marketable commodities, much like any other. In recent years, an increasingly large part of the corporate sector has engaged in the production and sale of social welfare goods and services. There are, for example, ten major child-care chains operating today, many on the franchise principle, running more than 1,000 child-care centers—about 5 percent of all centers nationwide. In more traditional child welfare areas like institutional and group-home care and residential treatment, more than half of all programs are run by proprietary establishments.[16]

The biggest profit-making operations of all are in the health field, where major corporations operate about 11 percent of all the hospital facilities in the country. Profit-making firms also own a major portion of the nursing home industry (thus the term "industry") and medical labs and clinics. The newest and fastest growing part of the U.S. health care system—free-standing emergency centers—is almost entirely a commercial enterprise. Major private corporations such as Upjohn Labs have also expanded into the home health field and drug and alcohol treatment services.

We do not want to give the impression that the profit sector is entirely the domain of major corporations. At the smaller end of the marketplace continuum are thousands of individual and small-group entrepreneurs who directly provide health and social services. These include private practice psychiatrists, social workers, marriage and family counselors, and lay people who operate family day-care and board and care homes. Currently, it is estimated that as many as 25 percent of the members of the National Association of Social Workers are in private practice for at least part of their work week.[17] It is clearly the hope of many social workers to go "solo," hang out their shingle, and "do good" providing services that clearly are in demand—most of which revolve around personal relationships; individual insecurities; and sex, alcohol, and drug problems.[18]

Mutual assistance.   The fourth major institution of modern society—mutual assistance—is perhaps the most explicitly focused on social welfare activities. Variously characterized as charity, philanthropy, informal help, or social support, these arrangements express society's need for mutuality, its recognition of interdependence. Whether seen as a function of altruism or self-interest, they constitute an essential part of community life.

Most mutual assistance represents society's natural response to everyday need. Although traditions of self-help go far back in American history, they increasingly constitute a critical resource for millions of people. One of the most notable developments of the past decade has been the reawakened interest in informal helping systems along with a reconceptualization of the ways in which professionals and lay helpers can work together.

How do friends, neighbors, and peers help? Neighbors check in on the sick and disabled, making sure all is well, sometimes helping with housework, cooking, shopping, and babysitting. Friends provide loans and emergency living arrangements. Self-help groups—small, nonbureaucratic, nonprofessional—assist people facing common emotional problems. Working face to face with others who share and understand their predicament, millions of people achieve a positive sense of themselves and learn realistic strategies for problem solving.

It is estimated that 12 to 15 million Americans belong to self-help groups.[19] Among the most common are

> Parents Without Partners (for single parents and their children)
> La Leche League (for nursing and other new mothers)
> Candlelighters (for the parents of children with cancer)
> Alcoholics Anonymous (for recovering alcoholics)
> Al Anon (for family members of alcoholics)
> National Alliance for the Mentally Ill (for families and friends of the seriously mentally ill)

Among the more esoteric are

> I Pride (for interracial couples)
> Parents of Near Drowners (POND)
> Incompletes Anonymous (for students unable to finish their course obligations)
> Beauties Anonymous
> Helping After Neonatal Death (HAND)

Beyond self-help and informal support is the extensive and multifaceted system of voluntary social welfare that provides formal expression to the philanthropic impulse. Organized on a nonprofit basis and aimed at community welfare needs, over 41,000 voluntary agencies today provide an array of social services for disadvantaged children, families, adults, the elderly, and a variety of special-need populations. These agencies, generally small in size compared to government bodies and governed by citizen boards of directors, coexist with a vast population of other nonprofit groups serving educational, health, research, and cultural purposes.[20]

Politics.   Political institutions, according to the *Encyclopedia of the Social Sciences,* deal with the "control of the use of force within a society and the maintenance of internal and external peace . . . as well as control of the mobilization of resources for the implementation of various goals and the articulation and setting up of certain goals for the collectivity."[21] Among the most important functions of the modern state, of course, is the mobilization and distribution of resources for welfare purposes. So important, and so huge, is the role of public activity in this area that the modern state is often defined principally as a welfare state. And today's polity, at least in the industrial world, *is* organized to support welfare. Broadly, the modern state is organized to ensure economic prosperity and social stability and, more specifically, material security; minimum standards of health, education, and housing; and protection against the contingencies of modern life that interfere with people's well-being.

Evolving Institutions and the Welfare State

Although social welfare activities are distributed among all the major institutions of society, the balance among them varies considerably. In a historical context, welfare functions evolved separately, institution by institution. In the simplest societies, most aspects of life revolve around the family—with religious, governance, economic, and mutual aid activities all organized through the kinship structure. As societies grow in complexity, individuals and groups begin to take on discrete social functions, and with increasing specialization there is an evolution of independent religious, government, economic, and mutual aid organizations.

If each of the major social institutions of society serve at least some welfare functions, is it possible to think in terms of social welfare itself as an institution? This question, it turns out, is of fundamental conceptual importance, although it is only in recent times that it has been posited. Before the current century, welfare was a subject of relatively modest scope. It was only when prevailing social arrangements became unable to deal with the emerging needs of modern industrial life that the publicly organized system of social welfare enlarged. The first major spurt of government social welfare activity in the United States resulted from the recognition that the family, religious and economic institutions, and instruments of voluntary mutual aid and local government were unable to address the enormous social distress caused by the Great Depression of the 1930s. This realization resulted in new demands being placed on government, especially national government. This change—frequently described as a shift from a residual model of social welfare to an institutional one—corresponded to the emergence of the American welfare state.

The traditional (i.e., residual) view is that social welfare itself is not a significant societal institution but rather a supplemental activity necessary only when the "normal" channels fail to perform appropriately. Viewed as a residual, temporary response to the failures of individuals and major institutions, social welfare is seen as a set of activities that although needed at times, is undesirable and expendable. Residualists argue that it is inappropriate to place social welfare on an equal standing with the primary institutions shown in Table 1–1.

Speaking at the Conference of Charities and Corrections in 1914, Dr. Abraham Flexner expressed one aspect of the residual conception of social welfare in comparing social work with other professions:

> A good deal of what is called social work might perhaps be accounted for on the ground that the recognized professions have developed too slowly on the social side. Suppose medicine were fully socialized; would not medical men, medical institutions, and medical organizations look after certain interests that the social worker must care for just because medical practice now falls short? The shortcomings of law create a similar need in another direction. Thus viewed, social work is, in part at least, not so much a separate profession as an endeavor to supplement certain existing professions *pending their completed development.*[22] [Emphasis added.]

Competing with this conception is the institutional view of social welfare as a distinct pattern of activities serving not as a safety net to catch the victim after all else has failed but rather as an integral and "normal 'first line' function of modern industrial society."[23] Perceived as a basic social institution, social welfare carries none of the stigma of the "dole" or of "charity." It is seen, instead, as a primary means by which individuals, families, and communities fulfill their social needs.

Much of our understanding of these competing models depends on how we comprehend both the causes and the incidence of unmet needs in society. In both models, the major institutional structures of society are viewed as ineffective to some degree in meeting people's needs. The fundamental issues are these: To what extent is this an anomaly reflecting mainly the deficiencies of some individuals and a small margin of institutional malfunctioning? To what extent is it a normal consequence of institutional limitations and individual failure? An answer of "very much" to the first question and "very little" to the second relegates social welfare to the status of a residual safety net. Reverse these answers, and social welfare emerges as a basic and distinct social institution.

The answers to these questions, however, remain equivocal. In this regard, Wilensky and Lebeaux's 1958 assessment is still accurate:

> While the two views seem antithetical, in practice American social work has tried to combine them, and current trends in social welfare present a middle course. Those who lament the passing of the old order insist that the [institutional conception] is undermining individual character and the national social structure. Those who bewail our failure to achieve utopia today argue that the

residual conception is an obstacle which must be removed before we can produce the good life for all. In our view, neither ideology exists in a vacuum; each is a reflection of broader cultural and societal conditions. With further industrialization the [institutional conception] is likely to prevail.[24]

While the debate continues, it is difficult to ignore the vast importance of the social welfare enterprise in modern society and the primary role of government in it. Although the development of social welfare as a separate institution does not entirely equate welfare with government, the national government in particular, there is no denying that modern societies demand a major public role for social welfare, a role that is most frequently conceptualized in terms of the welfare state.

The modern welfare state, in its most prosaic terms, conveys the idea of significant government responsibility for social protection. Perhaps its best known definition posits a government obligation to act when society's private institutions do not properly function. For Asa Briggs, then, the welfare state is intended to "modify the play of market forces," to improve the well-being of citizens who are not able to manage on their own.[25]

Briggs specifies three particular roles for the welfare state. The first is helping people maintain their incomes when various "life contingencies," such as unemployment or divorce or old age, make normal self-support impossible. This goal is often described as "offsetting income loss." The second goal is making sure that people receive at least a minimum level of subsistence income. This is the antipoverty goal of the welfare state. The third goal is helping people secure the basic, minimum essentials of life, such as health care, education, and adequate nutrition.

These three objectives serve to define the public policy agenda in all the developed countries of the world; in this sense, every modern industrial state is a welfare state. All modern states utilize public intervention to ensure that neither bad luck nor economic distress nor social disadvantage fully determine the life chances of citizens. All have programs explicitly directed to combating misfortune and advancing opportunity and, as the U.S. Constitution states, providing "for the general welfare."

This is not to say that the institutional model has won the day. Despite its significance in contemporary life, the welfare state is an ambiguous enterprise. Although it is an essential political and economic institution in western Europe, the United States, Canada, New Zealand, Australia, and Japan, the welfare state is nevertheless subject to sustained criticism from both the right and left. Criticism from the right, extraordinarily potent during the 1980s, expresses the traditional unease of conservatives with state welfare. For conservatives, government undermines welfare by weakening the traditional instruments of private, personal well-being—the family, the church, and the community. Instead of protecting the poor from misfortune, conservatives argue that public programs provide incentives for young men to remain idle and for young women to have children out of wedlock. Securing the poor from responsibility, the argument continues, the welfare state creates dependency, poverty, and needless expense. According to Charley Murray, the best-known representative of this viewpoint, the welfare state "tried to provide more for the poor and produced more poor instead. It tried to remove the barriers to escape from poverty, and inadvertently built a trap instead."[26]

Whereas conservatives believe that government has gone too far, producing "unintended consequences," the left maintains that government should extend further its efforts to ensure the important first principles of genuine welfare—"fair shares," universal income maintenance, adequate health and social services, and full employment. For the left, a progressive welfare state is one in which the government guarantees that all people are treated as equals; in which all have access to quality education, housing, health care, and jobs; and in which all children have an equal chance to dignity and well-being.[27]

The disagreement between left and right over the appropriate level of government intervention, in part, reflects the fact that despite a broad commitment to mutual support and critical programs of assistance to citizens in all walks of life, the welfare state retains important elements of residualism. Eligibility requirements, for example, often reflect the concept of public intervention as a last resort, available only when personal resources have been exhausted.

The Scope of the Welfare State

Although means testing and other poor-law remnants are not likely to be eliminated, the enormous scope of the welfare state in all the rich nations of the world attests to its fundamental role in late twentieth-century society. The clearest way of indicating this scope is to examine trends in government spending. Although this approach significantly understates the size of the welfare institution, since it omits private expenditures and indirect tax benefits, it nonetheless yields an impressive picture.

As Figure 1–1 indicates, public social welfare spending in 1965 amounted to $77.1 billion, some 11.5% of the gross national product (GNP). A quick glance at the figure reveals that spending between 1960 and 1988 increased eleven-fold, whereas the proportion of GNP devoted to welfare (which gives a real, inflation-corrected picture of change) almost doubled—from 11.5% to 18.5%.

The primary welfare state programs—Medicare, Medicaid, food stamps, Social Security, public housing, public education, child welfare, veterans assistance—are spending programs, programs that provide people with money or goods or services. Although public policy also encompasses outlays for things like defense, transportation, and agriculture, the

[Dollar amounts in billions]

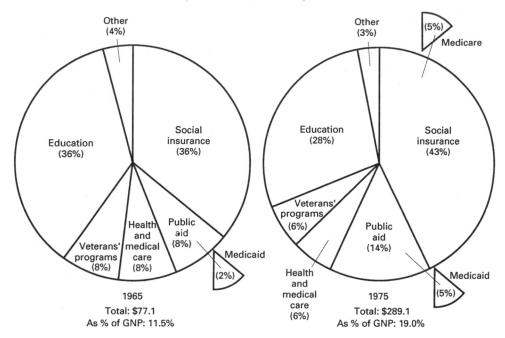

1965
Total: $77.1
As % of GNP: 11.5%

1975
Total: $289.1
As % of GNP: 19.0%

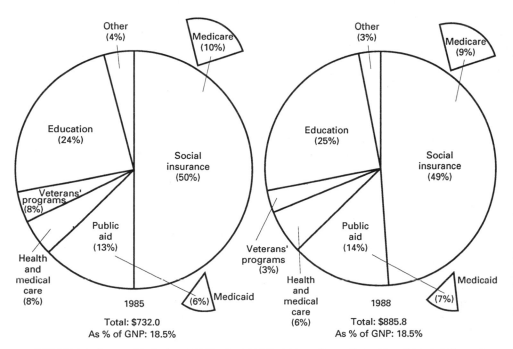

1985
Total: $732.0
As % of GNP: 18.5%

1988
Total: $885.8
As % of GNP: 18.5%

FIGURE 1-1 Percent Distribution of Public Social Welfare Expenditures. Expenditure Totals in Billions of Dollars.

Source: Ann Kallman Bixby, "Social Welfare Expenditures, Fiscal Year 1988," *Social Security Bulletin,* May 1991/Vol. 54, No. 5, p. 18.

$886 billion spent for social welfare in 1988 comprised more than half of all government allocations at all levels.

Private expenditures for social welfare remain considerably less, as is indicated in Figure 1–2, but they are far from inconsequential. Private responsibility has been predominant in certain welfare fields such as health, in which private physicians, hospitals, and insurance schemes remain the principal components of organization and finance. What is notable is that the great rise in government welfare activity since the 1960s has not come at the expense of private spending. Indeed, private outlays rose from 7.7% of GNP in 1972 to 12.3% in 1988.

Despite the overwhelming importance of public outlays, then, contemporary social welfare remains a pluralistic, multi-institutional enterprise. It is not simply a matter of government. Social welfare is more than the sum total of activities carried on by organized agencies, programs, and specialized personnel. It involves both formal and informal, public and private, and profit-making and altruistic endeavors. This welfare pluralism is illustrated in many areas of activity. Day care, for example, is provided by grandparents, relatives, hired nannies and au pairs, neighborhood family-care facilities, on-site corporate centers, church centers, and publicly funded agencies. A woman abused by her husband or boyfriend can turn to family or clergy for help and take refuge in the home of relatives, in a shelter, or with friends. She may seek help from the police; she may require emergency care in a hospital.

The nature of society's helping arrangements is critically influenced by the balance that exists among the institutional sectors we have described. That is, the various systems of provision have distinctive characteristics and distinctive costs and benefits. The help that families provide, for example, is immediate, empathic, caring, and unbureaucratic. However, family help can be onerous, emotionally exhausting, and costly for the caregivers. Families can be wiped out financially by the needs of sick and dependent relatives. Family care, of course, is also limited by ties of marriage and blood: It provides nothing for the needy who are strangers without families of their own, and it cannot do the job alone when complex technological procedures, such as kidney dialysis, are required to sustain life.

Public services, however, have their own pluses and minuses. Although they can be impersonal, inefficient, and bureaucratic, they can also ensure that isolated individuals are helped and that no one is allowed to fall below a certain minimum level of living. They can redistribute societal resources and promote equality. They can reduce the stigma of private charity, making benefits a right rather than a handout.

Whatever their distinctive characteristics, it is clear that in today's world, public, voluntary, and for-profit forms of social welfare are substantially interdependent. Particularly important are the public influences on

[Dollar amounts in billions]

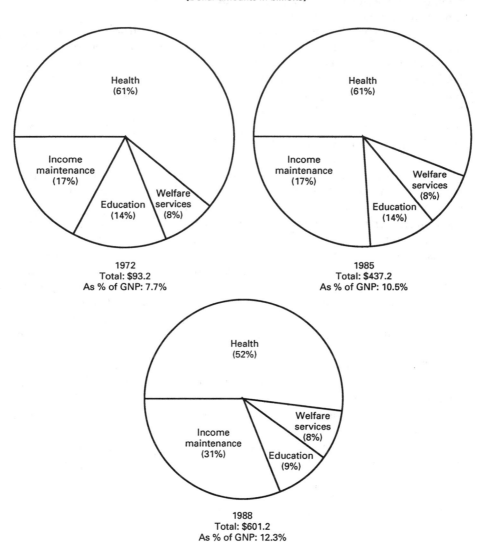

FIGURE 1-2   Percent Distribution of Private Social Welfare Expenditures. Expenditure Totals in Billions of Dollars.

Source: Wilmer L. Kerns and Milton P. Glanz, "Private Social Welfare Expenditures, 1972–88," *Social Security Bulletin,* February 1991/Vol. 54, No. 2, p. 3.

private action. Corporate practice is powerfully affected by laws and regulations governing parental leaves and minimum wages. Family care is facilitated by special tax credits and publicly provided respite care. Voluntary agencies are not taxed, contributions to them are deductible, and they often receive major grants and contracts from the government to carry on and expand their activities.

THEORETICAL EXPLANATIONS FOR THE EVOLUTION OF SOCIAL WELFARE AS AN INSTITUTION

The idea of social welfare as a primary societal institution draws on the theoretical perspective of *functionalism*. This perspective is a useful means of describing a social institution in terms of its contribution (i.e., its function) to the whole society. Social welfare fulfills an integrative social functions; it sustains morale and cohesiveness in society and thereby contributes to efficiency, stability, and order. However, functionalism (sometimes called social systems theory) is very abstract. (C. Wright Mills derisively refers to it as "Grand Theory.")[28] For example, the concept of social integration does not enable one to deal with questions about why different patterns of social welfare develop and the varying consequences that may occur when similar approaches are used in different contexts. A more pointed critique of functionalism is that because the theory is concerned with how institutions contribute to stability, everything is seen in positive terms, including inequality. (This condition, some functionalists would say, provides necessary incentives for people to work hard and aspire to improve their social condition.)[29] Finally, because functionalism is supposedly value free, it accepts the status quo and fails to provide a critique of society.

Although functionalism provides a plausible explanation for the development of social welfare as an institution, other theoretical perspectives offer different views and insights on the question. Mishra identifies several of the main theoretical schools of thought, including welfare as citizenship, technological determinism, and Marxism.[30]

The *welfare as citizenship* view is exemplified in the work of T. H. Marshall.[31] As industrial society develops, the bonds that tie people to their communities change. In traditional, preindustrial societies, human relationships are based on ascribed statuses; the individual's place in society is determined at birth and usually does not change. The social mobility and rapid change of modern societies, however, require a different form of social solidarity; and citizenship provides a "direct sense of community membership based on loyalty of free men endowed with rights and protected by common law."[32] Civil, political, and social rights, according to Marshall, constitute the elements of citizenship. Marshall perceives these rights as developing through an evolutionary process. Civil rights (e.g., the right to trial by jury) develop first, political rights (the right to vote) next. These, in turn, lay the groundwork for social rights (the right to education and welfare). Interestingly, Marshall does not believe that citizenship rights necessarily eliminate inequality; in fact, it can be argued that these rights develop in industrial society for the purpose of ensuring stability to the social systems within which they develop. The classic illustration is Bismarck's concession of social rights to German workers in the 1870s and 1880s. Bismarckian social legislation was quite explicitly intended to reduce the force of socialist demands for full civil and political rights.[33]

Technological determinism is similar to the citizenship perspective in that the origins of social welfare are perceived to lie in industrialization. However, whereas citizenship stresses the political aspects of industrial society, technological determinists focus on the structural aspects. For example, industry's "need" for a highly educated, well-trained, reliable work force leads to health, welfare, and educational legislation to ensure the development and protection of that work force. This view, sometimes referred to as convergence theory, posits that both socialist and capitalist societies will eventually narrow their differences and move toward a middle position, mixing individual freedom and state controls. Critics of technological determinism believe that it is overly deterministic and provides no explanation for the great variation in the social welfare systems of different countries.[34] Technological determinism is represented in the works of Galbraith[35] and Wilensky and Lebeaux.[36]

The *Marxist* view of social welfare is based on an analysis of how economic systems develop and change. Social welfare, from this perspective, is fundamentally a way to regulate and control the conditions under which work is organized and wealth is distributed. Piven and Cloward's book, *Regulating the Poor*,[37] is an analysis of the American system of social welfare from this perspective. In the extreme, Marxists perceive the ideal state to be one in which there is no institution of social welfare because the distribution of goods and services is based exclusively on need rather than deed. Marxists view social welfare in Western society as the handmaiden of capitalism, a mechanism to pacify the working class and keep it subservient. Marxism, like functionalism, is "grand" theory, useful for analyzing entire systems; it is less useful for looking at parts. And because Marxism is primarily focused on economics, it tends to ignore the independent influence of values, beliefs, and ideologies in the development of social welfare programs.

In summary, there are a variety of theories about social welfare and how it develops. No one theory, by itself, can illuminate all of the facets, problems, and issues with which we must deal in attempting to understand the institution.

ANALYTIC APPROACHES TO THE STUDY
OF SOCIAL WELFARE POLICY

Analysts tend to approach social welfare policy in several interrelated ways. The major approaches to analysis can be characterized as studies of the three *p*'s: *process, product,* and *performance.* Each approach examines social welfare policy questions that are primarily relevant to the professional roles of planning, administration, and research. Professionals engaged in these activities devote most of their resources and energies to questions concerning the process, product, and performance of social welfare policy. In actual agency practice, all three roles may be performed by the same worker. In such cases the worker tends to draw equally on the knowledge and insights generated by all three modes of study. However, in most large agencies and programs, planning, administration, and research tasks are specialized, and practitioners tend to be more interested in the insights of one analytic approach than in others. Even when the roles of planner, administrator, and researcher are highly compartmentalized, however, requirements for handling "outside" tasks seep into the job.[38]

Similarly, it is important to underscore that these three approaches are overlapping and interrelated. This is a shorthand way of saying that conceptual distinctions tend to capture the core qualities of a phenomenon but, by their very nature, do not well portray subtle and relative characteristics. Frequently, policy analysts may employ different combinations of approaches in their investigation. In *Fiscal Austerity and Aging,* for example, Estes and others trace the process of legislative development concerning the needs of the aged, describe the various programs that were products of this legislation, and evaluate their performance.[39]

Whatever the practice, however, it is theoretically useful to distinguish among these analytic approaches to the study of policy because each, at its core, addresses different types of questions, and the knowledge and insights generated are differentially applicable to major practice roles related to social welfare policy. At the conclusion of this section we will describe what we believe to be the policy-relevant tasks of the direct-service practitioner. And in the final section of the chapter we will tie the process of policy formulation to these professional tasks, illustrating how they are related to one another in practice.

Studies of Process

Studies of process in social welfare policy focus on the dynamics of policy formulation with regard to sociopolitical and technical-methodological variables. Political science and history are two of the major academic disciplines on which process studies are based. Process study is most concerned with understanding how the inputs of planning data and the relationships and interactions among the various political, governmental, and other organized collectivities in a society affect policy formulation.

Studies of process are employed as points around which policy assessments are organized, usually in the form of case studies of the political and technical inputs to decision making. Process studies may vary in the time dimension and levels of analysis with which they deal. That is, they may be long-range studies of the development of an entire social welfare system or studies of the development of specific circumscribed programs. Examples of the former are James Leiby's historical analysis, *The History of Social Welfare and Social Work in the United States*;[40] Heffernan's political and economic analysis, *Introduction to Social Welfare Policy: Power, Scarcity, and Common Human Needs*;[41] and Piven and Cloward's sociopolitical analysis, *Regulating the Poor: The Functions of Public Welfare*.[42] One analysis of a specific program is Martha Derthick's *Uncontrollable Spending for Social Service Grants*.[43]

Regardless of the time perspective, however, process studies generally deal with such questions as the societal context in which policy decisions are made; the behaviors, motivations, and goals of various actors who participate in the process; and the stages of the process of policy development. Process studies help illuminate how social context, social roles, and stages of development contribute to policy outcomes.

Studies of Product

The product of the planning process is a set of policy choices. These choices may be framed in program proposals, laws and statutes, or standing plans that eventually are transformed into programs. The analytic focus of such studies is on issues of choice: What is the form and substance of the choices that make up the policy design? What options did these choices foreclose? What values, theories, and assumptions support these choices?

Essentially, the analytic approach employed in this book is that of product study. Although widely used in a variety of academic disciplines, product study is the least systematically developed form of social welfare policy analysis. Analyses usually focus on one or another issue of choice that is germane to a specific policy, but there is no systematic framework for placing the generic issues of policy design in a broad context. Examples of these issue-specific studies are cited in the following chapters as we attempt to explicate a generic view of social welfare policy from this analytic perspective. In the next chapter we will address the development and utility of this approach in greater detail.

Studies of Performance

Performance studies are concerned with the description and evaluation of the programmatic outcomes of policy choices. Studies of program outcome are more amenable to objective, systematic observation than studies of process and product because program boundaries are more sharply delineated. Performance can be measured through the collection of qualitative and quantitative data and through the application of a wide range of methodological tools from various academic disciplines. Research methodology as taught in the social science disciplines and in professional schools provides the major technological and theoretical knowledge and skill for these kinds of studies.

From this perspective, investigators ask two types of questions: First, how well is the program carried out? Second, what is its impact? With regard to the former, programs are monitored to see what they consist of, whether they are reaching their target population, how much they cost, and so on. Impact is measured as "the difference between pre-program behavior and conditions and post-program behavior and conditions which can legitimately be attributed to the invention."[44] Some examples of performance studies are Rein's *Work or Welfare: Factors in the Choice for AFDC Mothers*,[45] Segal and Aviram's *The Mentally Ill in Community-Based Care*,[46] and Gilbert and Specht's *Dynamics of Community Planning*.[47]

Intellectual debate is generally more vigorous in the arena of process studies than in work concerned with product performance. That is not to say that there is no controversy concerning product and performance studies. Rather, the issues at stake in the latter two arenas most frequently stem from the political, economic, and social context within which programs are developed, whereas the issues that underlie process studies are more likely to be related to intellectual and philosophical assumptions about the social context itself. For example, an analysis that is focused on a particular program's outcomes might deal with such issues as whether there is utility in charging a fee for the use of a social service (as in Chapter 5) or whether there are advantages or disadvantages to offering benefits in cash versus in kind (as in Chapter 4). Analyses of performance seek to measure the effects, effectiveness, and efficiency of social welfare programs. In such studies, the purposes and objectives of the policies and programs are taken as a starting point. But in studies of process, analysts attempt to come to grips with such questions as these: What large political and economic forces in society brought about these social welfare policies and programs? What are the factors that determine how communities meet changing social needs? How analysts deal with these questions is strongly influenced by their own cultural and philosophical values and by their *welt anzicht*, or worldview.

The concepts used in this book to analyze the products of policy can be applied to social welfare programs in all societal contexts—capitalist, socialist, post-communist, or whatever. Similarly, the analytic methods used in the study of social welfare policy products (i.e., separating the components of choice in program design and examining the values and theories associated with these choices) do not vary in any considerable way from one social context to another. However, the study of process is heavily dependent on the analyst's basic intellectual and philosophical assumptions about the social context. Frequently the analyst is guided by overarching ideas about the nature of human society; frequently, analysts may not even be aware of how these assumptions influence their own thinking.

Why Policy Analysis Is Relevant to Practitioners in Direct Services

We have observed that the study of social welfare policy may serve the interests of planners, administrators, and researchers. Another group of professionals is also responsible for important policy-related functions. These are people who devote the major portion of their energies and resources to direct-service activities, such as caseworkers, probation officers, and group workers.

The practitioner directly involved in the provision of services to clients can play an important role in the formulation and execution of social service policies. Indeed, it is well recognized that the separation of policy formulation from policy execution is a delicate division, more characteristic of a porous membrane than of the solid line of bureaucratic hierarchy. Experienced practitioners often exercise considerable discretion in executing broad directives, and so shape as well as discharge organizational policies.

The importance of practitioner discretion for policy interpretation increases as organizations grow larger and more complex. Too frequently, however, the charge to the practitioner is delivered in oversimplified clichés to "get into the political arena" or to deal more effectively with "community elites."[48] Such demands can be demoralizing to professionals, particularly to those whose major energies are devoted to dealing with the problems of individuals and families. At best, a general call to arms without more specific instructions about which arms to use and how to use them is only temporarily inspiring; at worst, it is likely to leave many feeling inadequate.

A second reason for the direct practitioner's sense of inadequacy in policy formulation is that this task is not as well defined as others. In casework or probation, for example, the actual doing (counseling) and the objects of one's work (cases) are relatively clear. Many of the methods used in direct practice allow professionals to work within a series of fairly well-defined roles that usually have a high degree of consonance. The process by which policy is formulated, however, involves a wide range of roles that often strain against one another. Direct service, finally, tends to be individual practice—one social worker handling one case. Policy formulation, by contrast, involves the efforts of many people.

In addition, the transmission of knowledge and skills in the field of social welfare policy is neither well organized nor sharply defined. Participation in policy formulation requires expertise in a major area of service and a comprehensive and extensive knowledge of a field. It also requires certain general analytic skills that may be taught to all in the helping professions. If policy formulation is seen as a process that entails many different tasks, roles, and transmissible analytic skills, all professionals can learn to utilize the process and contribute to it in the most appropriate ways.

The fact that the direct-service practitioner's major functions are remote from the final decision points in the process of policy formulation makes many students less than enthusiastic for courses in social welfare policy. Direct-service practitioners are more inclined to concentrate on the development of interactional skills, on learning how to conduct themselves as professionals and how to engage themselves with clients, colleagues, and community leaders and groups. The study of social choices and social values seems, to many, abstract and theoretical. But professionals who ignore social choices and social values in favor of developing practice skills are like musicians playing background music to a melody that seems to come from nowhere. Like musical themes, the directions and goals that are reflected in social welfare policy are neither accidental nor aimless: They develop because people make choices. One has to understand what the range of choices is, what values are implied in the alternatives, the framework within which these choices are made, the various means by which they are implemented, and the methodological tools that can be used to assess their consequences.

Although direct-service workers may be unconcerned with policy design, they are affected by it in important ways. In the long view, policy choices affect the technologies direct-service workers will use. Consider, for example, the ways in which changes in federal policies have affected the character and extent of the social services. The 1962 amendments to the Social Security Act placed great value on the provision of supportive casework services to welfare clients, and this choice was supported with substantial financial resources. In 1967 social welfare policy changed, and along with the push for the separation of income and services, individualized therapeutic interventions were deemphasized.

The federal government, however, did support social services to reduce and prevent financial dependency. This goal was accomplished on a "matching" basis, whereby the federal government paid $3 for every $1 spent by the states. Federal expenditures, in addition, were "open-ended," meaning unlimited. As a result, federal social services costs by the early 1970s had soared to more than $2 billion annually, up from almost nothing a decade earlier. Federal policy changed once more in 1974 with the enactment of the Title XX amendments to the Social Security Act. This title placed a cap (financial limit) on federal expenditures for social services, and states had to meet certain requirements to receive Title XX funds.

They were required to offer protective services to children and adults without regard to income, and they were required to expend at least 50 percent of their Title XX funds on people in the "categorical" programs (i.e., those receiving public assistance, such as Aid to Families with Dependent Children or Supplementary Security Income). In 1981, federal policy changed again—allocations for Title XX were reduced, and states were given virtually free reign in designing programs and targeting beneficiaries.

We will examine some of the factors that were related to these changes in social choices later and assess some of the values, theories, and assumptions underlying them. At this point we only want to illustrate how the kinds of social services that professionals offer, their clientele, and the conditions under which they are provided are affected by public social policy. The direct-service practitioner who has the conceptual tools to analyze the dimensions of policy is more likely to be a participant in these changes rather than merely a product or victim of them.

Whether or not the direct practitioner is conversant with social welfare policy, the public assumes that those engaged in the provision of services can provide useful information about social welfare programs and their consequences. Legislators, politicians, and community groups turn to child welfare workers, probation officers, and mental health case managers for advice, and their advice is treated seriously—whether ill or well informed—because of their status as professionals. There is, then, at the very least, a professional obligation to be knowledgeable about policy matters.

Finally, many students now being trained as direct practitioners will, later on, become planners, administrators, and researchers because these positions are frequently filled within agencies on the basis of seniority. Direct-service professionals who will ultimately perform policy-related roles would be wise to link some part of their formal education to planning, organization, and analysis.[49] From a career point of view, it is essential that the direct practitioner have at least an appreciation of the dimensions of the field of social welfare policy, if not an intimate knowledge of its specializations.

THE PROCESS OF POLICY DEVELOPMENT

Many authors have developed models of policy formulation as a series of unfolding stages, the number of which vary according to the author's purpose. In most cases the neat sequential ordering of the process is qualified by the recognition that in reality these stages are in a state of dynamic readjustment, feeding back data that alter the preceding information while forming the groundwork for data to follow.

TABLE 1–2   Comparison of Models of Policy Development

MODEL A (KAHN) PLANNING PROCESS	MODEL B (DINITTO) POLICY-MAKING PROCESS	MODEL C (FREEMAN & SHERWOOD) SOCIAL POLICY-DEVELOPMENT PROCESS
1. Planning instigators		
2. Explorations	1. Identifying policy problems	1. Planning
3. Definition of planning task	2. Formulating policy alternatives	
4. Policy formulation	3. Legitimizing public policy	2. Program development and implementation
5. Programming	4. Implementation of public policy	
6. Evaluation feedback	5. Evaluating policy	3. Evaluation

For students new to the field of social welfare policy these models are sometimes confusing because they vary not only in the number of stages and the terminology used to describe them but also in the general labels under which they are presented. Nevertheless, there is much similarity. To illustrate this point, Table 1–2 compares three process models found in the literature. Model A contains six stages under the heading "Planning Process";[50] Model B delineates a five-step policy-making process;[51] Model C contains three stages under the heading "Social Policy-Development Process."[52] Whatever the number of stages, these models relate a process of rational progression, although each differs in the level of generalization employed.

Our model, presented in Table 1–3, divides the policy-formulation process into eight separate stages, providing a sense of the rich variety of tasks and professional roles involved. Five social-welfare-related roles are identified: direct service, research, community organization, management, and planning. As indicated, these roles are often filled by the same worker; a planner, for example, may have both research and community organization responsibilities.

The policy-formulation process outlined in Table 1–3 serves both to uncover incipient and unmet social needs and to identify methods of meeting them. The process might occur in a variety of settings—a small private agency, a large institution, or a nationwide bureaucracy. The model, like the others, does not reflect the complex feedback interactions among stages nor does it specify who generates the initiative for carrying the process forward.

TABLE 1–3   Professional Roles and Policy Formulation

STAGE	PROFESSIONAL ROLES
1. Problem identification	1. Direct service
2. Problem analysis	2. Research
3. Informing the public	3. Community organization
4. Development of policy goals	4. Planning
5. Building public support and legitimacy	5. Community organization
6. Program design	6. Planning
7. Implementation	7. Management and direct service
8. Evaluation and assessment	8. Research and direct service

Problem Identification

The impetus for policy change usually reflects a recognition of an unmet or poorly met need in the community. The perception of particular needs and the formulation of appropriate responses are related to numerous political, economic, social, and institutional forces. What people define as problems, for example, commonly reflect their institutional positions. So, for example, concerns for organizational economy and harmony might guide the perceptions of agency managers more than their feelings of responsibility for improving services to clients.[53]

Tasks that must be completed during this stage are case-finding, recording examples of unmet needs, and discovering gaps in services. These are tasks that direct-service practitioners are singularly well positioned to perform. It is through their functions as advocates and social brokers for their clients that they will most likely be involved in the policy-formulation process. Scott Briar has discussed these functions as part of direct-service workers' professional role, noting that these individuals bring to the task "a substantial body of knowledge with which to understand the dynamics of the welfare system and its constituent agencies."[54] However, to use such knowledge in this process requires a professional orientation that views service to one's client as the foremost professional responsibility. For the practitioner, a major dilemma arises when (as discussed in Chapter 5) the requirements of bureaucratic conformity clash with this responsibility.

Problem Analysis

Having identified a problem, it is necessary to develop factual data about its magnitude and severity and the number of people it affects. The kind and quality of information-gathering may change as the process evolves. Consider the following hypothetical case. A probation officer observes that children are being physically mistreated in the county's residential institution. Unable to make headway with the agency administrator (who is defensive and unwilling to recognize that order can be maintained without occasional physical coercion), the probation officer brings the problem to the attention of a group of citizens who have organized to advocate for the needs of children. This citizens' committee sets up meetings throughout the county, inviting youths who have been at the institution to relate their experiences.

In this case, a fairly informal procedure—the community meeting—is used early in the process to generate raw data for the work of the citizens' committee. As these meetings progress and the nature of the issues becomes clear, the committee might direct its energies toward bringing in a professional standard-setting agency or research unit to examine more systematically the probation program. Whatever the method employed, the basic task at this stage is to move from an expression of concern about unmet needs to an organized (frequently complicated and expensive) program of information gathering and analysis. Research skills are primary to this task.

Informing the Public

The public includes the various subsystems in the community that must be informed of a problem if improvements are to occur. The size of the public—as big as the community at large or as limited as an institution's top leadership—depends on the nature of the problem. The task is to present the problem in a form that will capture the interest and attention of the relevant parties. Such a task requires organizing skills and the use of appropriate media channels.

As in the analysis stage, no clear-cut time frame divides information gathering from informing the public. The use of testimony at community meetings, for example, interweaves public information with information gathering and analysis. Neighborhood surveys by resident volunteers can similarly uncover unmet needs while informing the public. Both research and organizing skills are required to implement such a survey.

Informing the public necessarily precedes developing policy goals even though the parties initiating change may have specific policy goals in mind. Such goals can have little meaning to a public that is unaware that a problem exists.

Development of Policy Goals

The preceding stages create public awareness of a problem and information concerning its dimensions. Now the discussion turns to addressing the problem and meeting the need. At this stage many solutions may be suggested, all of which must be sifted, analyzed, and shaped in order to develop concrete policy goals. In the case of the probation department, these goals might include changing the attitude and behavior of residential center staff, moving residents out of the facility into community-based half-way houses, or attacking the need for incarcerating children and adolescents in the first place.

The key professional function at this stage is social planning. According to Kahn,

> The planner's most serious decision and major contribution is what may be called the *formulation or definition of the planning task.* The "task" is formulated through a constant playing back between an assessment of the relevant aspects of social reality and the preferences of the relevant community. Each of these two factors affects and modifies the perceptions of the other. The task definition appears as an integration of the two. Much else in social planning follows from the outcome of such integration.[55]

The outcome of this stage is a general statement of the broad-based objectives or goals to be achieved.

Building Public Support and Legitimacy

During and after the process of goal formulation, efforts must be made to maintain public support for the general course of action proposed. Those initiating the policy must identify groups in the broader system—political figures, professional groups, voluntary social agencies, and the like—that can lend support and legitimacy to the change objectives and can assist in translating those objectives into instruments for action.

Major tasks at this stage include the cultivation of leadership, coalition formation, and negotiation of agreement among potential supporters. Compromises may be made at this stage that modify the goal statement. Here, the organizer's skills in bargaining, exchange, and persuasion are essential to forge the support base. The culmination of this stage is the creation of a consensus platform containing the goals and objectives of the supporting constituencies.

Program Design

Once a general direction has been determined, the task of actually drafting a program design rests on the drawing board of the social planner. At this point, goals and objectives are transformed into operational guidelines for action—whether in the form of statutes for the agenda of a legislative body or program proposals for consideration by an agency board of directors.

The plan of action or policies that are products of this stage describe the allocation of responsibility for the proposed program and the organizational structure, financing, and personnel requirements of program operations. These program elements vary in the amount of detail they contain.

Frequently, a program is designed to leave considerable room for interpretation by those responsible for its implementation.

Implementation

Depending on how detailed the program design is, a large part of the process of policy formulation may be left for this stage, when the concrete translation of action principles to programmatic elements is accomplished through practice, precedent, and experimentation. The 1974 Title XX amendments to the Social Security Act, which required each of the states to develop a Comprehensive Annual Services Plan involving social planning, problem analysis, and citizen participation, are a good illustration. The specific ways in which these requirements were to be implemented were quite vague, leaving the substance of implementation decision making to state administrators. In Chapter 8 we will discuss some of the different ways this policy design was interpreted and their implications for program development.

The chief tasks at this point—getting the program organized, clarifying policy, producing the service or benefit, and delivering it to the client group—relate to administrative and direct-service functions. The courts may also enter the process at this stage and play a major role in the clarification of policy. It is by establishing a system of rights and guarantees through appeals and judicial precedents that a body of administrative procedure and law evolves.

Evaluation and Assessment

In a sense, the goals of social welfare policy are always receding. New programs create new expectations and uncover additional unmet needs. Programs themselves become a major element in the "demand environment" of policy. This continuing process may be based in part on faulty assumptions of policy design concerning the resources needed to implement programs and the availability of resources and supportive services in the external system.

SUMMARY

In this chapter we examined the field of social welfare policy in four different contexts, summarized as follows:

1. *The institutional context.* The field of social welfare policy consists of policies related to the institutional settings structuring social welfare activities.
2. *The theoretical context.* Several theories explain how and why the institution of social welfare developed. Prominent schools of thought include functionalism, welfare as citizenship, technological determinism, and Marxism.

3. *The analytical context.* The field of social welfare policy is studied by various academic disciplines from viewpoints that coalesce around issues of process, product, and performance.
4. *The developmental context.* The development of social welfare policy involves a series of practice roles including administrator, planner, community organizer, direct-services practitioner, and researcher. Each of these roles may serve primary functions at different stages of the policy-formulation process.

In general, this overview illustrates some of the breadth and depth of the field. We have suggested why the study of policy is of central importance to students training for professional positions that serve the institution of social welfare. Effective participation in the field requires basic knowledge about social welfare policy. Such knowledge includes an understanding of the process of policy formulation and the technical tools and sociopolitical knowhow required to move policy along. It also includes the methodological techniques of descriptive and evaluative research required to assess performance. Finally, this knowledge entails insight into the abstract entity—those principles or guides to action that constitute social welfare policy—that is the culmination of process and the prelude to performance. The development of such insight hinges on understanding the fundamental choices that determine the design of social welfare policies.

We turn now to a discussion of these choices.

NOTES

1. Martin Rein, *Social Policy* (New York: Random House, 1970), pp. 3–20; Kenneth Boulding, "The Boundaries of Social Policy," *Social Work*, Vol. 12, no. 1 (January 1967), 3–11; Richard Titmuss, *Essays on "The Welfare State"* (London: Unwin University Books, 1963).
2. See, for example, David A. Gil, "A Systematic Approach to Social Policy Analysis," *Social Service Review*, Vol. 44, no. 4 (December 1970), 411–426.
3. Alfred Kahn, *Theory and Practice of Social Planning* (New York: Russell Sage, 1969), p. 13; Rein, *Social Policy*, p. 211; Garth Mangum, *Emergence of Manpower Policy* (New York: Holt, Rinehart & Winston, 1969), p. 130.
4. See Neil Gilbert and Barbara Gilbert, *The Enabling State: Modern Welfare Capitalism in America* (New York: Oxford University Press, 1989), pp. 18–19.
5. Robert Lampman, *Social Welfare Spending* (Orlando, FL: Academic Press, 1984), p. 27.
6. U.S. Bureau of the Census, *Who's Helping Out? Support Networks Among American Families* (Washington, DC: U.S. Government Printing Office, 1988).
7. National Center for Health Services Research and Health Care Technology Assessment, *Research Activities*, no. 87 (July 1986), 1–2.
8. Sheila Kamerman and Alfred Kahn, *Helping America's Families* (Philadelphia: Temple University Press, 1982), pp. 25–32.
9. "Mormons and the 'Sin' of Being Poor," *San Francisco Examiner*, December 19, 1982, p. A16.
10. Ibid.
11. Kamerman and Kahn, *Helping America's Families*.
12. Estimates based on U.S. Chamber of Commerce figures for 1986, reported in Sylvia Porter's money column, *San Francisco Chronicle*, January 16, 1987, p. A18.

13. Gilbert and Gilbert, *Enabling State*, p. 20.

14. U.S. General Accounting Office, *"An Overview of the Working Uninsured,"* Report GAO/HRD–89–45, February 1989, p. 2.

15. Gilbert and Gilbert, *Enabling State*, pp. 20–21.

16. C. E. Born, "Proprietary Firms and Child Welfare Services," *Child Welfare*, Vol. 62, no. 2 (1983), 109–118.

17. Harry Specht, "Social Work and the Popular Psychotherapies," *Social Service Review*, Vol. 64, no. 3 (September 1990), 345.

18. Available evidence reflects a shift in professional social work toward private practice. National survey data reveal that the proportion of social workers reporting employment under profit-motivated auspices, mainly private practice, increased fourfold (3.3 percent to 12 percent) between 1972 and 1982. Findings from a Massachusetts survey in the mid-1980s indicate that 19 percent of the Licensed Independent Clinical Social Workers (the state's highest level of license for social work) were in private practice on a full-time basis and 26 percent on a part-time basis. See Gilbert and Gilbert, *Enabling State*, p. 73; and Thomas McGuire et al., "Vendorship and Social Work in Massachusetts," *Social Service Review*, Vol. 58, no. 3 (September 1984), 372–383.

19. Phyllis R. Silverman, "Mutual Aid Groups," *Encyclopedia of Social Work*, 18th ed., Vol. 2, 1987, (Silver Spring, MD.), 171–175.

20. Ralph Kramer, "Voluntary Agencies and the Personal Social Services," in *The Nonprofit Sector*, ed. Walter W. Powell (Yale University Press, 1987), pp. 240–45.

21. Roy Wallis, "Institutions," *International Encyclopedia of the Social Sciences*, Vol. 14, p. 410, 1968. Macmillan, N.Y.

22. Abraham Flexner, "Is Social Work a Profession?" Paper presented at the Conference of Charities and Corrections, May 17, 1915.

23. Harold Wilensky and Charles Lebeaux, *Industrial Society and Social Welfare* (New York: Russell Sage, 1958), p. 138.

24. Ibid., p. 140.

25. Asa Briggs, "The Welfare State in Historical Perspective," in *The Welfare State*, ed. Charles Schottland (New York: Harper Torchbooks, 1967), p. 29.

26. Charles Murray, *Losing Ground* (New York: Basic Books, 1985), p. 9.

27. Alvin Schorr, *Common Decency* (New Haven: Yale University Press, 1986).

28. C. Wright Mills, *The Sociological Imagination* (New York: Grove Press, 1961), pp. 25–49.

29. Kingsley Davis and Wilbert E. Moore, "Some Principles of Stratification," in *Class, Status, and Power: Social Stratification in Comparative Perspective*, 2nd ed., eds. Richard Bendix and Seymour Martin Lipset (New York: Free Press, 1966), pp. 47–53.

30. Ramesh Mishra, *Society and Social Policy: Theoretical Perspectives on Welfare* (London: Macmillan, 1977). For a somewhat different analysis of these theoretical perspectives, see James Midgely, "Social Welfare Implications of Development Paradigms," *Social Service Review*, Vol. 58, no. 2 (June 1984), 181–190.

31. T. H. Marshall, *Sociology at the Crossroads and Other Essays* (London: Heinemann, 1963).

32. Ibid., p. 96.

33. Koppel S. Pinson, *Modern Germany* (London: Macmillan, 1966), pp. 156–160, 245–246.

34. Reinhard J. Skinner, "Technological Determinism," *Comparative Studies in Society and History*, Vol. 18, no. 1 (January 1976), 2–27.

35. J. K. Galbraith, *The New Industrial State* (London: Hamish Hamilton, 1967).

36. Wilensky and Lebeaux, *Industrial Society and Social Welfare*.

37. Frances Fox Piven and Richard A. Cloward, *Regulating the Poor: The Functions of Public Welfare* (New York: Pantheon Books, 1971).

38. For example, in Robert Perlman and Arnold Gurin, *Community Organization and Social Planning* (New York: Wiley, 1972), an entire chapter is devoted to various ways in which the administrator of a direct-service agency is engaged in community organization and social planning tasks.

39. Carroll L. Estes et al., *Fiscal Austerity and Aging* (Beverly Hills, CA: Sage Publications, 1983).

40. James Leiby, *The History of Social Welfare and Social Work in the United States* (New York: Columbia University Press, 1978).

41. W. Joseph Heffernan, *Introduction to Social Welfare Policy* (Itasca, Il.: F. E. Peacock, 1979).

42. Piven and Cloward, *Regulating the Poor.*

43. Martha Derthick, *Uncontrollable Spending for Social Service Grants* (Washington, DC: Brookings Institution, 1975).

44. Howard Freeman and Clarence Sherwood, *Social Research and Social Policy* (Englewood Cliffs, NJ: Prentice Hall, 1970), p. 13.

45. Mildred Rein, *Work or Welfare: Factors in the Choice for AFDC Mothers* (New York: Praeger, 1970).

46. Steven P. Segal and Uri Avirum, *The Mentally Ill in Community-Based Care* (New York: Wiley, 1978).

47. Neil Gilbert and Harry Specht, *Dynamics of Community Planning* (Cambridge, MA: Ballinger, 1977).

48. Alan D. Wade, "The Social Worker in the Political Process," *Social Welfare Forum 1966* (New York: Columbia University Press, 1966), pp. 52–67.

49. For a more detailed discussion of these curriculum issues see Neil Gilbert and Harry Specht, "The Incomplete Profession: Commitment to Welfare vs. Commitment to Social Work," *Social Work*, Vol. 19, no. 6 (November 1974), 665–674.

50. Kahn, *Theory and Practice of Social Planning*, p. 61.

51. Diana M. DiNitto and Thomas R. Dye, *Social Welfare: Politics and Public Policy* (Englewood Cliffs, NJ: Prentice Hall, 1983), p. 13.

52. Freeman and Sherwood, *Social Research and Social Policy*, pp. 3–16.

53. Organizational maintenance and direct-service needs frequently make competing claims on social welfare administrators. Etzioni suggests that this type of position constitutes a case of institutionalized role conflict. Amitai Etzioni, *Modern Organizations* (Englewood Cliffs, NJ: Prentice Hall, 1964), pp. 82–85.

54. Scott Briar, "Dodo or Phoenix? A View of the Current Crisis in Casework," *Social Work Practice 1967* (New York: Columbia University Press, 1967); see also Gordon Hamilton, "The Role of Social Casework in Social Policy," *Social Casework*, Vol. 33, no. 8 (October 1952).

55. Kahn, *Theory and Practice of Social Planning*, p. 61.

Chapter Two
A FRAMEWORK FOR SOCIAL WELFARE POLICY ANALYSIS

Even when armed with this much greater scientific knowledge, contemporary societies will, of course, face difficult choices between simultaneously held but competing values or objectives. . . . The precise balance between adequacy and equity in the determination of social insurance benefits, between equal access to minimum security and retention of the principle of local autonomy, between the interests of different social classes in allocating the costs of social security measures, or between the claims of family obligation and responsibilities to the wider community illustrate the nature of these ultimate and difficult value choices. Yet while there is no guarantee that democracies will act rationally in formulating their social policies, it is also abundantly clear that they cannot even be expected to do so unless they are made aware of the full implications of the choices available to them.

Eveline M. Burns
Social Security and Public Policy

Traditionally, courses in social welfare policy have emphasized the study of process and performance. In courses organized around process, students have learned about social, political, and technical processes in policy formulation; and in courses organized around performance, they have learned about the details of social welfare programs in operation. A major advantage of the study of performance is its focus on factual and substantive material: It describes and evaluates programs. Here, too, lies its major shortcoming: The substance of social welfare programs is continually changing. Moreover, these programs are so numerous that one or two courses can cover only a segment of the field.

As indicated in Chapter One, a third approach to the study of this field is to focus on the set of policy choices that evolves from the planning process. From this perspective the analytic task is to distinguish among and to dissect the essential components of policy design rather than to examine the sociopolitical processes through which policy is developed or to evaluate policy outcomes. The basic components of policy design to which this task is addressed may be seen as dimensions of choice. In this chapter we present a framework for analyzing basic choices in the design of social welfare policy.

With this analytic approach, we will use program descriptions as examples to formulate and substantiate general concepts. Because we are interested mainly in illustrating the concepts that are useful in the analysis of social welfare policy, rather than in understanding the details of specific programs, there will be a certain eclecticism in their selection: We include large and small programs; pieces of programs; existing programs; and proposed programs, some of which may never leave the drawing boards and others of which have not yet arrived on the public agenda.

As Eveline Burns has suggested, the major advantage of this approach is that it equips students with a convenient set of concepts that can usefully explain and illuminate a wide range of policies.[1] To accomplish this, however, we must simplify reality somewhat—which is the price of any effort to cull and distill the essential elements of any complex phenomenon.

An analytic framework is an intellectual tool to order reality. It directs our attention to certain elements in a field while it filters out others. Before elaborating on the analytic framework around which this book is organized, let us say a few words about certain features of the field of social welfare policy that our framework screens out. These features concern levels of comprehensiveness and realms of policy. This brief detour is taken to underline the complexities of the reality with which we are dealing.

LEVELS AND REALMS

Although social welfare policies are formulated at different geographical levels within society, much of the field is identified with the broad policy choices that are made by public and private agencies at the national level. Social Security legislation is a primary example. However, we should not forget that policy-making also includes agency activities at the local level. For example, the director of a neighborhood settlement house planning to offer teen parenting classes is as fully engaged in the design of social welfare policy as the task force member assigned to help draft national strategy for day-care reform. This view of policy as pertaining to micro- and macro-level program development, although widely held, is not universal.

Occasionally the term *policy*, as found in the literature, designates an overall strategy or master plan focused on a geographic or functional sector of society. Moynihan's observation that "programs do not a policy make" reflects this point of view, distinguishing program from policy according to levels of comprehensiveness.[2] But the point at which programs end and policies begin is inexact, and the question of what constitutes comprehensive policy rather than fragmented programs is open to a range of interpretations. There is the distinction between macrosystem and microsystem, wherein policy formulated at the macro level, usually national in scope, is identified as comprehensive.[3] There is also the American Institute of Planners, which defines comprehensive planning as efforts to identify and order the physical, social, and economic relationships implicit in development programs within a delimited geographic area ranging from a neighborhood to an international region.[4] And finally, to add spice to the issue, there is the view that at whatever level it is preached, comprehensive planning is rarely practiced. As Lindblom argues, most policy formulation is achieved by "muddling through" via successive limited comparisons between *what is* and a series of incremental alternatives of *what might be*.[5]

In this book we make little effort to sort out or distinguish social welfare policy in terms of comprehensiveness. Our treatment of policy is impartial on the issue; it includes analyses of designs to guide implementation of programs of limited scope at the micro level as well as broader national-level strategies. Although many of the specific examples we employ focus on the macro level, the concepts and issues are equally applicable to the choices addressed by planners and administrators in local agencies.

In addition to the different levels of comprehensiveness, social welfare policies are often classified according to functional fields (e.g., health, criminal justice, education), problem areas (e.g., domestic violence, homelessness, unemployment), population groups (e.g., children, adolescents, the aged), or some combination thereof.[6] There is considerable overlap among these realms. The line between functional fields and problems is rather fuzzy; it appears to be less substantive than definitional. The U.S. Department of Health and Human Services' classification of social welfare expenditures indicates a functional division in terms of social insurance and public aid (i.e., income maintenance), health, education, and housing programs. But there is one special classification based on group affiliation (veteran's programs) and a residual category of "other" social welfare, which includes a problem area (juvenile delinquency) as well as group-classified programs like child welfare.[7]

TABLE 2–1   Social Welfare Expenditure under Public Programs (in Billions of Dollars)

PROGRAM	1960	1965	1970	1975	1980	1985	1988
Social Insurance	$19.3	$28.1	$54.7	$123.0	$229.8	$369.6	$432.2
Public Aid	4.1	6.3	16.4	41.4	72.0	98.2	120.4
Health, Medical	4.5	6.2	9.6	16.7	27.3	39.1	52.6
Veterans Programs	5.5	6.0	9.1	17.0	21.5	27.0	29.3
Education	17.6	28.1	50.8	80.8	121.1	172.0	219.4
Housing	0.2	0.3	0.7	3.2	6.9	12.6	16.6
Other Social Welfare	1.1	2.1	4.1	6.9	13.6	13.6	15.5
Total	$52.3	$77.1	$144.6	$289.1	$492.0	$732.0	$885.8
As percent of GNP	10.3%	11.5%	14.7%	19.0%	18.4%	18.5%	18.5%
As percent of all government spending	38.4%	42.4%	46.5%	56.6%	57.1%	52.2%	52.8%

Source: Ann Kallman Bixby, "Public Social Welfare Expenditures, Fiscal Year 1988," *Social Security Bulletin,* Volume 54, No. 5, May, 1991, pp. 4–8.

Note: Medicare spending is included in Social Insurance; Medicaid spending is included in Public Aid.

When defined in terms of these areas, the field of social welfare has grown considerably over the last several decades. As indicated in Table 2–1, public expenditures for social welfare rose from 10.3 percent to 18.5 percent of the gross national product (GNP) between 1960 and 1988. This increase is particularly notable in comparison to the relatively steady state from 1940 to 1960, when social welfare expenditures hovered around 10 percent of the GNP. In hard currency the magnitude of this growth amounts to a rise from $52.3 to $885.8 billion.

If we attempt to chart the various viewpoints concerning the levels of comprehensiveness on a vertical axis and the realms of policy on a horizontal axis, a singular fact emerges from the matrix. The field does not lend itself to a conceptually neat and orderly mapping. What one person may consider to be a comprehensive policy in a functional area another person may perceive to be a fragmented program in a problem area.

Social, Occupational, and Fiscal Welfare

The realms of social welfare policy may be seen from another angle, first designated by Richard Titmuss in terms of three complimentary systems of welfare: social, fiscal, and occupational.[8]

The *social* component discerned by Titmuss corresponds to the "direct expenditure" approach utilized by the Social Security Administration to organize the spending data in Table 2–1. Basically, it equates social welfare with the provision of a range of publicly sponsored goods and services—income support, health, social services, and the like. *Fiscal* welfare, on the other hand, involves the reverse—the income side—of the budget coin. Specifically, it identifies those features of the tax-raising system, such as special tax deductions and credits, that advance explicit social objectives. The *occupational* system, finally, comprises the system of welfare associated with employment—chiefly the fringe benefit arrangements identified in the previous chapter.

According to Titmuss, all three systems of welfare share a fundamental social character and goal. That is, each constitutes a primary area of collective intervention aimed at meeting individual and societal needs. Although many question the appropriateness of defining the welfare system in such broad terms, there is increasing recognition among policy scholars and analysts, as well as among policymakers themselves, of the role that each of these separate arrangements plays in affecting citizens' well-being and of the varying ways in which the three systems affect one another. There is also considerable evidence that over the past three decades the scope of fiscal and occupational welfare has grown at least as rapidly as traditional social expenditures.

The importance of the Titmuss model is that it explicates the broad range of organized welfare and shows the artificiality of equating welfare narrowly with government outlays. For Titmuss, analyses of welfare that limit themselves to public outlays present distorted—and overly sanguine—views of the true character of the welfare state.

One of the most obvious distortions can be seen in how we identify the beneficiaries of organized welfare activities. Because occupational welfare generally mirrors employment status, its benefits are distributed in much the same way as wages and salaries. That is, health, pension, and other perquisites of employment are first and foremost a function of job status. One must be employed—or related to someone who is employed—to receive them. And since their value generally increases with income, managerial and professional workers are eligible for broader and more lucrative benefits than blue-collar or intermittently employed workers.

Although occupational welfare is restricted in scope, and inversely related to need, it is nevertheless extremely important to a broad segment of the population. In 1983, for example, 56 percent of all nonfarm workers and 85 percent of all workers in large firms had pension plans. Although these plans may take years to mature, fully one-third of the 65-plus population today receives regular employee pensions. In addition, 51 percent of all firms offer life insurance to employees' dependents, 85 percent cover their retirees' medical insurance, and 27 percent offer full hospital room and board.[9] Smaller numbers of firms offer programs such as adoption services, health promotion, legal assistance, child and elder dependent care, and drug and alcohol counseling and treatment.

For Titmuss, occupational welfare is a form of "collective intervention" since its scope and character reflect public policy. In other words, despite their nominal "private" character, job benefits are significantly influenced by government; they are hardly fully private matters. Public policy in the form of special tax arrangements—notably the deductibility of employee benefit costs as a regular business expense—has been a powerful inducement for private employers to sponsor health and welfare programs. From the employees' point of view, fringe benefits are also specially advantageous. Benefits like health insurance are not taxed, whereas an equivalent cash payment—provided as salary—would be. Other employer-provided fringe benefits, such as pension contributions, are tax deferred until retirement, at which time they are subject to several tax advantages. Thus, although these benefits have a cash value that is the equivalent of wages in the employment contract, this cash value is substantially tax exempt. To the extent that these benefits escape taxation they constitute government subsidies, "welfare," in the same manner as other social provisions.

Although powerfully influenced by public policy, occupational welfare is less "public" than the core realm of government social welfare. Clearly, occupational benefits are an established part of the reward structure of the market economy. The distribution of these benefits is motivated less by collective strivings for security and equality than by entrepreneurial inducements, which vary from firm to firm. For this reason, Mishra suggests that occupational benefits should be classified not as social welfare but as "part of the 'social policy' of private enterprise."[10]

The chief idea of Titmuss's third classification—fiscal welfare—is that the tax system itself acts as an important instrument of social policy, above and beyond its role as a source of revenue. Acting through a number of special tax measures, fiscal welfare advances welfare objectives in much the same fashion as direct spending. Federally financed public housing and housing allowances for the poor, clearly within the realm of direct social welfare, are akin to benefits derived from such fiscal measures as the income tax deduction for interest payments on home mortgages. Similarly, deductions and credits for charitable contributions, occupation-based health and pension plans, and child care are substantially equivalent to direct subsidies. As Titmuss stated, "The tax saving that accrues to the individual is, in effect, a transfer payment. In their primary objectives and their effects on individual purchasing power there are no differences. Both are manifestations of social policies in favor of identified groups in the population."[11]

In an effort to quantify the value of such fiscal measures and increase public awareness of their importance, Stanley Surrey, a one-time Treasury Department official, invented the concept of the tax expenditure. According to Surrey, these are deviations from the normal tax code that serve to affect the private economy in ways that normally are achieved by spending. Surrey estimated the value of these deviations, which were not counted in ordinary budget tabulations, to be about one-quarter of the regular federal budget.[12] As a result of Surrey's work, Congress ordered a regular accounting of tax expenditures to accompany the regular federal budget. Since 1975 it has been compiled annually as one of several special analyses prepared by the executive branch.

The large number of people that benefit from tax expenditures, and the view that these provisions amount to a form of public subsidy, has led some analysts to claim that "everyone is on welfare."[13] For others, however, there are important differences between a system of fiscal measures such as tax expenditures and traditional social welfare. Irving Kristol, for example, challenges the view that these benefits are similar to direct social welfare provisions. To think of tax deductions as subsidies "implicitly asserts that all income covered by the general provisions of the tax law belongs of right to the government, and what government decides, by exemption or qualification, not to collect in taxes constitutes a subsidy."[14] In other words, allowing citizens to keep money they earned that is spent or invested in ways that benefit the individual or society is not the moral or functional equivalent of taking money from those who can afford to pay taxes and distributing it as cash benefits to those in need.

Tax expenditures—"loopholes" to their detractors—are, of course, different in many ways from direct spending. For one thing, like occupational welfare, they tend to benefit better-off taxpayers the most. Often described as upside-down subsidies, they generally provide the greatest dollar value to those in the highest tax brackets. The deductibility of charitable contributions, for example, clearly helps voluntary hospitals, universities, and social service agencies, but it just as clearly reduces the tax liability of the rich far more than of ordinary taxpayers. Further, because the poor usually pay no federal income taxes at all, they get no immediate benefit.

private sector, lessening public intrusion, and foregoing public income to promote private action—all conservative preferences—Titmuss is clearly correct in his contention that tax policies constitute critical elements in social policy. Although the overall distribution of these indirect outlays does not help those most in need, taxation remains a key instrument for implementing public aims. Fiscal welfare and occupational welfare are analogous to regular spending, and all three systems must be assessed if one is to understand, or to affect, the nature of contemporary social welfare. Occupational, fiscal, and social welfare can each be assessed as a distinct phenomenon, but their interactions have a major bearing on the nature of the overall welfare system.

The occupational system, for example, frequently supplements public provisions, as with retirement pensions. In areas such as health insurance, it often provides support where government action is absent. Of course, meeting social needs through the occupational system discourages the development of public policy to meet the needs of those who are not employed. The repeal of the short-lived Catastrophic Medicare Bill of 1988 reflected, in large measure, the broad coverage provided by private "medigap" policies to retired workers. A major concern on the left, therefore, is that occupational welfare—welfare principally for the middle classes and well-to-do—undermines support for the mainline welfare state. Public provision is already a dubious public objective; an expanded occupational system, it is feared, may further reduce the constituency for positive government.

The provision of social welfare transfers through indirect tax expenditures, such as deductions for mortgage interest and exclusions on employee benefits, has grown dramatically in recent decades. Between 1970 and 1988, for example, the number of tax expenditure items in the federal code increased by almost one-third, from 71 to 94. In the area of income maintenance, the value of benefits funded through indirect outlays grew at a faster rate than benefits financed through direct expenditures. Rising from $25 billion in 1978 to $93 billion in 1986, the cost of these benefits rose from 16 percent to 32 percent of direct federal outlays.[15]

Regulatory Transfers

There is a significant limitation in utilizing a conception of social welfare that is restricted to concrete benefits—be they occupational or public; income, goods, or services; or funded directly or through tax arrangements—since they ignore the importance of other sorts of social interventions. At all levels of government, public activities that enhance community well-being involve more than the direct and indirect allocation of income or service tangibles.

Social welfare objectives are also advanced by the regulatory powers of government. Regulatory powers, of course, have long been used to pursue health, safety, and welfare goals in employment and housing; the licensing and certification of publicly funded residential facilities and hospitals; and the financing, planning, budgeting, and staffing arrangements governing the implementation of federal aid programs. Today's social regulation, far broader in scope, advances a variety of explicit social objectives, many of which cannot otherwise be pursued because of budgetary restrictions.

One such area of regulation imposes obligations on the private sector to help needy groups such as children and the handicapped—thus reducing the need for direct public programs. Thus, for example, many state and local governments have enacted child-care ordinances affecting developers of commercial properties. In San Francisco, a typical instance, major developers must either provide on-site care for employee's children or else pay one dollar per square foot into a special fund to support centers throughout the city.[16] At the state level, Massachusetts has extended access to health care throughout the commonwealth by requiring private businesses to provide medical insurance to all their employees. Other states require private insurance plans to cover a variety of populations and procedures. For example, employers may be obligated to extend insurance coverage to family dependents, such as newborns, as well as to handicapped workers, those needing alcohol treatment, and those requiring home health care. California, in the early 1980s, prohibited insurance companies from denying coverage for the services of social workers, dentists, podiatrists, speech and hearing therapists, and professional counselors and psychologists.

Such mandated benefits—benefits by regulation—permit government to address social and health problems without having to spend money or raise taxes. Regulation, of course, is not free. The private sector pays in one fashion or another, either through higher insurance costs or higher prices for consumers or, occasionally, by withdrawing benefits. It has been argued, for example, that state-mandated programs have caused many small employers to drop health coverage altogether.[17] In a similar vein, many contend that stringent rent control ordinances lead to a decreasing number of available rental units.

In public assistance, a broad political consensus emerged in the 1980s in support of federal regulations to ensure fair child-support payments from absent parents. To increase payment levels and to enforce compliance with court-ordered child-support rulings, federal enactments powerfully strengthened the influence of government over family behavior. The 1984 Child Support Enforcement Amendments required states to establish procedures for withholding support payments from the wages of delinquent (i.e., nonpaying) parents. Later enactments required paternity determinations at birth and compelled states to establish and utilize uniform standards for child-support payments. Perhaps most important, the 1988 Family Support Act required states to withhold wages in cases in which court child-support orders were violated.[18] Since the vast majority of absent fathers are not currently paying support for their children on a regular basis, these federal regulations are likely to increase the income level of lone-parent households.

Such regulatory interventions can advance welfare-state goals. Although someone winds up paying for each measure—be it employers, employees, or separated parents—such approaches substantially broaden the range of ways in which government can address problems. Regulatory substitutes for spending programs, especially attractive in an era of fiscal constraint and tax and spending limits, are likely to expand in importance in the years ahead.

CONCEPTUAL CONTEXT: THE SOCIAL MARKET
AND THE MIXED ECONOMY OF WELFARE

Social welfare policies operate at different levels of comprehensiveness and through various direct, indirect, and regulatory measures. Aside from providing a heightened respect for the complexities of the field, where does all this discussion leave us? In trying to construct an analytic framework, we must grapple with this question: What are the common elements in social welfare policies? There is no single answer with which everyone engaged in policy analysis will agree. Obviously, the apparent commonalities in the design of social welfare policy vary according to the level of abstraction on which the analysis is conducted. In this respect, an analytic framework is somewhat like a microscope: It provides a conceptual lens through which the phenomena under investigation may be studied. Unlike the microscope, however, most analytic frameworks do not have a wide range of focus. Rather, they tend to lock onto some level of abstraction that magnifies and draws our attention to the phenomenon being examined in the context of a distinct conceptual set. The analytic framework we use in this book places social welfare policy in the context of a *benefit-allocation mechanism functioning outside the economic marketplace.* As Marshall has observed,

> In contrast to the economic process, it is a fundamental principle of the Welfare State that the market value of an individual cannot be the measure of his right to welfare. The central function of welfare, in fact, is to supersede the market by taking goods and services out of it, or in some way to control and modify its operations so as to produce a result which it would not have produced itself.[19]

To say that social welfare allocations are made outside the economic marketplace offers a rather nebulous picture of the conceptual domain within which social welfare policy operates. To clarify this domain we must draw a distinction between social and economic markets. This distinction rests on the principles and motives that guide the allocation of provisions. The social market of the welfare state allocates goods and services primarily in response to financial need, dependency, altruistic sentiments, social obligations, charitable motives, and the wish for communal security. In contrast, benefits in a capitalist society are distributed through the economic market, ideally on the basis of individual initiative, ability, productivity, and a desire for profit.[20] As illustrated in Figure 2–1, the social market contains both a public and a private sector. The public sector encompasses federal, state, and local governments and accounts for the largest portion of goods and services distributed in the welfare state. Provisions allocated through the private sector of the social market include the informal efforts of family and friends and the services provided by voluntary agencies and, occasionally, by profit-oriented agencies. The last overlap with the activities of the

THE SOCIAL MARKET OF THE
WELFARE STATE

THE ECONOMIC MARKET OF
CAPITALIST SOCIETY

Public Sector	Private Sector			
Direct provision of transfers by Federal, state, and local government. Indirect transfers through tax expenditures Regulatory transfers	Informal supports by family and friends	Services by voluntary (non-profit) agencies	Services by profit-making agencies	Goods and services produced and distributed by profit-making enterprises

FIGURE 2-1 Social and Economic Markets of Welfare.

economic market, which to some extent blurs the boundary between the private social welfare sector and the economic market.

The allocation of provisions in the social market involves both the financing and the delivery of benefits, and these roles are not always performed by the same unit. A public agency, for example, can hire its own staff to provide day-care services for low-income mothers, or through purchase-of-service arrangements, it may pay to have the service provided by a voluntary agency, by a profit-making enterprise, or by members of the client's family. In this manner the roles of public, voluntary, profit-oriented, and informal units are variously combined. The resulting variety in the modes of benefit allocations constitutes what Ken Judge refers to as the "mixed economy of welfare."[21]

Although profit-oriented agencies still constitute only a small segment of the social market, their numbers have been growing since the mid-1960s. Proprietary agencies are now prominently represented in many social service program areas including homemaker/chore, day care, transportation, meals-on-wheels, and employment training. The most conspicuous area of growth has been in nursing home care. About one-half of nursing home costs are paid with public (mainly Medicaid) funds, although close to 82 percent of all nursing homes are operated on a for-profit basis.[22] This area of service is typically referred to as the nursing home "industry"; the child-care "industry" looms just over the horizon. The penetration of profit-oriented agencies into the welfare state imbues the social market with the spirit of capitalism and inclines the modus operandi of social welfare allocations toward that of the market economy.

During the 1980s, proposals for the expansion of profit-oriented enterprises in the social market gained serious consideration. Robert Reich, for example, advanced a scheme for government and business partnerships aimed at integrating social welfare and economic development. Under this arrangement, he says, "We can expect that a significant part of the present welfare system will be replaced by government grants to businesses that agree to hire the chronically unemployed."[23] Public funds for social services such as day care, health care, and disability benefits would be allocated to businesses, eliminating the need for government administration. Joined in this way to business institutions, social welfare provisions would serve an important purpose by contributing to the formation of "human capital". Herein lies what is certainly the strongest attraction of such mergers: They confer on welfare activities the legitimacy and value of a productive force promoting growth in the market economy.

However, there is an aspect of mixing welfare services with the market economy that runs counter to the communal and charitable ethos that typifies the humanistic character of social welfare. The merger of welfare programs and private enterprise assumes a harmony among social and economic purposes that is not self-evident. Reward for merit and productivity is hardly consonant with support for benefits based on need and dependency. A system that encourages taking risks for financial gain is unlikely to invest serious effort in the pursuit of equality and security. The fundamental issue is how a capitalist society deals with conflicting objectives such as meeting needs versus rewarding merit, promoting freedom versus providing security, and providing equality of opportunity versus ensuring equality of outcome.

The functioning of the social and economic markets in industrialized capitalist societies is based on a complex relationship between individual ambitions and collective responsibilities. It is a relationship filled with tensions and contradictions. Marshall suggests that these tensions help maintain a constructive balance between charitable and profit impulses (or need and merit) and so contribute to a healthy society.[24] It is difficult to imagine that such a balance might be improved by an influx of profit-oriented agencies to commercialize the social market.

Some analysts believe that because social welfare policies entail benefit allocations outside the market system, they provide for unilateral exchange, or *social transfers,* (from society to the individual) rather than reciprocal or *market exchanges* (from buyer to seller).[25] Although we will analyze social welfare policies as unilateral designs for allocating benefits that are usually free or well subsidized, it should be recognized that those on the receiving end often incur stringent obligations. As Zald points out, "Although many welfare recipients may not pay money for the service that they receive, they may pay much more: gratitude, political acquiescence, and the like. Thus the lack of reciprocity depends on specification of coin."[26]

ELEMENTS OF AN ANALYTIC FRAMEWORK: DIMENSIONS OF CHOICE

Within the benefit-allocation framework, social welfare policies can be interpreted as choices among principles determining what benefits are offered, to whom they are offered, how they are delivered, and how they are financed. The elements of this framework, of course, are not physical structures of the sort a microscope might reveal. Rather, they are social constructs that are used in the intellectual process of making choices. The major dimensions of choice in this framework may be expressed in the form of four questions:

1. What are the bases of social allocations?
2. What are the types of social provisions to be allocated?
3. What are the strategies for the delivery of these provisions?
4. What are the ways to finance these provisions?

A few words are in order about the genesis of this approach. Eveline Burns utilized this general framework in her seminal study *Social Security and Public Policy,* focusing on four types of decisions that informed program design in the realm of social security: (1) those related to the nature and amount of benefits, (2) those concerned with eligibility and the types of risks to be covered, (3) those regarding the means of finance, and (4) those relevant to the structure and character of administration. Our analytic approach in this book seeks to extend the pathways of policy analysis charted by Burns and others.[27] These dimensions of choice cut across the entire field of social welfare policy rather than simply delineating choices specific to a single program sector.

We treat the bases of social allocations, types of social provisions, strategies of delivery, and modes of finance as dimensions of choice because each will be examined along three axes: (1) the range of alternatives within each dimension, (2) the social values that support them, and (3) the theories or assumptions that underlie them. This framework is illustrated in Figure 2–2.

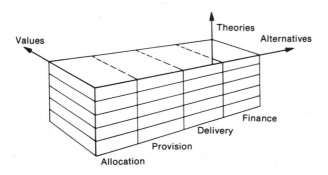

FIGURE 2-2 Dimensions of Choice.

Allocations and Provisions

The first two dimensions of choice are expressed in the question "Who gets what?" The bases of social allocations address the "who" of social welfare policy.

Social welfare policies always include some designation of beneficiaries, those whose welfare is to be enhanced through policy implementation. Although these policies are supposed to serve the abstract interests of society as a whole—the elusive "public interest"—direct and immediate benefits are usually distributed differentially among segments of the population. We will have more to say about notions of the public interest in Chapter 8. For now, it is enough to say that few social welfare policies help everybody equally. Choices are required, and they are continually made as trade-offs among what policy planners think is desirable, what circumstances necessitate, and what the public will countenance.

Numerous criteria are used to determine who is eligible for social provisions. These criteria include marital status, employment status, residence, family size, IQ, health, age, education, length of military service, ethnicity, gender, disability status, and income. Our concern in examining the bases of social allocations, however, is not to catalog the many possibilities that may be employed to define eligibility. Rather, the issues of choice we address focus on a set of general principles that informs the design of eligibility criteria. *The bases of social allocations refer to the choices among the various principles on which social provisions are made accessible to particular people and groups in society.*

The bases of social allocations are the guidelines for the operational definition of eligibility criteria. *What* people become eligible to receive involves policy choices about the nature of the social provision. In policy analysis the traditional choice has been between whether benefits are offered *in cash* (money) or *in kind* (goods or services). There are, however, other types of benefits that are commonly distributed through social welfare policy, such as power, vouchers, and opportunities, which permit different degrees of consumer sovereignty than the in cash/in kind dichotomy. In Chapter 4 we analyze the range of alternatives in this dimension of choice. Our objective is to distinguish the various forms of social provision and their implications for consumers of social welfare benefits. Thus *questions about the nature of social provisions refer to the kinds of benefits that are delivered.*

Delivery and Finance

The third dimension of choice addresses alternative strategies for delivering social provisions. Here the choices are not about who and what but rather about *how.* That is, after decisions about the who and what of policy are resolved, arrangements must be made for getting the provisions selected to the eligible consumers. The ways in which delivery systems are designed to achieve this objective are of crucial significance to the first two dimensions of choice because it is through the delivery mechanism that policy guidelines regarding eligibility and the nature of provision are operationally expressed. Consider, for example, a proposal for new employment counseling services. Should they be centrally located in a downtown facility or dispersed in small neighborhood units? Should counselors be trained professionals or local residents? Should the services be offered if they duplicate others that already exist? Should they be incorporated under a unified administrative umbrella that includes health and legal aid? These choices influence who gets served and the type of benefits they receive, policies about the nature of provisions and bascs of allocations notwithstanding. Included among these design elements are overall composition of the service system, linkages among service units, location of facilities, and caliber and adequacy of personnel.

In examining the design of delivery systems, one usually discusses strategies to enhance the flow of services from providers to consumers, a point to which much of the literature in this area is addressed. Since the federal social service cutbacks of the 1980s, however, increasing attention has been given to strategies for restricting or rationing services. When we examine this dimension of choice in Chapter 5 we will analyze strategies both for facilitating and for rationing service delivery. *Delivery strategies refer to the alternative organizational arrangements among providers and consumers of social welfare benefits in the context of local community systems (i.e., neighborhood, city, and county), the level at which the overwhelming majority of providers and consumers come together.*

If social welfare policies are viewed as benefit-allocation mechanisms functioning outside the marketplace, choices must be made concerning the sources and types of financing. It is important to recognize the distinction between funding benefits and delivering them. To clarify where funding ends and delivery begins, it is helpful to think in terms of a simple flowchart. *Funding choices involve questions concerning the source of funds and the fashion in which funds flow from the point of origin to the point of service provision.* Delivery choices involve the organizational arrangements that move social provisions, either in cash or other forms, from providers to consumers.

Some of the major financing alternatives concern whether money is derived from public, private, or mixed sources; the level of government involved; and the types of taxes levied. Financing also involves the administrative conditions that govern funding arrangements such as grant-in-aid formulas, specification of purpose, and timing. This dimension of choice will be examined in Chapters 6 and 7.

Although the dimensions of allocation, provision, delivery, and finance will be analyzed separately in the following chapters, each with its own range of alternatives, it should be emphasized that in the design of social welfare policies most decisions are interdependent. For instance, a decentralized delivery system results when the social provision is in the form of power, as in policies for greater parental control of local education that transfer decision-making authority from middle-class professional bureaucracies to service consumers. Similarly, the bases of social allocations and methods of finance are closely interwoven when eligibility for benefits involves some form of payment, as in subsidized user charges and contributory social insurance.

These four dimensions of choice encompass fundamental issues in the design of social welfare policies. The process through which these issues are resolved raises a different set of choices, choices that concern the design of decision-making arrangements. In Chapter 8 we explore the implications of alternative arrangements for social welfare planning.

AN EXAMPLE: THE TRANSFORMATION
OF SOCIAL SERVICES

At this point we will tie the dimensions of choice to a concrete case so the reader can see how the framework is applied. The case selected involves the evolution of social services over the last three decades.[28] The focus is on social service provisions originally established under several titles of the Social Security Act: Titles I (Old-Age Assistance,), IV-A (Aid to Families With Dependent Children, AFDC), X (Aid to the Blind), and XIV (Aid to the Permanently and Totally Disabled). Incorporated into Title XX of the Social Security Act in 1974, these provisions were refashioned in their current form in 1981 as the Social Services Block Grant. There are, of course, other sources from which social services emanate, such as the Adoption Assistance and Child Welfare Act of 1980; the Older Americans Act, first legislated in 1965; and the Anti-Drug Abuse Act of 1988. The Social Services Block Grant has been selected as the focal point of analysis because it provides the largest single source of social service funds. In the most concrete sense, it represents the cornerstone of the structure of social services in the United States.

Any discussion of developments in the social services over the last 30 years must take into account the substantial increase in federal spending in this area. Between 1963 and 1971 federal grants to states for social services grew more than threefold, from approximately $194 million to $740 million. That was a moderate rate of growth compared with the precipitous rise from $740 million to $1.7 billion that occurred between 1971 and 1972. Of course, $1.7 billion is no trifling sum; but when state estimates for 1973 indicated a potential increase in expenditures to $4.7 billion, Congress enacted a $2.5 billion ceiling on federal expenditures for social services.[29]

This ceiling on social service funding rose to $2.9 billion by 1981 but was reduced to $2.4 billion in that fiscal year when Title XX was redesignated as the Social Services Block Grant. Since then, federal spending on social services has gradually risen, reaching $2.8 billion in 1990.

Although it is important to appreciate the growth of federal funding as a force in the general development of social services, the focus of this case study is on the substantive program changes that have accompanied expanded federal support. In this analysis, the rise in federal expenditures can be seen as a quantitative backdrop to a qualitative transformation in the nature of the social services.

Social services experienced several significant changes since they first gained solid financial support in the 1962 Social Security amendments. There has been a consistent broadening of eligibility standards and an enlargement of the population receiving services. In 1962, eligibility was limited to public assistance recipients, former recipients, and others who in light of their precarious life circumstances were potential candidates for public assistance. The Bureau of Family Services defined "potential recipients" as those who might reasonably be expected to require financial aid within one year of their application for services. Whereas these standards offered the possibility of extending services beyond the immediate public assistance population, it was not realized in practice. At that early stage, both program funds and trained social service workers were in relatively short supply. Since political support for the 1962 amendments was predicated on the idea that intensive social work services would reduce the size of public assistance rolls, the recipient population clearly held first priority on service allocations. Despite those immediate limitations, the possibility of extending service eligibility was established in principle.

This principle was applied in the Social Security amendments of 1967, under which persons became eligible for social services if it was determined that they might become welfare recipients within the next five years. Even more significant was the introduction of the concept of *group eligibility*, whereby residents of low-income neighborhoods and other groups (such as those in institutional settings) could become eligible for service.

By 1972, people who were not receiving welfare were well represented among the social service clientele, and their number was growing. One reason for this growth was that the 1967 amendments had provided a loophole through which states could squeeze many locally funded services into federally funded programs, eligible for 75 percent cost reimbursement.

The Title XX Social Service amendments of 1974 ushered in a new set of eligibility criteria that further extended entitlements. Under the enactment, the federal government designated three categories of people who were eligible for services: (1) income-maintenance recipients, (2) income eligibles, and (3) universal eligibles. *Income-maintenance* recipients were those receiving public assistance, including Supplementary Security Income (SSI) and Medicaid; these recipients were poor according to already-existing means-tested standards. Title XX regulations required each state to target at least 50 percent of its federal funds for people in this category. *Income-eligible* recipients included those who earned up to 115 percent of their state's median income. States could offer services free of charge to those whose income did not exceed 80 percent of the state median. For those earning between 80 and 115 percent of the median, services could be offered on a subsidized basis for reasonable income-related fees. The *universal* category referred to services that were available free of charge to all, without regard to income: information and referral services, protective services for children and adults, and family planning. In 1978, a fourth category, *group eligibility*, was added. This category allowed states to designate groups of people with similar characteristics—for example, the elderly and the institutionalized mentally ill—as eligible if it could be shown that 75 percent of the group's members had incomes less than 90 percent of the state's median income.

When Ronald Reagan's 1981 Omnibus Budget Reconciliation Act superseded Title XX with the Social Services Block Grant (SSBG), federal eligibility requirements were eliminated altogether, leaving states free to exercise whatever standards of eligibility they desired. Despite the discretion afforded them, however, most states continue to employ much the same eligibility standards as before.[30]

As eligibility restrictions were eliminated, the scope and content of social provisions changed. Social services were originally advanced in 1962 as a way to prevent and reduce dependency—through intensive social casework services that presumably would rehabilitate the poor, changing their behavior in ways that would help them become economically independent.[31] Although social services also included other basic forms of provision such as homemakers and foster home care, the essential feature was the provision of social casework. Although it was not specified in the law, "welfare professionals in the Bureau of Family Services knew more or less what they meant by 'services.' Fundamentally and at a minimum, it meant casework by a trained social worker."[32]

There is an intangible quality about casework service that makes the exact nature of the provision difficult to specify. This vagueness has led to the cynical observation that such service "is anything done for, with, or about the client by the social worker. If a social worker discusses a child's progress in school with an AFDC mother, a check is made under 'services related to education. . . .' When the discussion turns to the absent father and possible reconciliation, a check is made under 'maintaining family and improving family functioning.'"[33] In a similar vein, Handler and Hollingsworth characterize public assistance services as "little more than a relatively infrequent, pleasant chat."[34]

At its best, social casework is certainly a more skillful and nurturing enterprise than these comments suggest. But large caseloads, the demands of eligibility certification (while trying to establish a casework relationship), the diversity of clientele (many of whom did not need or want casework services but were forced to accept them), and the omnipresent bureaucratic regulations of public assistance were hardly conducive to effective practice.[35] In any event, whatever its powers and benefits, social casework was not a cure for poverty. The addition of almost 1 million recipients to the public assistance rolls between 1962 and 1966 dramatically proved this point.

The failure to reduce economic dependency combined with social casework's intangible quality made these services a prime target of congressional disillusion, a disillusion that was reflected in the 1967 Social Security Act amendments, under which casework services were deemphasized. The 1967 amendments opened the way for a broader conception of social services. Before, federal grants for services were used mainly to pay the salaries of social caseworkers.[36] In contrast, the regulations implementing the 1967 amendments "created such a comprehensive array of specific services that literally almost any service was federally reimbursable."[37] At the same time, greater emphasis was placed on the delivery of services far more tangible than social casework. According to Derthick, "A distinction soon began to develop between 'soft' and 'hard' services. Advice and counseling from a caseworker were 'soft' . . . and presumably less valuable than daycare centers, or drug treatment centers, or work training, which were 'hard,'" and which soon became much more widely available. "The changed conception and changed social context helped lay the basis for granting funds for a much wider range of activity than the daily routines of caseworkers."[38]

With the passage of the 1974 social service amendments, the movement toward diversification reached new heights. Under Title XX, each state was free to support whatever social services it deemed appropriate for its communities. The only requirement was that these services be directed to one of five federally specified goals, which were so broadly stated as to encompass almost anything the imagination of social service planners could devise. In the first year of implementation, Title XX plans for the 50 states and the District of Columbia specified a total of 1,313 services.[39]

The substantive range of services today is illustrated in Table 2–2, which shows services grouped into the 25 categories devised by the federal government in 1990 for tabulation and analysis. Although many federal reporting requirements and regulations were eliminated in the 1981 conversion from Title XX to SSBG, there have recently been new requirements mandating annual reports, uniform definitions of services, and specific information on the number of people receiving services, the amount of SSBG funds going for each service, methods of service delivery, and criteria

TABLE 2–2   Title XX Service Categories

Adoption Services
Case Management Services
Congregate Meals
Counseling Services
Adult Day Care Services
Child Day Care Services
Employment, Education, and Training Services
Family Planning Services
Foster Care Services for Adults
Foster Care Services for Children
Health Related and Home Health Services
Home Based Services
Home Delivered Meals
Housing Services
Information and Referral Services
Legal Services
Pregnancy and Parenting Services for Young Parents
Prevention and Intervention Services
Protective Services for Adults
Protective Services for Children
Recreational Services
Residential Treatment Services
Special Services for the Developmentally Disabled,
    the Blind, and the Physically Disabled
Special Services for Juvenile Delinquents
Transportation Services
Other Services

Source: *Social Legislation Information Service,* Vol. 31, no. 32 (April 23, 1990), 125–126.

for eligibility. Today, some states offer over 20 services, whereas two states use all of their funds to support just one or two services. Some states have also attempted to mesh Title XX funds with other federal, state, and local social service dollars to consolidate their services and budgetary planning.[40]

Along with the increasing emphasis on tangible services and the diversification of social service content, a profound change in the purpose of the social services was taking place. The 1962 amendments were aimed almost exclusively at reducing poverty; under Title XX there developed a service network largely concerned with maintenance and care and directed more at enhancing human development and the general quality of life than at reducing economic dependency.[41] The first major step in this direction was the 1967 divorce of income-maintenance functions from social service functions in the public assistance program.[42] In 1977, this administrative separation was reinforced at the federal level by placing income-maintenance programs under the Social Security Administration and joining social service and human development programs under the Office of Human Development Services (OHDS). This trend is reflected in SSBG's current emphasis on services that are not associated with notions of personal deficiency or inadequate character, such as transportation and meals on wheels for the elderly, home-based services for the disabled, and child day care.

Along with the separation of financial aid from the provision of social services, responsibility for the delivery of services became more dispersed through the increasing use of purchase-of-service arrangements between public agencies and social service providers in the private sector. Under the 1962 amendments, state public assistance agencies were enjoined from using federal funds to purchase services directly from voluntary agencies. It was possible, however, to purchase these services indirectly with grants to other public agencies, which could then "contract out." Opportunities for purchase of services from private sources were broadened significantly when the 1967 Social Security amendments authorized purchase arrangements for a wide array of activities. Although the amendments allowed state agencies to purchase services directly from private agencies, private agency donations could not be used as the states' 25 percent matching share if those contributions reverted to the donor's facility.[43] This restriction was lifted in 1974.

Over the last three decades these developments have generated an enormous expansion in the systematic use of public funds to purchase private and/or voluntary services. Given the virtual elimination of federal reporting requirements in the 1981 SSBG, it is difficult to calculate the precise magnitude of purchase arrangements. It is estimated, however, that nonprofit providers receive about 50 percent of all federal social service dollars.[44]

These changes in the scope and delivery of provisions were accompanied by basic reforms in federal financing. Under the 1962 laws, federal financing was open-ended, with the states reimbursed for 75 percent of costs for recipients in the four public assistance categories: the aged, the blind, the disabled, and families with dependent children. The 1967 amendments expanded the range of services and clientele that might qualify for federal funds. With this expansion the definitions of social services and client-eligibility standards were loosely drawn. Whether a particular service for certain clients qualified for federal reimbursement depended in large part on local interpretation rather than on a clearly defined statutory formula. The most enterprising states made the boldest interpretations, claimed the greatest need, and received the largest proportional share of federal grants for social services. In the states' scuffle for federal funds, grantsmanship was the name of the game. Three states—New York, Illinois, and California—were the biggest winners, together receiving 58 percent of federal grants in 1972.[45]

This open-ended approach to financing underwent fundamental revisions with the 1974 Title XX amendments. The new legislation incorporated the social service provisions originally financed under the four public assistance categories (Titles I, IV-A, X, and XIV of the Social Security Act) into a single grant (Title XX) program. With the $2.5 billion ceiling that Congress placed on social services, financing was no longer open-ended. This limitation ushered in a change in allocative procedures that tied federal allotments to a formula based strictly on a state's population. Each state was thereby entitled to a proportional share of Title XX funds, but the receipt of the funds was contingent on meeting certain regulations and supplying a local matching share. When the SSBG was enacted in 1981, the local share requirement was dropped along with most other federal regulations. The SSBG allocations continue on a population basis, spreading funds in a way that yields a rough form of interstate equalization. However, this mode of finance is not sensitive to the greater needs of poorer states.

APPLICATION OF THE FRAMEWORK

Now let us superimpose the dimensions of choice on the complex social service program changes that have occurred over the last three decades. Our approach to policy analysis provides a way of thinking about this program that extracts and organizes its major elements, making the whole more readily comprehensible. Using the framework we have outlined, the substance of social service policy may be divided into our four choice categories and summarized as follows:

1. *The bases of social allocations: Selective to universal.* In 1962, eligibility for social services was means-tested, effectively limited to recipients of the four categorical aid programs—Aid to Families with Dependent Children, Aid to the Blind, Old-Age Assistance, and Aid to the Permanently and Totally Disabled. By 1974, eligibility criteria were broadened by the Title XX amendments to include many middle-income beneficiaries. The Social Services Block Grant, which revised Title XX in 1981, gave the states latitude to impose any eligibility criteria they wished. Since most states continue to employ the limited requirements of earlier years, it would be an exaggeration to say that in the 1990s there is universal access to social services. Nevertheless, there has been a pronounced trend from selective to universal access.

2. *The nature of social provision: Intangible and limited to concrete and diversified.* In 1962, social services consisted primarily of social casework to help families improve their functioning and gain economic independence. What these services entailed, beyond some form of psychotherapeutic counseling, was only vaguely defined. More tangible forms of service were established in 1967, emphasizing employment training, day care, and family planning. By 1975, diversification of social services had grown to include 41 categories of provision. Under the 1981 conversion to the SSBG, states may offer any kind of social service imaginable.

3. *The delivery system: Public and income maintenance linked to public, private, and free-standing.* Up to 1967, social service and income-maintenance functions were combined and were delivered by the same administrative unit. Caseworkers distributed financial aid and also provided social services. After 1967 these functions were administratively divorced and performed by different workers, with an emphasis on hiring AFDC recipients to perform certain service roles related to day care and eligibility determination. Also, since 1975, an increased reliance on purchase-of-service arrangements by state and local governments has drawn an increasing number of private nonprofit agencies into what was originally a delivery system of public agencies.

4. *Finance: Open-ended categorical grant to fixed-amount block grant.* In 1962 the federal government reimbursed states for 75 percent of all social service costs for recipients in the public assistance categories. When these services were incorporated into Title XX, a $2.5 billion expenditure ceiling was established, with grants allocated to states according to a formula based strictly on population size. To qualify for grants, states were required to supply a 25 percent local match. For all practical purposes, Title XX amounted to a block grant. In 1981, the SSBG gave states almost complete discretion in the use of these grants and no longer required matching funds or reporting or planning.

In specifying the dimensions of choice—the first step of a two-step process in social welfare policy analysis—we asked these questions: What benefits are to be allocated and to whom? How are these benefits to be delivered and financed? These questions may be answered without reference to purpose. Now we turn to the second step in the analysis process—the "why" question, addressing the values, theories, and assumptions that inform social choices.

SOCIAL VALUES AND SOCIAL CHOICE IN PUBLIC ASSISTANCE

Some answers to the why of social choice can be found through the explication of underlying values. The importance of illuminating the values embedded in policy designs is stated by Alva Myrdal:

> An established tendency to drive values underground, to make analysis appear scientific by omitting certain basic assumptions from the discussion, has too often emasculated the social sciences as agencies for rationality in social and political life. To be truly rational, it is necessary to accept the obvious principle that a social program, like a practical judgment, is a conclusion based upon premises of values as well as upon facts.[46]

The analysis of values and social welfare policy may be approached from at least two levels. At the upper level the analytic focus is on policy in the generic sense. Rather than examining each of its dimensions of choice and the values expressed therein, this level of analysis addresses broad purposes. Specifically, to what extent does the policy achieve distributive justice? At this level of generality three core values shape the design of policy: equality, equity, and adequacy. As we will see by examining the changing arrangements for financial aid under public assistance, these values are not always in harmony.

In addition to providing social services, the main function of categorical public assistance programs has been to provide financial assistance to the needy. When these programs were established under the Social Security Act of 1935, three categories of needy people were eligible for aid: the elderly under Title I, Old-Age Assistance (OAA); dependent children under Title IV, Aid to Dependent Children (ADC); and the blind, under Title X, Aid to the Blind (AB). A fourth category was added in 1950 under Title XIV, Aid to the Permanently and Totally Disabled (APTD).

In 1961, Aid to Dependent Children was changed to Aid to Families with Dependent Children (AFDC), reflecting an emphasis on maintaining the family unit. Temporary legislation, made permanent and universal in 1988, required the states to provide financial aid to children of unemployed parents (AFDC-UP).

These four categorical programs were financed by the federal government and administered by the states, with each state contributing a variable matching share, the size of which was based on its wealth. A fifth public aid option, General Assistance (GA), is available for individuals who do not qualify for support under the federally financed programs. Funded entirely by states and localities, General Assistance is usually more parsimonious than the federal categories in the duration and amount of assistance.

In 1965 a broad program of medical assistance for the poor was enacted, unifying the various arrangements for meeting medical costs that existed under the four categorical programs. Popularly known as Medicaid, this program also allows the states to offer payments to the medically indigent, people whose economic resources are insufficient to pay all their medical costs but who do not otherwise qualify as needy for cash assistance.

Up through the early 1970s, Medicaid and the five categorical programs (OAA, APTD, AFDC, AB, and GA), along with food stamps, formed the general core of public assistance in this country. Within the framework established by federal legislation, the states had considerable latitude to design programs according to their own local norms and preferences. One reflection of this policy is the 20-odd different agency names used by the 50 states to designate the bureaucracies administering the public assistance programs: Public Welfare, Social Services, Family and Children Services, Institutions and Agencies, Human Resources, and Economic Security, to name only a few. There are more profound variations concerning standards of eligibility and levels of assistance. For example, in 1989, AFDC benefits for a family of four ranged from $824 in California to $221 in Texas, with the U.S. median around $430.[47] In more than half the states,

AFDC payments equalled less than the minimum required to meet basic needs according to cost standards that these states themselves had set.

The structure of categorical public assistance was dramatically altered by the Social Security Act amendments of 1972, under which OAA, AB, and APTD were replaced by the consolidated Supplemental Security Income (SSI) program, which went into operation in 1974. In contrast to the incorporation of the categorical social services under Title XX, which increased state administrative authority, the replacement of the financial aid categories by SSI brought these programs entirely under federal control (see Figure 2–3).

Not included in SSI, AFDC continues to be administered by the states and jointly financed through federal-state matching. Administered by the Social Security Administration and supported totally by federal funds, SSI provides uniform cash assistance to the needy, blind, aged, and disabled throughout the country. (Most states currently supplement SSI with modest additional state-funded payments.) Average monthly payments to SSI recipients more than doubled from $114 in 1975 to $260 in 1988. The highest amounts go to the blind, whose monthly payment averaged $306 in 1988.[48]

In allocating financial aid outside of economic markets, public assistance represents an effort to alter the distribution of resources from that produced by the market economy. In this effort the aim of public assistance is to further distributive justice in society—an undertaking that must come to grips with the values of equality, equity, and adequacy.

Equality

Although it is one of the foundation stones of distributive justice, equality is a value open to interpretation. At least two salient notions were differentiated by Aristotle: numerical equality and proportional equality.[49] These concepts represent the egalitarian and meritarian elements of distributive justice. *Numerical equality* implies the same treatment of everyone—to all an equal share. *Proportional equality* implies the same treatment of similar persons—to each according to his or her merit or virtue. These interpretations of equality offer conflicting prescriptions for the treatment of dissimilar persons. With the concept of proportional equality, Vlastos points out, "The meritarian view of justice paid reluctant homage to the egalitarian one by using the vocabulary of equality to assert the justice of inequality."[50] To clarify this distinction and to reduce the definitional awkwardness, we will use the term *equality* in its numerical sense and will subsume the meaning of proportional equality under the value of *equity*.

Social welfare policy is influenced by the value of equality with regard to the outcome of benefit allocations. Specifically, the value prescribes that benefits should be allocated to equalize the distribution of resources and

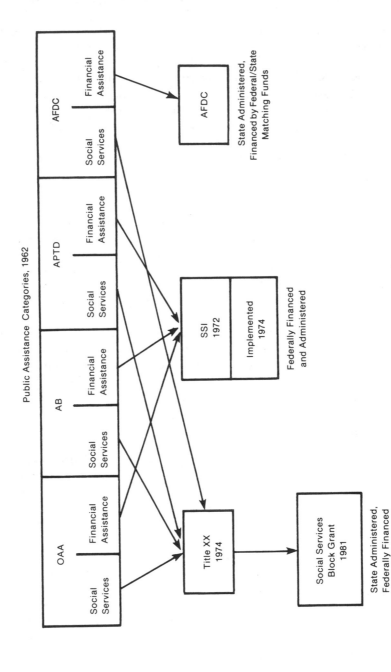

FIGURE 2-3 Reorganization of Public Assistance: Social Services and Financial Aid.

opportunities. In some policies this value is predominant, for instance, in the development of quota hiring plans for the equal allocation of work roles among different groups of people. In a modified version there are opportunity-oriented policies whereby the equal shares objective is recast in terms of equal opportunity. Fair housing legislation, for example, demands that people, whatever their racial and ethnic characteristics, receive the same treatment in their quest for shelter. It does not, however, ensure equal results for everyone.

In public assistance, the introduction of uniform federal grants under SSI was, in part, a measure to promote greater equality in financial aid across the country. The influence of the equality goal in shaping the design of public assistance is also evident in the extent to which money is shifted from wealthy states and individuals toward those that are poor. Although such redistribution takes place through public assistance, it falls considerably short of creating even a roughly equal share for all because distributive justice is also responsive to other values.

Equity

Equity denotes a conventional sense of fair treatment. There is a proportional quality to notions of fair treatment—if you do half the work you deserve half the reward. People's deservedness should be based on their contributions to society, modified only by special considerations for those whose inability to contribute is clearly not of their own making. Accordingly, there are many "equitable inequalities" that are normatively sanctioned, as in preferential treatment for veterans and unemployment benefits that vary in proportion to prior earnings.

In public assistance, equity is stressed through the doctrine of "less eligibility," first formulated by the English Poor Law Commissioners in 1834. In the commissioners' words,

> It may be assumed that in the administration of relief, the public is warranted in imposing such conditions on the individual relieved, as are conducive to the benefit either of the individual himself, or of the country at large, at whose expense he is to be relieved.
>
> The first and most essential of all conditions, a principle which we find universally admitted, even by those whose practice is at variance with it, is that *his situation on the whole shall not be made really or apparently so eligible as the situation of the independent laborer of the lowest class.* [Emphasis added.][51]

One reason for the extremely low level of public assistance in most states is the ingrained belief that aid should not elevate the conditions of recipients above those of the poorest workers. Here, the emphasis on equity supports the maintenance of incentives to work. It is interesting to note that some proponents for increasing AFDC levels argue their case in the name of equity. They do not ask that dissimilar people, those who work and those who do not work, be treated equally and awarded similar standards of living. Rather, the argument is made that motherhood itself should be considered an occupation—one, indeed, that is more trying than most. This view was expressed by a ten-member panel (nine of whom were men) commissioned by the federal government to study the problem of American workers. The panel recommended, among other things, that welfare mothers be subsidized to stay home and care for their children.[52] The case for this policy gains momentum when we calculate the substantial per capita costs of day-care services necessary to allow AFDC mothers to work.[53]

Adequacy

Adequacy refers to the desirability of providing a decent standard of physical and spiritual well-being, quite apart from concerns for whether benefit allocations are equal or differentiated according to merit. Thus, as Frankena explains, the quest for distributive justice involves

> a somewhat vaguely defined but still limited concern for the goodness of people's lives, as well as for their equality. The double concern is often referred to as respect for the intrinsic dignity or value of the human individual. This is not the position of the extreme egalitarian but it is essentially egalitarian in spirit; in any case it is not the position of the meritarian, although it does seek to accommodate such principles.[54]

Standards of adequacy vary according to time and circumstances. In medieval times, serfs were usually given enough to keep them healthy and productive. At the turn of the twentieth century, $624 a year was estimated as a living wage for a family of five in New York City.[55] By 1990, the poverty level for a family of four was $12,700. In addition to the economic aspects of material existence, standards of spiritual well-being also vary. In the Middle Ages these standards had a basically religious connotation: The vicissitudes of life on earth were suffered for spiritual salvation in the hereafter. Today, spiritual well-being is more a secular concern; it involves, for instance, the sense of being able to control one's destiny, freedom of expression, self-realization, security, and happiness.

The value of adequacy is expressed rather faintly in public assistance and honored more in the breach than in reality. Nevertheless, its presence is reflected in the fact that grant levels are not set arbitrarily but are based on state estimates of the costs of basic needs (even though the grants rarely approach the levels of these estimates).

Overall, as a benefit allocation mechanism, public assistance is more responsive to concerns for equity than for adequacy and equality. This emphasis stems, at least in part, from the broader societal context in which the program operates. In capitalist society the value of equity is generally accentuated—those who work hard deserve to be rewarded. According to normative standards, the capitalists are those reaping the just fruits of their labor. Socialist societies theoretically place greater stress on the value of equality. As Marx wrote, "The secret of the expression of value, namely that all kinds of labour are equal and equivalent, because, and so far as they are human, labour in general cannot be deciphered, until the notion of human equality has already acquired the fixity of a popular prejudice."[56] Once the notion of human equality has achieved the status of a popular prejudice, differential treatment of dissimilar people is significantly reduced if not completely abolished because, judged by the most important of characteristics—their humanness—everybody is the same.

From this somewhat lofty perspective, the why of policy design may be analyzed in terms of the quest for distributive justice as it is manifested in the differential realization of adequacy, equity, and equality.[57] Although a policy may emphasize any one of these values, the emphasis is often tempered by the demands of the other two values as efforts are made to approximate distributive justice.

Value Preferences

Moving down a rung, a much larger range of social values enters into the consideration of choice. For instance, the values of privacy, dignity, work, and independence may influence the criteria of eligibility, the forms of social provision, and the design of delivery and finance arrangements. To illustrate, we list in Table 2–3 our four dimensions of choice and some of the competing values that influence them. These four value dichotomies are suggestive and hardly exhaust the range of possibilities. They were selected because the range of values represents variations on central issues of policy choice exemplified in the polarity of individualism versus collectivism. These issues concern the ways and extent to which expressions of individual interests are given free rein or are harnessed in the service of the common good. As Marshall explains,

> The claim of the individual to welfare is sacred and irrefutable and partakes of the character of a natural right . . . but the citizen of the Welfare State does not merely have the right to pursue welfare; he has the right to receive it, even if the pursuit has not been particularly hot. . . . But if we put individualism first, we must put collectivism second. The Welfare State is the responsible promoter and guardian of the welfare of the whole community, which is something more complex than the sum total of the welfare of its individual members arrived at by simple addition. The claims of the individual must always be defined and limited so as to fit into the complex and balanced pattern of the welfare of the community, and that is why the right to welfare can never have the full stature of a natural right. The harmonizing of individual rights with the common good is a problem which faces all human societies.[58]

TABLE 2–3   Dimensions of Choice and Competing Value Orientations

INDIVIDUALIST ORIENTATION	DIMENSIONS OF CHOICE	COLLECTIVIST ORIENTATION
Cost effectiveness ←————————→	Allocation ←————————→	Social effectiveness
Freedom of choice ←————————→	Provision ←————————→	Social control
Freedom of dissent ←————————→	Delivery ←————————→	Efficiency
Local autonomy ←————————→	Finance ←————————→	Centralization

Cost effectiveness may be applied to each dimension of choice. When applied to the bases of social allocations it is measured by the extent to which each dollar of benefit is allocated to those most in need, that is, those least able to purchase what they need in the open marketplace. The guiding thought is that there be no waste of resources. With the cost-effectiveness criterion, individual treatment varies according to individual circumstances. Implementing this value requires a high degree of selectivity in determining those who are eligible for benefits. Applied in the extreme, this value can produce invidious distinctions among people, dividing the community into groups of the dependent and the independent, the incompetent and the self-sufficient.

Social effectiveness may take different forms. One way it is measured in allocative decisions is by the extent to which all individuals are treated as equal members of the social body. Here the notion of effectiveness is related to the fact that nobody who is potentially eligible will feel inhibited about applying for benefits because of shame, stigma, or the organizational rigmarole that is often required to implement selective procedures. Allocations are universal: An individual's special need or defect need not be exposed for scrutiny in order to become eligible for benefits. The "badge of citizenship" is sufficient basis for entitlement. In the AFDC program, for example, the basis of social allocations—a thorough and probing means test of every applicant—is clearly influenced more by concerns for cost effectiveness than social effectiveness.[59]

Titmuss has observed that the apparent strain between cost effectiveness and social effectiveness may be a function of the short-range perspective of using cost-effectiveness calculations, especially for medical benefits, where policy objectives include prevention as well as treatment. For example, if access to medical care entails a means-test investigation that is demeaning, time-consuming, or otherwise inconvenient, clients may procrastinate about seeking aid until their symptoms are so advanced that they can no longer be ignored. At this stage the cost of treatment is usually more expensive. In the long run, cost effectiveness and social effectiveness can be brought into harmony when the universal allocation of medical care saves more through prevention than selective allocations save by limiting treatment only to those in dire need.[60]

Freedom of choice is reflected in provisions that offer recipients considerable latitude in exercising their individual preferences. Thus, for example, when social provisions are in the form of cash, a high degree of consumer sovereignty is preserved. *Social control,* in contrast, is reflected in provisions that limit individual choice. With in-kind provisions, recipients are limited to whatever specific items (housing, medical care, counseling, therapy, advice, information, etc.) are offered. Of course, they have the freedom to take it or leave it, but that is where the choice ends. In some social welfare programs, social provisions are linked so that freedom of choice in one area of provision is bought at the price of social control in another. For example, in AFDC, recipients are given cash grants and may exercise a degree of choice in meeting their daily requirements for material existence. However, under the Family Support Act of 1988, cash assistance in AFDC is linked to participation in work training programs and, in some states, to educational programs as well.[61]

Freedom of dissent and efficiency are values that influence the design of the delivery system whether it is structured primarily along democratic or bureaucratic lines. Blau states the choice succinctly:

> Bureaucratic and democratic structures can be distinguished . . . on the basis of the dominant organizing principle: efficiency or freedom of dissent. Each of these principles is suited for one purpose and not for another. When people set themselves the task of determining the social objectives that represent the interests of most of them, the crucial problem is to provide an opportunity for all conflicting viewpoints to be heard. In contrast, when the task is the achievement of given social objectives, the essential problem to be solved is to discover the efficient, not popular, means for doing so.[62]

In the AFDC program, the delivery system is organized primarily along bureaucratic lines. Clients do not vote to establish the level of their grants or eligibility criteria. In other social welfare programs, however, social provision is so loosely formulated that the local delivery system is charged with the dual purpose of deciding on specific objectives and then carrying out those decisions. For instance, the War on Poverty and Model Cities programs of the 1960s required substantial citizen participation in program planning and implementation. These systems thus incorporated democratic as well as bureaucratic elements in their structure. The problem, it often turned out, is that neither value was served very well, or one value was emphasized at the expense of the other.[63]

Local autonomy and centralization are values that find expression in the financing and administration of programs. Strains between these values are most likely to emerge when costs are shared intergovernmentally or, in the private sector, between nationwide and local voluntary organizations. Cost-sharing arrangements are implemented through federal grants-in-aid that vary along a continuum from broad-purpose block grants to special-purpose categorical grants. The block grant is a lump-sum national contribution for local programs. It carries few specifications or requirements on how the money should be spent beyond that it be applied to a general program realm such as health, community development, or education. This aspect ensures a high degree of local autonomy. At the other end of the continuum is the special-purpose grant with detailed standards. Here, local discretion regarding the use of funds is restricted according to precise federal criteria. In most cost-sharing arrangements, the methods of finance fall somewhere midway on the continuum, reflecting the mutual desirability of local autonomy and national planning.

For example, although based on categorical principles, AFDC contains elements of both values. This grant-in-aid program defines quite specifically the category of the poor the central government is interested in. Various conditions are attached to these grants concerning citizenship, "statewideness," and the provision of services. Yet local autonomy prevails in at least two crucial aspects of the program. States are free to exercise broad discretion in defining both the criteria of need and the amount of financial assistance that is provided. The centralist thrust of the program is mitigated in part because, as Burns explains, "To prescribe in the federal act both the standards of needs which determine eligibility and the minimum level of living to be assured all eligible applicants raises major issues regarding federal interference in an area which traditionally has been thought of as peculiarly a matter for local determination."[64]

THEORY AND SOCIAL CHOICE

The subtle and complex relationships between value preferences and social welfare policies offer one level of insight into the why of social choice. Another dimension of analysis that has a bearing on this question involves theories and assumptions about how clients, delivery systems, methods of finance, and types of social provisions function, both independently and in concert. Much of this kind of theory-derived knowledge is fragmented and only partially verified. This is not to deny the effect of social science knowledge on choice, but rather than overestimate what is known, we use the term *theory* to cover the influence and support that social science insights render to policy choices. We classify as *assumptions* those suppositions for which there has been little systematic effort to obtain and codify evidence. In the general sense the term assumptions is used to designate theories "writ small."

To illustrate, let us look at public assistance. At least three assumptions underpinning major policy choices in this program ,have been seriously challenged by subsequent evidence. First, the 1962 "service" amendments were supported by the belief that the clinical model of casework service would bring about change in the economic dependency of individuals in poverty. Implicit is the theory that poverty is mainly a function of individual deficiencies, deficiencies that can be transformed and alleviated through the casework process. This theory was relatively new. Until the 1950s, assistance recipients were generally considered "victims of external circumstances, such as unemployment, disability, or the death of the family's breadwinner," who "needed to be 'relieved'—not treated or changed."[65] In 1971, after reviewing studies of casework efforts to treat and rehabilitate those on public assistance, Carter concluded,

> It becomes clear that it is time to reassess the purpose of casework services offered welfare recipients and other low income groups for whom problems identified for alleviation are complex and interrelated with other personal, family, and community or societal problems . . . . There are serious questions as to what behavioral changes can be set in motion without provision first being made for a decent level of living and access being provided to a range of social resources within the agency and the community.[66]

Second, the separation of income maintenance from the administration of social services was predicated on the assumption that services would be improved because the caseworker-client relationship would no longer be tinged by the coercive undertones emanating from the worker's discretionary authority over the client's budget. Clients, presumably, would be free to accept or reject services as needed, and caseworkers, released from the task of administering grants, would have more time to engage in a voluntary service enterprise. This is a plausible line of reasoning but one open to critical examination. Neither the strength of the caseworker's coercive powers, and their effects on relationships with clients, nor the extent of client initiative to seek services when routine caseworker visits were terminated was clearly discernible. It is quite possible, as Handler and Hollingsworth suggest, that the coercion argument was exaggerated and, more important, that in the absence of routine home visits welfare clients would be reluctant to seek help from an unknown official. Thus, "requiring welfare clients to take the initiative may have the effect of cutting off a reasonably valuable service that most clients, in their own words, seem to like."[67] Indeed, research findings on this issue reveal that AFDC recipients made higher demands for services and expressed greater satisfaction when service and income maintenance were combined.[68]

As a final example, the 1967 Social Security amendments established a work incentive program to provide training and employment to "all appropriate individuals," which included welfare mothers with young children. (Previously, work programs had been available on a much smaller scale mainly to fathers of families receiving aid under AFDC-UP.) In addition, the provision of day-care services was authorized so that mothers would be free to work, and for an incentive, the first $30 of monthly earnings plus one-third of the remainder were exempted from determination of continued eligibility for assistance. In 1981, "30 plus one-third" was limited to only the first four months of employment, and in 1988 it was replaced altogether with the workfare provisions of the Family Support Act.

The perversely accurate acronym for the Work Incentive Program, WIP, conveys the image of an instrument used to drive beasts of burden. Through some creative bureaucratese it was quickly transformed to WIN. An objective of the 1967 amendments was to swing AFDC services away from traditional social casework toward more practical and concrete work-oriented provisions. This shift from welfare to workfare reflected then, and continues to reflect, the assumption that jobs are available for anyone who really wants to work. The problem is seen primarily as individual deficiency—the lack of skills and adverse attitudes toward work—although of a different nature than those amenable to psychiatric casework. The solution is to equip people for jobs and motivate them to seek employment.

Although facts about WIN are not decisive, what is known suggests that its assumptions, and the assumptions of workfare approaches more generally, are unrealistic. Levitan and Taggart indicated that of the 167,000 people who enrolled in WIN through March 1970, more than one-third dropped out of the program and, all told, only 25,000 got jobs. Those who found jobs were "creamed" from the pool of applicants; that is, those moving into jobs were those best prepared for jobs. This group included a high percentage of unemployed fathers receiving AFDC-UP, who probably would have found employment sooner or later without social assistance. In light of the program's "conspicuously unspectacular performance," the study observes, "the wisdom of expanding WIN is questionable, and the theoretical arguments for such a move are even more dubious."[69]

A more recent analysis of the WIN experience suggests that the program's shortcomings endured to the end. In 1982 only 3 percent of the AFDC clients registered for the WIN program in New York State were placed in a job; an additional 5 percent found employment through their own efforts. In a distinct echo of Levitan and Taggart's findings, the 1982 study observed, "Those who eventually are served generally represent the easiest to employ—those most likely to get jobs without the help of special services."[70] Although recent findings on workfare programs in the five states that formed a model for the Family Support Act of 1988 are somewhat more encouraging, a substantial proportion (from 40 to 80 percent) of participants remained unemployed after 6 to 15 months. The extent to which this type of program can ameliorate the circumstances of welfare recipients, therefore, remains uncertain.[71]

We should point out that in these examples the influences of value and theory on policy have been treated separately as a matter of analytic convenience. In reality, theory and value do not separate quite so neatly. Social facts do not organize themselves into a coherent framework simply by being observed; a theoretical viewpoint is required. But if theory informs the ordering of social facts, what is it that informs theory? On this issue Gunnar Myrdal's insight is worth noting:

> Prior to answers there must be questions, and the questions we raise stem from our interests in the matter, from our valuations. Indeed, our theories and all our scientific knowledge are necessarily pervaded by valuations. . . . Value premises are required not only in order to enable us to draw practical and political inferences from observations and economic analysis, but . . . in order to formulate a theory, to direct our observations, and to carry out our analysis.[72]

SUMMARY

In this chapter we have outlined an analytic approach to the study of social welfare policy. The essence of this approach may be summarized as follows:

1. Viewing social welfare policy as a benefit allocation mechanism requires four types of choices, those pertaining to allocations, provisions, delivery, and finance.
2. Understanding these four dimensions of choice requires knowing the basic alternatives associated with each.
3. Understanding why given alternatives may be preferred over others requires explicating the basic values, theories, and assumptions implicit in policy design.

The implication here is not that certain choices are inherently preferable to others. Different preferences will be registered by different policy planners, depending on the values, theories, and assumptions given the most worth and credence. Our objective in the following five chapters is to take each dimension of choice, delineate the basic policy alternatives, and examine the interplay of relevant values, theories, and assumptions.

NOTES

1. Eveline M. Burns, *Social Security and Public Policy* (New York: McGraw-Hill, 1956), p. ix.
2. Daniel Moynihan, "Toward a National Urban Policy," *Public Interest*, no. 17 (Fall 1969), 5.
3. H. Wentworth Eldrige, "Toward a National Policy for Planning the Environment," in *Urban Planning in Transition*, ed. Ernest Erber (New York: Grossman Publishers, 1970), p. 8.

4. Louis B. Wetmore, "Preparing the Profession for Its Changing Role," in *Urban Planning in Transition,* ed. Ernest Erber (New York: Grossman Publishers, 1970), p. 235.

5. Charles E. Lindblom, "The Science of 'Muddling Through,'" *Public Administration Review,* Vol. 19 (Spring 1959), 79–88.

6. For example, see Alfred Kahn, *Theory and Practice of Social Planning* (New York: Russell Sage, 1969), pp. 18–20; and Diana DiNitto, *Social Welfare: Politics and Public Policy* (Englewood Cliffs, NJ: Prentice Hall, 1990).

7. Ann Kallman Bixby, "Social Welfare Expenditures, 1981 and 1982," *Social Security Bulletin,* Vol. 47, no. 12 (December 1984), 14–22. There are various other schemes for classifying the realms of social welfare policy. For example, Romanyshyn divides welfare programs into three functional types, which he describes as offering social provisions, social service, and social action. John Romanyshyn, *Social Welfare: Charity to Justice* (New York: Random House, 1971), pp. 153–154.

8. Richard Titmuss, *Essays on the "Welfare State,"* 2nd ed. (London: Unwin University Books, 1958), pp. 34–55.

9. *San Francisco Chronicle,* October 11, 1989, p. 6.

10. Ramesh Mishra, *Society and Social Policy* (London: Macmillan, 1977), p. 107.

11. Titmuss, *Essays on the "Welfare State,"* p. 44.

12. Stanley Surrey, *Pathways to Tax Reform* (Cambridge, MA: Harvard University Press, 1973).

13. See, for example, Mimi Abramovitz, "Everyone Is on Welfare: The Role of Redistribution in Social Policy Revisited," *Social Work,* Vol. 28, no. 6 (November/December 1983), 440–445.

14. Irving Kristol, *Two Cheers for Capitalism* (New York: Mentor, 1978), p. 194.

15. For a more detailed analysis, see Neil Gilbert and Barbara Gilbert, *The Enabling State: Modern Welfare Capitalism in America* (New York: Oxford University Press, 1989).

16 *San Francisco Chronicle,* October 8, 1985, p. 10.

17. "How Mandated Benefits Boondoggle the Little Guys," *San Francisco Chronicle,* October 23, 1989, p. 1.

18. Robert Reischauer, "The Welfare Reform Legislation: Directions for the Future," in *Welfare Policy for the 1990s,* eds. Phoebe Cottingham and David Ellwood (Cambridge, Mass: Harvard University Press, 1989) pp. 10–40.

19. T. H. Marshall, "Value Problems of Welfare Capitalism" *Journal of Social Policy,* Vol. 1, no. 1 (January 1972), 19–20.

20. For further discussion of social and economic markets, see Neil Gilbert, *Capitalism and the Welfare State;* and Gilbert and Gilbert, *The Enabling State* (New Haven, CT: Yale University Press, 1983).

21. Ken Judge, "The Mixed Economy of Welfare: Purchase of Service Contracting in the Personal Social Services," Discussion Paper (Canterbury, England: Personal Social Services Research Unit, University of Kent, 1981), p. 195.

22. Gilbert and Gilbert, *The Enabling State,* p. 129.

23. Robert Reisch, *The Next American Frontier* (New York: Times Books, 1983), p. 247.

24. Marshall, "Value Problems of Welfare Capitalism."

25. For example, see Richard Titmuss, *Commitment to Welfare* (New York: Pantheon Books, 1970), p. 124; and Martin Wolins, "The Societal Function of Social Welfare," *New Perspectives,* Vol. 1, no. 1 (Spring 1967), 5.

26. Mayer Zald, ed., *Social Welfare Institutions* (New York: Wiley, 1965), p. 4.

27. The analytic questions with which we will deal have also been explored by Martin Rein, *Social Policy* (New York: Random House, 1970); Titmuss, *Commitment to Welfare,* pp. 130–136; Kahn, *Theory and Practice of Social Planning,* pp. 192–213; and Gilbert Steiner, *The State of Welfare* (Washington, DC: Brookings Institution, 1971), pp. 1–30.

28. This case analysis draws substantially on material originally presented in Neil Gilbert,

"The Transformation of Social Services," *Social Service Review,* Vol. 51, no. 4 (December 1977), 624–649.

29. Martha Derthick, *Uncontrollable Spending for Social Services Grants* (Washington, DC: Brookings Institution, 1975), p. 8.

30. Alan Pardini and David Lindeman, *Eight State Comparative Report on Social Services,* Working Paper no. 21 (San Francisco: Aging Health Policy Center, University of California, 1982).

31. A prominent example of the extreme faith on which the movement for intensive services by trained caseworkers relied is expressed in the design of a study that compared special intensive services by professional caseworkers with 50 multiproblem families over two and one-half years to a control group receiving routine services by staff without professional training. The primary assumption on which the study is based is that some degree of variation in social casework skills can have a significant impact on the severe problems created by economic deprivation. The results of this study showed no significant differences between the two client groups and was deemed inconclusive because of methodological flaws. But it is in the methodological design that faith is revealed. The goals of the service and how workers' activities related to these goals were defined in such general terms as to be unmeasurable. See Gordon E. Brown, ed., *The Multiproblem Dilemma: A Social Research Demonstration with Multiproblem Families* (Metuchen, NJ: Scarecrow Press, 1968).

32. Derthick, *Uncontrollable Spending,* p. 9.

33. President's Commission on Income Maintenance, *Background Papers* (Washington, DC: U.S. Government Printing Office, 1970), p. 307.

34. Joel F. Handler and Jane Hollingsworth, *The Deserving Poor: A Study of Welfare Administration* (Chicago: Markham Publishing, 1971), p. 127.

35. Whereas efforts were made to upgrade services, the results were seriously limited by the dearth of trained social workers available for these jobs and turnover difficulties in departments of public assistance. A study of turnover in public assistance agencies in New York City during 1964 indicates that 30 percent of the workers resigned within nine months of their appointment. Lawrence Podell, "Attrition of First-Line Social Service Staff," *Welfare in Review,* Vol. 5, no. 1 (January 1967), 9–14. In 1966 the national turnover rate for public assistance agencies was 22.8 percent. This figure is almost double the national turnover rate of all professionals in civil service positions on a federal, state, and local level at that time. Further comparisons along these lines are reported by Irving Kermish and Frank Kushin, "Why High Turnover? Social Work Staff Losses in a County Welfare Department," *Public Welfare,* April 1969, p. 138. A survey of 766 AFDC recipients in the summer and autumn of 1967 gives evidence of a very low level of social service activity in the field. "For the majority of AFDC families, social services means a visit of a caseworker a little more than once every three months for a little more than thirty minutes per visit, with an occasional client's call to her caseworker." Joel F. Handler and Ellen J. Hollingsworth, "The Administration of Social Services and the Structure of Dependency: The Views of AFDC Recipients," *Social Service Review,* Vol. 43, no. 4 (December 1969), 412. For some observations on the lack of trained personnel, see Chapter 4.

36. Derthick, *Uncontrollable Spending,* p. 19.

37. Mildred Rein, "Social Services as a Work Strategy," *Social Service Review,* Vol. 49 (December 1975), 519.

38. Derthick, *Uncontrollable Spending,* p. 19.

39. Social and Rehabilitation Service, Department of Health, Education, and Welfare, *Social Services U.S.A.,* Publication no. SRS 76–03300 (Washington, DC: National Center of Social Statistics, 1975), p. 7.

40. *Washington Social Legislation Bulletin,* Vol. 31, no. 32 (April 23, 1990), p. 125.

41. The evolution of caretaking services is discussed in Robert Morris and Delwin Anderson, "Personal Care Services: An Identity for Social Work," *Social Service Review,* Vol. 49 (June 1975), pp. 157–174.

42. Gilbert Y. Steiner, *The State of Welfare* (Washington, DC: Brookings Institution, 1971), pp. 106–110.

43. There were ways to circumvent this restriction. In practice, for example, it was not uncommon for a donation to be made by a United Fund organization with the request that the contribution be used to support a particular type of activity in a specified community, one performed only by an agency affiliated with the United Fund organization. In this fashion, private donations could be covertly earmarked as the local share for a designated agency. See, for example, Booz, Allen, and Hamilton, "Purchase of Social Service—Study of the Experience of Three States in Purchase of Service by Contract Under the Provisions of the 1967 Amendments to the Social Security Act," Report Submitted to the Social and Rehabilitation Service, January 29, 1971 (distributed by National Technical Information Service, U.S. Department of Commerce), pp. 40–42.

44. Lester Salomon and Alan Abramson, *The Federal Budget and the Non-Profit Sector* (Washington, DC: Urban Institute Press, 1982), p. 44.

45. Derthick, *Uncontrollable Spending,* pp. 100–101.

46. Alva Myrdal, *Nation and Family* (Cambridge, MA: MIT Press, 1968), p. 1.

47. *San Francisco Chronicle,* May 21, 1990, p. A5.

48. U.S. Bureau of the Census, *Statistical Abstract of the United States 1990* (Washington, DC: U.S. Government Printing Office, 1990), p. 367.

49. Aristotle, *The Politics* (New York: Random House, Modern Library, 1943), pp. 260–263.

50. Gregory Vlastos, "Justice and Equality," in *Social Justice,* ed. Richard Brandt (Englewood Cliffs, NJ: Prentice Hall, 1962), p. 32.

51. Cited in Karl de Schweinitz, *England's Road to Social Security* (New York: A. S. Barnes, Perpetua, 1961), p. 123.

52. U.S. Department of Health, Education and Welfare, *Work in America* (Washington, DC: U.S. Government Printing Office, 1972).

53. See, for example, William Shannon, "A Radical, Direct, Simple, Utopian Alternative to Day-Care Centers," *New York Times Magazine,* April 30, 1972; and Sheila M. Rothman, "Other People's Children: The Day Care Experience in America," *Public Interest,* no. 30 (Winter 1973), 11–27.

54. William Frankena, "The Concept of Social Justice," in *Social Justice,* ed. Richard Brandt (Englewood Cliffs, NJ: Prentice Hall, 1962), p. 23.

55. See Robert Hunter, *Poverty,* ed. Peter d'A. Jones (New York: Harper & Row, Torchbook, 1965), pp. 51–52.

56. Karl Marx, *Das Kapital,* ed. Freidrich Engels, Vol. 1 (Chicago: Henry Regnery, Gateway, 1959), pp. 33–34.

57. For example, see Richard Titmuss, "Equity, Adequacy, and Innovation in Social Security," *International Social Security Review,* Vol. 2 (1970), 250–267.

58. T. H. Marshall, *Class, Citizenship, and Social Development* (New York: Doubleday, Anchor Books, 1965), pp. 258–259.

59. An analysis of cost effectiveness as it is expressed in different income-maintenance strategies is provided by James Cutt, "Income Support Programmes for Families with Children: Alternatives for Canada," *International Social Security Review,* Vol. 23, no. 1 (1970), 100–112.

60. Titmuss, *Commitment to Welfare,* pp. 69–71.

61. "Learnfare: Policy Implications," *Youth Law News,* May/June 1989, pp. 12–13.

62. Peter Blau, *Bureaucracy in Modern Society* (New York: Random House, 1956), p. 107.

63. Various studies on the War on Poverty and Model Cities have documented this result. See, for example, Ralph Kramer, *Participation of the Poor* (Englewood Cliffs, NJ: Prentice Hall, 1969); Neil Gilbert, *Clients or Constituents* (San Francisco: Jossey-Bass, 1970); Neil Gilbert and Harry Specht, *Dynamics of Community Planning* (Cambridge, MA: Ballinger, 1977).

64. Burns, *Social Security and Public Policy,* p. 231.

65. Davis McEntire and Joanne Haworth, "Two Functions of Public Welfare: Income Maintenance and Social Services," *Social Work,* Vol. 12, no. 1 (January 1967), 24–25.

66. Genevieve Carter, "Public Welfare," in *Research in the Social Services: A Five Year Review,* ed. Henry S. Maas (New York: National Association of Social Workers, 1971), p. 224.

67. Handler and Hollingsworth, "Administration of Social Services," p. 418. For a comprehensive historical review of the "separation" issue see Winfred Bell, "Two Few Services to Separate," *Social Work,* Vol. 18, no. 2 (March 1973), 66–77.

68. Irving Piliavin and Alan Gross, "The Effects of Separation of Services and Income Maintenance on AFDC Recipients," *Social Service Review,* Vol. 51 (September 1977), 389–406. See also Bill Benton, Jr., "Separation Revisited," *Public Welfare,* Vol. 38, no. 2 (Spring 1980), 15–21.

69. Sar Levitan and Robert Taggart, III, *Social Experimentation and Manpower Policy: The Rhetoric and the Reality* (Baltimore: Johns Hopkins University Press, 1971), p. 53.

70. Mary Bryna Sunger, "Generating Employment for AFDC Mothers," *Social Service Review,* Vol. 58, no. 1 (March 1984), 32.

71. Judith Gueron, "Reforming Welfare with Work," *Public Welfare,* Fall 1987, pp. 13–25.

72. Gunnar Myrdal, *Value in Social Theory,* ed. Paul Streeten (London: Routledge & Kegan Paul, 1958), pp. 254–255.

Chapter Three
BASIS OF SOCIAL ALLOCATIONS

"I suppose you mean that you have no money to pay wages in," said I. "But the credit given the worker at the government storehouse answers to his wages with us. How is the amount of the credit given respectively to the workers in different lines determined? By what title does the individual claim his particular share? What is the basis of allotment?"

"His title," replied Doctor Leete, "is his humanity. The basis of his claim is the fact that he is a man."

Edward Bellamy
Looking Backward

In his 1888 utopian novel, *Looking Backward,* Edward Bellamy views the "good society" as a place where every individual can claim an equal share of the goods and services produced by the nation. Citizens are guaranteed a comfortable standard of living from, as Bellamy puts it, "cradle to grave." Entitlement does not depend on being rich or poor, single or married, brilliant or dull, healthy or ill—a person's entitlement is his or her humanity.[1] In Bellamy's vision, social allocations are arranged according to the principle that everyone deserves an equal share, with one exception: "A man able to do duty [i.e., work] and persistently refusing is sentenced to solitary imprisonment on bread and water 'til he consents."[2] Although this may seem rather harsh, in Bellamy's society work roles are structured to dignify every task and to allow a choice of occupations broad enough to suit individual preferences. Nevertheless, as an introduction to the allocative dimension of choice in social welfare policy, there is perhaps some small comfort in noting that even in a utopian world of rationality, harmony, and consensus, problems of social allocation are not entirely amenable to neat solutions based on unqualified principles.

In the real world few social welfare policy issues engender more vigorous debate than who shall benefit and the manner in which entitlement is defined. The rules used to determine who will benefit from any social welfare policy may be predicated on a variety of specific criteria ranging from the esoteric (American Indian blood quantum) to the mundane (amount of money earned). We refer to the general principles that underlie these criteria as the bases of social allocations. In this chapter we examine some of the fundamental alternatives among these general principles.

Attempts to develop principles of eligibility usually begin with the distinction between universalism and selectivity. *Universalism* denotes benefits made available to an entire population as a social right. Examples are Social Security for the elderly and public education for the young. *Selectivity* denotes benefits made available on the basis of individual need, usually determined by a test of income. Examples include public assistance and public housing for the poor.

The social policy literature contains an ongoing debate between proponents of universal and selective principles. Universalists view social policy as society's proper response to those common problems faced by all members of the community—not just the poor, the disabled, or those facing special hardships. For universalists, all citizens are "at risk" in the sense that all of us, at one time or another, face a variety of problems and needs. The proper aim of the welfare state, accordingly, is to organize broad programs of response, without differentiating among rich or poor, men or women, or other categories of citizens. Young people, for example, need care and education. Those who are ill need health care. The elderly, disabled, and unemployed need income support. Universalists favor public arrangements that address these needs on the basis of a general entitlement, as a social right comparable to the political rights we take for granted. Social insurance, public education, health care for the aged— programs available without regard to income—stand as the models for a proper welfare society.

Universalists emphasize the value of social effectiveness as manifest in the preservation of dignity and social unity that result when people are not divided into separate groups of givers and receivers. In their view, programs based on economic determinations are divisive, accentuating differences in society which frequently take on moral as well as economic meanings. Those who receive benefits often feel demeaned—even when their rights to benefits are clear. Receiving Aid to Families with Dependent Children (AFDC), for example, or being assigned to a special class for the educationally impaired, is for many people a sign of failure, an embarrassing, stigmatizing experience. "Invidious rationing for the poor," as Alvin Schorr puts it, "does not seem a sound principle for a welfare state."[3]

Selectivists disagree, of course. They view the appropriate scope of social policy in restrictive terms. Families or individuals requesting support, they believe, should have to demonstrate need. Rather than seeing benefits as universally available entitlements, selectivists favor benefits that are targeted on the poor. Underlying this perspective is the view that a proper social policy is a limited social policy, that people who can afford to meet their own needs should not receive government handouts, and that taxpayers should provide help only for that margin of the population legitimately unable to fend for themselves.

Means-testing, obviously, is a direct way of confining social benefits to "exceptional" groups. Selectivists argue that such a circumscribed approach to eligibility reduces overall spending while ensuring that available funds focus on those most in need. Why, after all, should money be wasted on people not in great need, or in no need at all?

But neither side is quite satisfied to let the debate rest there. Each lays claim to at least a share of the values that support the opposition. Universalists, for example, claim cost effectiveness since broad prevention programs such as comprehensive prenatal health care or generally available prekindergarten programs can avoid future problems—and their associated costs—in a way that case-by-case eligibility determination cannot. In the long-run cost accounting of "an ounce of prevention," then, universalists infer an economic saving to the larger community. As a bonus, universal allocations are said to be less expensive to administer than selective allocations since they do not require constant screening, checkups, and benefit adjustments to ensure the proper level of assistance.

Universalists also argue that broad scope policies can, in fact, be redistributive, concentrating assistance on those with the greatest needs. For example, "tax backs" can be employed to shift the cost of universal benefits to the economically better off. By including the value of universal benefits in their taxable income, richer individuals and families wind up supporting a disproportionate part of the costs involved.[4] In this way a program for everyone is substantially financed by those most able to pay. Universal services, finally, can also provide a basic level of assistance to all while concentrating additional help on those in greatest need. In Great Britain, for example, public health home visits for new mothers are universal, with additional visits focused on those mothers, and children, at greater-risk.

The selectivists' rejoinder is to claim social effectiveness. That is, if society seeks to move toward greater equality, offering benefits to the poor alone is far more effective than allocations for which everyone is eligible.

Provisions targeted on the needy—whether through education, or health care, or child care, or housing—clearly reduce the inimical discrepancies that produce tension and hostility in our society. Given vast unmet needs, equity would seem to demand that the poor receive first call on scarce public resources.

These are some of the general issues that provide a framework for the universal-selective debate. To place this debate in a substantive context, we will illustrate how the choice between universal and selective principles translates to specific policy proposals. We will also examine the values and assumptions that underlie these principles when they are applied.

UNIVERSALITY AND SELECTIVITY
IN INCOME MAINTENANCE

In the continuing dialogue concerning federal income-maintenance programs, numerous reform measures have been put forth by academicians and politicians.[5] These proposals can be analyzed from different perspectives. For example, they can be placed along a continuum of generosity, depending on where they define the poverty level and the proposed amount of financial aid they offer. For purposes of this discussion, however, we are concerned with the bases of social allocations in these schemes. From this perspective, income-maintenance programs can be divided into two broad categories: guaranteed-income programs (sometimes referred to as negative income taxes) and children's allowances (sometimes called family allowances).

Guaranteed-income programs are defined by two characteristics—the provision of a defined minimum subsidy for families with little or no income and the utilization of a formula to determine how much this subsidy decreases as earnings increase. This formula represents what economists call a *negative tax*. Most proposals suggest administering such a system through the Internal Revenue Service, using the same procedures by which personal income taxes are collected and refunds distributed. Simply stated, the income tax structure would become a two-way operation, with money flowing to government from people with incomes above a certain level and money flowing from government to people with incomes below that level. In either case, the amount paid in or out would be graduated according to income. An essential feature of the plan is that the allocation of benefits is tied directly to an income test and is thereby based on the principle of selectivity.

Schemes for a children's allowance usually involve the provision of a *demogrant*, "a uniform payment to certain categories of persons identified only by demographic (usually age) characteristics."[6] More than 60 nations throughout the world, including all of the industrial West, except the

United States, offer some form of children's allowance as an integral part of their welfare system. (It is sometimes argued that in the United States the exemption for dependents on the federal income tax operates as a children's allowance.) The development of children's allowances has achieved widespread support for various reasons; among them is the fact that children represent a substantial proportion of the poor, and wherever one places the blame and however one perceives the causes of poverty, children are clearly innocent victims. An essential characteristic of the demogrant is that benefits are allocated to all families, regardless of economic circumstances, thereby reflecting the principle of universality.[7]

To illustrate the issues that arise in applying the universal-selective framework, we will describe the basic features of two specific income-maintenace proposals. The first is the negative tax program tested experimentally in the mid-1970s in Seattle and Denver.[8] The second is a proposal for a universal program, a children's allowance scheme developed by Martha Ozawa, one of the foremost advocates of this type of program in the United States.[9]

Seattle and Denver Income-Maintenance Experiments

The Seattle and Denver Income-Maintenance Experiments (SIME/DIME) were the largest and most carefully controlled such experiments in history. The sample enrollment included 4,706 families, 44 percent assigned to the control group and the remainder divided among 11 experimental groups. Each experimental group received one of three guaranteed levels of annual income—$3,800, $4,800, and $5,600—and was taxed at varying rates. Four negative tax rates were used: two constant tax rates, one of 50 percent and the other of 70 percent, and two varying tax rates that started at 70 percent and 80 percent and declined as income increased. With the 50 percent constant tax rate and the $5,600 subsidy, for example, a recipient family with no earned income would be paid $5,600 a year. For each dollar earned, the grant would be reduced by 50 cents. With this negative tax rate, an income of $11,200 is the break-even level, the point at which the grant drops to zero.

Children's Allowance

The Ozawa proposal, formulated in 1974, involves an allotment of $60 a month for each child, with payments independent of family income or other eligibility conditions. Under the proposal, the allowance itself constitutes taxable income. Thus, when translated into dollars and cents, families of equal size receive the same benefits. Depending on their income, however, these families end up returning different amounts of the allowance to the government through their federal income taxes. Under 1991 tax rates, a family with income low enough to fall below the federal tax threshold would not be taxed on the allowance at all. A family in the 15 percent bracket, however, would have a portion of the allowance "taxed back." Households with higher incomes, in the 28 percent and 31 percent brackets, would find their allowance reduced by greater amounts.

The overall effect of this scheme is to vary the net gain received by the allowance according to income. The significance of this arrangement is that it makes the children's allowance a benefit that is universal at the point of distribution but selective at the point of consumption. This is not an attribute only of the children's allowance. When we consider how benefits are financed, some form of selectivity creeps into virtually all universal schemes. As Reddin has demonstrated, universal benefits are "those in which the universal gene is dominant but where there are also variant forms of 'recessive' selective genes incorporated in the structure."[10]

CONSIDERATIONS OF SOCIAL EFFECTIVENESS AND COST EFFECTIVENESS

When the abstract principles of the universal-selective debate are applied to choices among concrete alternatives, such as the income-maintenance schemes just described, the discussion generally centers on considerations of social effectiveness and cost effectiveness, the definition of these values, and assumptions regarding policy elements that facilitate and impede their realization.

Measures of the relative cost effectiveness of income-maintenance proposals are usually arrived at by comparing the total costs of the alternative schemes, the extent to which the funds allocated fill the poverty gap, and the amount of "seepage" to the nonpoor. Implicit is a definition of income maintenance that relates to improving the lot of the statistically defined poor, those with an income below $12,700 for a family of four, according to official 1990 federal guidelines.

On the basis of these criteria, the negative income tax is clearly superior. That is, benefits akin to SIME/DIME provide higher levels of assistance to the poorest families with virtually no seepage to working- or middle-class income groups. However, this advantage is hardly impressive if the goal of income maintenance is to improve the lot of children in general, an important objective given the fact that working- and middle-class families, as well as the poor, can use additional income to improve the welfare of their members. From this viewpoint, cost effectiveness is defined quite differently and children's allowance schemes may be preferable. As Cutt points out,

> Universal schemes may be considered to be redistributive in a horizontal sense—from the childless to those with children—and therefore may be seen as having a broader objective than a selective scheme, specifically the allevia-

tion of need among children in any income group, rather than the more tightly focused alleviation of need in families defined as poor in a statistical sense.[11]

In addition, the Ozawa scheme contains at least an element of vertical income redistribution—from the wealthy to the poor—by imposing income tax on the allowance. Cost effectiveness, then, is not an unequivocal attribute of either the universal or the selective bases of social allocations, although it tends to be advanced more directly with the selective approach.

On the other side of the ledger, social effectiveness tends to be identified with the universal approach, although here, too, a definitive case is lacking. Estimates concerning the social effectiveness of income-maintenance schemes are based on certain assumptions about the potential consequences of the alternative approaches. These consequences include the effects on work, childbearing, family stability, stigmatization, and social integration. To illustrate some of these factors, let us review some relevant research findings.

Work Incentives

All social welfare benefits, to some extent, provide an incentive for the very circumstances they are established to ameliorate. Unemployment insurance makes it easier to be unemployed; Aid to Families with Dependent Children (AFDC) makes it easier to support a child. In this sense there is a germ of truth to the contention of Charles Murray and other conservatives that welfare "causes" dependency. Thus, for example, to the extent that they eliminate some degree of economic stress, both SIME/DIME and children's allowances have some negative effect on the incentive to work.

The engineers of welfare reform in the 1960s and 1970s were very much aware of these "perverse incentives" and sought to arrange payments in such a way as to minimize them. Since the disincentive to work in a guaranteed-income arrangement like SIME/DIME was great because the basic payment in a zero-work/zero-income situation was high, these programs sought to reduce benefits only fractionally in response to work earnings. That is, the "tax" on work implicit in the benefit formula was kept low so that recipients were not discouraged from getting jobs.

One of the most perplexing issues in the design of negative income tax schemes is the impact of different tax rates on work incentives. Simply put, how does a 50-, 60-, or 70-cent reduction in grant payments for each dollar of income earned affect a beneficiary's motivation to work? And how do these effects differ for grants offering low and high levels of support? The issue is more complicated than it first appears because the lines of influence may flow in both directions. That is, high tax rates may be an inducement as well as a deterrent to greater work effort. The popular belief is that the person who gets to keep only 50 cents on a dollar is less inclined to work than the person who keeps 90 cents. However, if we assume the desire for a certain standard of living, those who keep only 50 cents may work harder and longer just to maintain their position, whereas those who keep 90 cents initially have more money to spend and may opt to enjoy more leisure time rather than supplement their income by additional work. That is, except for extreme cases in which the tax rate approaches 100 percent, the point at which a worker may decide that the additional income is not worth the effort is indeterminate.

Regarding the ordinary federal income tax, for example, there is little evidence to support the belief that high tax rates necessarily have a deleterious influence on work. After reviewing a number of studies, economist George Break concluded, "Neither in Great Britain nor in the United States is there any convincing evidence that high levels of taxation seriously interfere with work incentives. There are, in fact . . . a number of good reasons for believing that considerably higher taxes could be sustained without injury to worker motivation."[12]

In the SIME/DIME experiments, however, the evidence is not quite so encouraging. In the first edition of this book we reported that the initial findings of one experimental negative tax program showed that "families receiving assistance worked just as hard as ever—and there were even some indications that they had been stimulated to work harder." The early findings also suggested that psychological barriers or disincentives to work were not evident even for those families whose earnings increased to the point where they were no longer eligible for assistance.[13] However, further research has revealed that these conclusions were somewhat premature. The preliminary findings reported in the early 1970s were sharply contradicted after a longer period of study of a much larger sample in the SIME/DIME programs.

Findings indicate that compared to the control group, families receiving the guaranteed income grant worked significantly fewer hours per year. Although changes in work effort varied with the amount of the grants and the negative tax rates, an estimate of the nationwide effects of a SIME/DIME program suggests that a guaranteed income at 75 percent of the poverty line and a negative tax rate of 50 percent would reduce work effort about 6 percent for husbands, 23 percent for wives, and 7 percent for female heads of families.[14]

There are a number of reasons to assume that these findings underestimate the work reduction that would actually take place. One cannot discount the possibility that simply knowing they were part of an important social experiment may have influenced the participants' behavior. The Hawthorne effect, a well-known phenomenon in social research, suggests that in the process of becoming actively engaged in an experiment, participants develop a commitment to its success and an inclination to behave in ways that do not disappoint the investigators.[15] Moreover, the limited scale of SIME/DIME could not simulate the effects of a nationwide program with millions of participants who might well organize to lobby for higher benefits. The relatively brief duration of the experiment no doubt inhibited tendencies to reduce work effort and risk losing a job that the participant would need when SIME/DIME grants ended. There is also a reasonable possibility that a guaranteed minimum income would invite early retirements. Compensating for these and other factors that might have biased the SIME/DIME measurements, Martin Anderson estimated that any such scheme, nationally implemented, would result in a minimum 29 percent reduction in the work effort of low-income workers.[16] Thus a guaranteed income for everyone would result in public money replacing a considerable amount of income that recipients would otherwise have earned themselves. This result means not only a costly program but also a morally questionable one. A society that prizes independent effort and initiative is not likely to value public policy that appears to undermine the work ethic.

Yet questions of the extent to which income guarantees affect work cannot be put to rest on the basis of a few studies. The economic variables involved in the SIME/DIME experiment must be checked against studies of other programmatic arrangements, different population groups, and varying economic and cultural conditions. Some of these variables are considered in a careful review of research by Mildred Rein into the effects of improved welfare benefits and various work-incentive features in the AFDC program. She notes that improved benefits and work incentives appear to have the effect of both encouraging some people to work and encouraging others to remain on, or to become eligible for, AFDC.

> The continually increasing welfare-benefit levels (now inflated by the disregards) [i.e., earned income that recipients do not have to report, like deductions for child-care expenses, and carfare] and the increasing income from mothers earnings while on AFDC should also add to the incentive to work and to choose work and welfare over work alone.[17]

Childbearing

Whereas the guaranteed income can be faulted for sapping the work effort, children's allowances are problematic in different ways. As Burns notes, a major objection "to the adoption of a children's allowance system—and to many people the most formidable—is the belief that it would stimulate procreation."[18] The assumption is that the children's allowance acts as a "baby bonus," encouraging population growth. On this issue, the experiences of Western industrial countries such as France and Canada is informative.

In the mid-1930s France's birthrate fell below the level necessary for replacement of the population, and thus emphasis was placed on the potential demographic impact of a number of social security measures. One result was the Family Code of 1939, which initiated children's allowances for the entire population with the explicit goal of increasing the birthrate. To what extent were the desired results achieved? Five years prior to World War II, France averaged 630,000 births a year. In the five years after World War II, the annual average increased to 856,000 births. Although there was a slight decline in 1953, the rate per thousand remained fairly constant through the mid-1960s, while the total population rose.

At first glance the data appear to support the contention that the family allowance successfully encouraged an increase in the birthrate.[19] However, as Schorr points out, during the same period the United States— with no children's allowance—also experienced a dramatic rise in the birthrate, and the birthrate in Sweden declined throughout the 1950s despite its allowance system.[20] Moreover, although families with three or more children gain the major benefits of the French arrangements, after World War II, more families in France had one to three children and the number of larger families decreased proportionately. French demographers, therefore, have been cautious in their interpretations of the influence of allowances on population growth. At best, they view the program as contributing "to a general natalist spirit which is now a force in itself."[21]

By the mid-1960s, however, this "natalist spirit" slackened and the French birthrate declined precipitously, even with a children's allowance among the most generous in the industrial countries. In 1983 the birthrate had fallen to 1.8 per woman, well below the 2.1 rate necessary to maintain a constant population size.[22] In the early 1990s, the "birth dearth" remained of considerable concern to French policymakers, despite even further liberalizations of the family allowance.

Turning to Canada, where a modest family allowance program was started in 1945, we see that the birthrate has virtually paralleled that of the United States. Although such parallels contradict the argument that the Canadian allowance significantly affected childbearing, Moynihan has observed that in the program's first year of operation "the monthly production of children's shoes rose from 762,000 to 1,180,000 pairs."[23]

The effect of children's allowances on family size, of course, depends to some degree on the magnitude of the allowance. Whereas almost all of the industrialized countries have some sort of payment, benefit levels tend to be small—generally about $500 to $1,000 per child per year in U.S. currency.[24] Although it is modest, it is not an inconsequential supplement for low-income families, but it is hardly likely to influence appreciably family-size decisions.

In light of existing evidence, then, assumptions about the effects of children's allowances on family size must be viewed with a healthy skepticism. Undoubtedly, such allowances provide some people with some incentive. However, to generalize from the few to the many underestimates the complexity of human motivation. Decisions concerning family size reflect fundamental conditions of human existence. In these matters the influence of allowance benefits must be weighed in the larger context of desires for self-betterment and a variety of other social and psychological factors (not the least of which is the need to be well thought of by others) that come to bear on people's decisions to have children.

Family Stability

Although children's allowances do not appear to constitute a potent stimulus to procreation, levels of financial support associated with guaranteed-income schemes can have other effects on family life. There are competing hypotheses about the exact nature of these effects. Since financial stress is one of the major factors increasing the risk of divorce,[25] access to reliable financial aid is likely to help stabilize family life. However, it has been suggested that giving mothers an assured source of support outside of marriage reduces the material incentives to get or stay married.[26]

These hypotheses were examined in SIME/DIME, with results that lend powerful credence to the proposition that a guaranteed income decreases marital stability. Compared to the control group, divorce in the experimental group at the $3,800 level of support was 63 percent higher for blacks, 184 percent higher for whites, and 83 percent higher for Chicanos. Overall the rate of marital dissolution for experimental families was approximately twice that of control group families.[27]

Amid these startling figures, however, there were some anomalies. It is puzzling, for example, that the marital dissolution rates at the highest support level ($5,600) were less than those at the lower levels of support. According to theory, the opposite should have occurred. That is, if the degree of economic independence available outside of marriage contributes to the risk of divorce, these risks should increase at higher levels of financial support.[28] Also, the SIME/DIME findings reflect the short-term consequences of guaranteed incomes, and the program's long-term effects on marital stability remain unknown. It is conceivable, for instance, that after the initial round of divorces the remaining pool of married couples and those who remarry would have lower divorce rates than the current level.[29]

Stigma and Social Integration

One of the most forceful claims for universal schemes is that they avoid stigmatizing recipients. The assumption of stigmatizing effects of the means test is held so firmly by so many that it has almost come to be considered fact. To achieve selectivity without stigma, Titmuss proposes the elimination of the means test and its "assault on human dignity" by employing, instead, a needs test applicable to specific categories, groups, and territorial areas.[30] To this suggestion, Kahn responds,

> It has yet to be demonstrated . . . that a needs test to open spécial services to disadvantaged and perhaps socially unpopular groups will not carry some of the consequences of the means test. Nor, apparently, have even the most egalitarian of societies found it financially or politically possible to completely drop means test selectivity. . . .[31]

Precisely what is it about the means test that presumably results in an assault on human dignity? Perhaps this result is inferred because means tests are frequently applied to socially unpopular groups, such as the poor, who may feel stigmatized even before they make an application for benefits. Certainly, college students, a privileged group, appear to carry the means-test burden lightly in making applications for financial aid. In some cases they have been known to express a strong preference for means-tested selection over other bases of allocation.[32] Moreover, average citizens experience a form of means test once every year, when their taxes are due, without apparent psychological damage to their sense of self-worth. Indeed, the social and psychological effects of the means test may be less inherently painful than is commonly assumed, even for the poor. Several studies have found that the means test per se is not a significant source of irritation to public assistance recipients.[33]

If this evidence is at all persuasive, and we think it is, why the dogged persistence of this assumption? Why is the means test so often the bugaboo of allocative choices? The answer is twofold: First, discussions of the means test tend to confuse the principle with the practice. Distinctions between the means test as an allocative principle and its actual administration are important considerations. As we have suggested, the principle may be quite innocuous where worth and self-esteem of individuals are concerned. It is in the application of this principle that the potential for denigration exists. For example, when the methods of determining eligibility include unscheduled home visits at all hours of the day and night, the message conveyed to the recipient is that he or she is untrustworthy and no longer entitled to a private life. Such procedures clearly are damaging to a person's sense of competence and self-respect.[34]

Practices of this nature support the belief in the stigmatizing effects of the means test and create much of the disapproval. However, what is actually at issue in these cases is not the principle but its application. There is no reason why the principle could not be operationally defined according to a simple and dignified procedure whereby applicants declare their needs and resources without fuss and prying. The means test need not be mean-spirited.[35] A distinction, for example, can be drawn between the typically probing means test, which demands a complete disclosure of income and assets, and the narrower, more dignified, income test, which is concerned only with the applicants' current income, usually verified through their tax returns.[36] Income-tested programs, such as the Earned Income Tax Credit, introduce selectivity without stigma.

The second reason that means-tested schemes frequently are maligned relates to their broader societal effects. By their very nature, means-tested programs divide society into distinct groups of givers and receivers. Although the argument against selectivity usually blends this divisive outcome with the notion that receivers are stigmatized, these effects can be weighed independently. That is, even if stigma did not attach to recipient status, the case remains that selective programs have a divisive influence on the social fabric, fracturing society along sharp lines according to income. The poor become a distinct recipient class, whereas the near poor, working class, and middle class fall together on the donor side of the transaction. This is an arrangement ill suited to the creation of social harmony. In contrast, universal schemes such as the children's allowance facilitate social integration by emphasizing the common needs families have in a variety of economic circumstances. Of the various issues we have discussed, this integrative function is one of the most frequently voiced arguments for the social effectiveness of the universal approach to social allocations.

Tax Exemptions and Credits

The pros and cons of negative income and child allowance proposals have been strongly argued for some time, but neither plan has proven politically popular. Rather than making sweeping changes in our system of social welfare, citizens and elected officials have been content to live with a variety of piecemeal programs geared to different needs and to different segments of the population and reflecting different principles and values. Although our political system has avoided grand new schemes of reform, both the guaranteed income and the children's allowance have been incorporated, in modest and camouflaged forms, into our ongoing social policies.

The personal exemption has already been noted. Taxpaying families have long received exemptions for each of their dependents, and this provides a meaningful form of income support that varies with family size. In 1991, for example, a lower-income family in the 15 percent tax bracket received tax relief of $322.50 for each child—15 percent of the $2,150 exemption.

The Internal Revenue Code also contains a viable negative income tax in the form of an Earned Income Tax Credit (EITC). The credit, enacted first in 1974, contains many of the key characteristics of guaranteed-income schemes. It provides a basic income subsidy to low-income families, it utilizes a formula to determine how subsidies decrease as earned income increases, and it is administered through the tax code. The EITC is different from a guaranteed-income plan, however, in that it covers only part of the population, that is, low-income wage-earning families with children. People who do not work are not covered; neither are single individuals or childless families.

Under EITC provisions, families with earnings under $6,810 a year (1991 figures) get roughly a 17 percent tax credit, that is, a 17-cent refund for each dollar they earn. The credit stays steady for families earning from $6,810 to $10,730 and begins to decline after that. What makes the arrangement a negative tax is its refundability. That is, when the value of the credit exceeds the amount of taxes owed, the worker receives a cash rebate. In 1991 the maximum credit/rebate was $1,178. As income rose above $10,730, the credit was reduced by 10 cents for each dollar earned, ultimately phasing out at $20,262.

The EITC covers only workers, so unlike the SIME/DIME demonstration, it has a salutary impact on employment. In this sense, it can be viewed as a wage subsidy, concentrating its benefits on those who are poor even though they work. Up to a point at least, the more people work, the more they get—quite the opposite of other negative tax and guaranteed-income plans. According to David Ellwood, the EITC avoids the "conundrums" of welfare:

> The rewards of work are increased, not diminished. Benefits go only to those with an earned income. People are helped without any need of a stigmatizing, invasive, and often degrading welfare system, and their autonomy is increased, not decreased. Since it truly would be part of the tax system, people would not be isolated. The negative impact on the work effort of the poor is likely to be small if it exists at all, but the benefits to the working poor may be large. And employers would have no reason to change their hiring practices. Their cost of doing business would essentially be unchanged except for slight additional administrative costs for employers who provided negative withholding.[37]

Since it is restricted to working families with children, the EITC is hardly the broad-brush measure proposed in the 1960s and 1970s by negative tax advocates. Moreover, EITC benefits are more modest than negative income tax payments are generally expected to be. Nevertheless, the EITC exists and the negative income tax does not. For all practical purposes, indeed, the latter idea has faded to near oblivion and is not likely to be revived as part of any universalist strategy in the near future. Refundable credits on the EITC model, however, constitute an antipoverty measure with substantial promise. When combined with the income tax exemption, they offer a mechanism for significant income support—especially for low-wage earners. Tying a liberalized EITC to family size, further could free many such families from the welfare system altogether. If the EITC could, in addition, be expanded to assist all adults, even those without children, it could reduce poverty even more broadly.

ANOTHER PERSPECTIVE ON ALLOCATIVE PRINCIPLES:
A CONTINUUM OF CHOICE

At the beginning of this chapter we suggested that the universal-selective dichotomy represents a preliminary effort to analyze the choices related to social allocations. For the remainder of this chapter we examine the bases of social allocations from other perspectives. Our purpose is to expand and refine the analytic concepts that may be brought to bear on this dimension of choice.

Although the universal-selective dichotomy serves as a useful starting point in conceptualizing eligibility, the bases of social allocations are more intricate than these ideas imply. In reality, abstract dichotomies are usually less useful than continua of choice. Thus, there are many instances of policies in which benefits are made accessible to people in selected categories, groups, or geographic regions without recourse to an individual means test. Until now we have used *selectivity* in the narrow sense to designate means-tested allocations. Yet as Titmuss points out, selectivity may be based on differential needs without the requirement of a means test.[38] The dilemma, however, is that once the concept of selectivity is pried loose from strictly economic means-tested considerations, its definition may be expanded to cover innumerable conditions, even some generally interpreted as universalistic, in which case the term's meaning is dissolved. For example, some veterans' benefits, housing relocation allowances, special classes for the handicapped, and affirmative action in employment involve selective benefits based on other than means-related criteria. In fact, once we yield to the broader definition of selectivity, even children's allowances may be included since they are limited to families with at least one child. To conceive of these as examples of "selectivity," however, adds little to our understanding.

The problem, then, is to identify a broader range of eligibility alternates than are provided by universalism and selectivity (in the narrow, means-tested sense) while still maintaining a degree of abstraction that permits generalizations that tell us something meaningful. Undoubtedly there are many ways to conceptualize allocative principles. Our view is to consider the different conditions under which social provisions are made accessible to individuals and groups in society. From this perspective, the bases of social allocations may be classified according to four allocative principles: attributed need, compensation, diagnostic differentiation, and means-tested need.

Attributed Need

Eligibility based on attributed need is conditioned on membership in a group of people having common needs that are not met by existing institutional arrangements in the economic market. Under this principle, *need* is defined according to normative standards. It may be attributed to as large a category as an entire population, such as in the case of health care in England, or to a delimited group, such as working mothers, children, or residents of "underclass" neighborhoods. The two conditions that govern this principle are (1) group-oriented allocations that are (2) based on normative criteria of need.

Compensation

Eligibility based on compensation is conditioned on membership in groups who have made special social and economic contributions—such as veterans or members of social insurance plans—or who have unfairly suffered harm at the hands of society, such as victims of discrimination or urban displacement. The two conditions that govern this principle are (1) group-oriented allocations that are (2) based on normative criteria for equity restoration.

Diagnostic Differentiation

Eligibility based on diagnostic differentiation is conditioned on professional judgments of individual cases in which special goods or services may be needed, as for the physically handicapped or mentally impaired. The two conditions that govern the principle are (1) individual allocations that are (2) based on technical diagnostic criteria of need.

Means-Tested Need

Eligibility based on means-tested need is conditioned on evidence regarding an individual's inability to purchase goods and/or services. The individual's access to social provisions is limited primarily by economic circumstances. The two conditions that govern this principle are (1) individual allocations that are (2) based on economic criteria of need.

ALLOCATIVE PRINCIPLES AND INSTITUTIONAL AND RESIDUAL CONCEPTIONS OF SOCIAL WELFARE

Before further examination of these allocative principles, let us return briefly to an issue raised in Chapter 1 concerning the competing conceptions of the institutional status of social welfare. We reintroduce this issue because the bases of social allocations are closely associated with the institutional and residual conceptions of social welfare. The purpose of this discussion is to help clarify how these conceptions are linked with policy design.

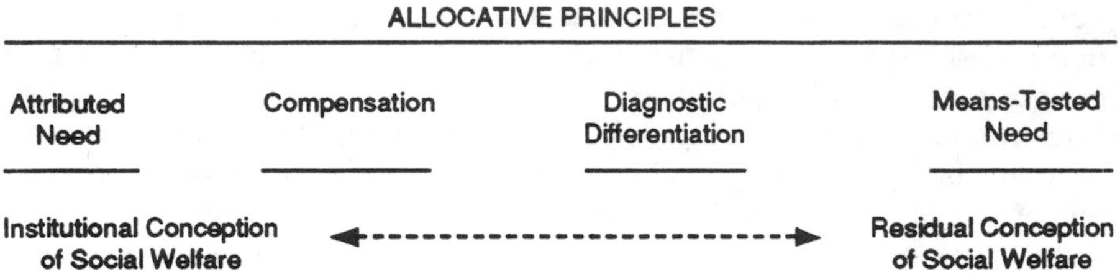

ALLOCATIVE PRINCIPLES

Attributed Need	Compensation	Diagnostic Differentiation	Means-Tested Need

Institutional Conception of Social Welfare ◄- -► Residual Conception of Social Welfare

FIGURE 3-1   Allocative Principles and Conceptions of Social Welfare.

As noted in Chapter 1, the institutional conception posits social welfare as a normal, ongoing, first-line function of society, whereas the residual view sees welfare as a temporary necessity when the normal channels for meeting needs fail to perform adequately. The fundamental distinctions concern the causes and incidence of unmet needs and problems in society. To what extent do these unmet needs represent a failure of the system and to what extent do they represent a failure of those afflicted? To what extent are these problems characterized as deviant or special cases rather than as normal occurrences? Answers to these questions are reflected in the choices regarding the bases of social allocations in Figure 3–1. Here the allocative principles are arranged along a continuum in terms of the degree to which they may be identified with institutional or residual conceptions of social welfare.

Allocations made on the basis of attributed need assume that needs are normal occurrences in society attributable to system inadequacies. Under these conditions, eligibility is determined according to an organic status, such as citizen, child, working mother, resident, and the like, rather than on the basis of an individual's attributes derived by a detailed examination of physical and psychological disabilities or evidence of special circumstances. Policies designed along these lines exemplify the institutional conception of social welfare in seeking to create stable, ongoing arrangements for meeting normal needs.

At the other end of the continuum, where means-tested need is used as the allocative principle, the problem being addressed is usually considered a special circumstance arising out of individual deficiency. To be poor is not an organic status defined in terms of an inherent set of rights and obligations, such as those for working mothers, but rather as a relative condition that is determined by calculating all of the income and resources available to an individual against an arbitrary level of economic well-being. Policies designed along these lines exemplify the residual safety-net conception of social welfare that affords temporary support until the individual is "rehabilitated"—educated, retrained, or otherwise made self-sufficient.

The allocative principles of compensation and diagnostic differentiation fall midway between the institutional and residual conceptions of social welfare. The principle of compensation is closer to the institutional view because it implies a systemic failure or "debt." Here eligibility is determined according to organic status. Diagnostic differentiation is closer to the residual view because it implies individual deficiencies and requires a more or less mechanical assessment of the applicant's special characteristics for eligibility.

This paradigm suggests that the residual conception of social welfare will persist as long as diagnostic differentiation and means-tested need (i.e., allocative principles that seek to differentiate among individuals) are incorporated into the design of social welfare policies. Under these principles, no matter how benign the operational mechanism for eligibility determination, unmet needs will be attributed more to chance or individual deficiency than to institutional strains or failure.

There will always be cases, of course, in which it is both necessary and desirable to differentiate among individuals in allocating social welfare benefits. Although the balance, over time, has shifted toward a larger institutional role for social welfare, it is unlikely that the residual functions will ever disappear. However, this does not mean that the negative aspects of the residual functions must endure. If attributed need and compensation are expanded as bases of social allocation, an adequate institutional core of social welfare may emerge. Then, as Shlakman suggests, the residual function becomes smaller and more manageable, and "It has a potential for emerging as the most flexible, most professionally oriented service, providing for the peculiarity of need and exceptional circumstances that cannot be met effectively by programs based on presumed average need."[39]

PROBLEMS IN OPERATIONALIZING THE ALLOCATIVE PRINCIPLES

This fourfold classification of allocative principles simplifies the structure of choice in the interest of order. To compensate for the distortions that occur whenever complex reality is compressed into theory requires at least a brief glimpse at some of the problematic facets of these principles. Differences among the conditions that govern the principles are not always self-evident. For instance, distinctions between normative definitions and technical assessments of need are often clouded. Is the allocation of special education slots for ethnic minority students with low IQ scores based on valid technical measurements of academic potential or on the cultural norms of white, middle-class groups? The technical assessment of social and psychological needs is a sensitive business in which science, art, and prevailing norms intermingle. Diagnostic differentiation encounters a serious dilemma when ostensibly objective individual assessments result in allocation patterns detrimental to minority populations.[40]

The principle of compensation is invoked to redress group inequities imposed by vagaries of the social structure and to reward contributions to society made by individuals and groups. But the restoration of equity to victims of society may be deferred because these cases are controversial or simply not recognized by the public. Are inner-city residents entitled to a special travel allowance if public transportation is not available to their areas of employment since the middle-class worker drives to work on publicly subsidized highways? To what extent are the hardships visited on past generations a legitimate debt to charge against present generations? Is it equitable to compensate past inequities through the creation of present inequities? These questions suggest some of the complex interplay among values and social choice that attach to the principle of compensation.[41]

Even the relatively straightforward principle of means-tested need becomes entangled in a web of a value-laden choices at the point of application. First, of course, a standard of need must be operationally defined. Here it is interesting to note how the "iron law of specificity" operates in matters of social policy. The iron law holds that policymakers (1) experience discomfort with the uncertainties that attach to broad problems, such as racism, unemployment, and poverty; (2) ease the discomfort by employing arbitrary but plausible specifications of such problems; (3) treat these specifications as literal substitutes for the problem in subsequent policy decisions; and (4) reinforce the substitutions through continued use, ignoring alternative problem definitions.[42]

Consider the notion of poverty and how closely it has become associated with the federal poverty index, $12,675 for a family of four in 1990. Based on the cost of a 1963 subsistence food budget multiplied by a factor of three and updated annually for inflation, the poverty line is concrete, plausible, and convenient to use, but it overlooks the existential quality of poverty as a condition of life.[43] Compare the poverty index to Robert Hunter's observation, "To live in misery we know not why, to have the dread of hunger, to work more and yet gain nothing—this is the essence of poverty."[44]

Here we need a major caveat lest the iron law of specificity be taken too literally. That is, specificity operates only if the issue of choice is one on which it is possible to achieve fundamental agreement among the parties involved (perhaps Congress, a presidential commission, a citizen's organization, or a local social agency board of directors). More precisely, it must be a question of choice when there is substantial uncertainty. (Such a situation is more likely to involve the definition of a problem such as poverty, crime, or unemployment than the character of its solution.) If the situation is marked not so much by uncertainty as by strongly opposing views, specification is likely to have the reverse effect, making agreement more difficult to achieve. In these cases, particularly when controversial solutions are being offered, there is a certain expedience to abstraction, which we will discuss in the next chapter.

Once the standard of need has been settled in means-tested allocations, there still remains the problem of determining how individuals measure up to this level. The scope of economic resources that are weighed in eligibility formulas is open to question. Should it include the value of assets as well as income? Should it include items of sentimental as well as economic value (e.g., wedding rings)? What about insurance payments, children's college accounts, the value of the tools of one's trade, or the income of relatives (distant or close)? When eligibility determination does include relatives' income as a resource and the relatives are held liable for support, in effect they, too, must be subjected to a means test. Under Medicaid, for example, nursing home eligibility requires that the value of certain assets be under a certain level—around $70,000. If the assets of the applicant— or the applicant's spouse—exceed this limit, they must be "spent down" until they qualify. (Certain property—such as a home, household possessions, and one car—are exempt from the valuation.)[45] For the most part, however, adult children are not legally responsible for their parents, and their own income and assets are not counted in the determination of their parents' aid eligibility.

The question of what resources should be included in a determination of income is one of the essential issues in measuring poverty. Specifically, should the dollar value of in-kind social welfare benefits (such as food stamps and public housing) be counted as a component of income? This issue gained currency during the 1970s and 1980s as the proportion of in-kind benefits in the federal budget more than doubled. Critics have argued that excluding the substantial value of these benefits in calculating the income of the poor inflates the poverty statistics. Estimates made by the Bureau of the Census for 1987, for example, indicate that that year's official poverty rate (13.5 percent) would have been considerably reduced (to 8.5 percent) if an expanded definition of income—one counting not only cash income but also the market value of noncash benefits such as Medicaid, food stamps, and housing subsidies—had been employed.[46]

However, there is another facet to the issue of specifying poverty. The poverty line is, in a very important sense, a *relative* measure. That is, people who have incomes below a certain level are perceived to be in poverty relative to those with incomes above that level. If in-kind benefits are to be figured into the incomes of those below the poverty line, perhaps they should be figured into the incomes of those above the line as well. After all, employer-paid benefits for working people, such as health and dental insurance, contributions to retirement plans, and paid vacations, are substantial portions of the "pay" of regular workers.

Having reviewed some of the problems associated with operationalizing the principles that underlie social allocations, we make one final qualification concerning this dimension of choice. That is, in practice these allocative principles are not mutually exclusive even though their underlying premises may seem incompatible, for example, in the joint employment of attributed need and means-tested need. On the contrary, various combinations of allocative principles are found in the design and application of social welfare policies, reflecting the tug, pull, and eventual compromise over competing values. We will illustrate this point with reference to two rather different types of social welfare programs: the Old-Age, Survivors, Disability, and Health Insurance program (OASDHI), created under the Social Security Act, and the Community Action Program, legislated under the Economic Opportunity Act.

In social insurance, eligibility for benefits is predicated on the dual principles of attributed need and compensation. A persistent issue is the balance between adequacy and equity in the benefit allocation formula.[47] The benefit to which a retired work is entitled under old-age insurance is designed, in part, to replace previous earnings as reflected in the contributions made to the social insurance system. To the extent that benefits reflect past contributions, a degree of equity is introduced into this system: Workers who paid in more over the years of their employment are entitled to larger benefits in the years of their retirement. However, eligibility is based also on the principle of attributed need. As Hohaus explains, social insurance "aims primarily at providing society with some protection against one or more major hazards which are sufficiently widespread throughout the population and far-reaching in effect to become 'social' in scope and complexion."[48] In the case of old-age insurance, the attributed need of the retired elderly is for an adequate standard of living.

Thus, whereas Social Security seeks to some extent to compensate retirees in proportion to their contributions, it also seeks to provide a level of adequacy for low-income workers whose contributions were minimal. For this group, strictly applying the principle of compensation would result in benefit levels far below even the meager standards to which the individual was accustomed before retirement. In most social insurance programs the dual allocative principles of attributed need and compensation result in a system in which the relationship between benefits and contributions exists in an ordinal sense but is limited in a proportional sense, as efforts to express equity are modified by concerns for adequacy.

In the development of the Community Action Program (CAP) during the 1960s, the principle of attributed need was employed widely as the basis for social allocations. Initially, people became eligible for a variety of CAP-funded goods and services by virtue of their residence in designated low-income neighborhoods.[49] Once the program began operating, however, these normative assessments of need were often modified. Levitan documents how CAP-funded neighborhood health centers that intended to provide free health care services to all target area residents eventually incorporated a means test into allocation procedures, as did CAP-funded Neighborhood Legal Aid, Head Start, and employment opportunities programs.[50] In certain instances neighborhood residents supported means tests as an additional basis for allocations, especially when the services were relatively inelastic. A limited number of slots for Head Start students in a summer program is a good example. Neighborhood applicants included large numbers of both poor and nonpoor residents. The poor were not convinced that attributed need was the most suitable allocative principle under such circumstances. For CAP, then, attributed need became a preliminary screening device, a necessary but not sufficient condition for determining eligibility.

Despite some of their untidy features, the four allocative principles—attributed need, compensation, diagnostic differentiation, and means-tested need—provide a useful framework for the conceptualization of policy alternatives. Consider, for example, the provision of preschool day-care center services, a program increasingly demanded by students, working parents, and feminists. To whom and on what basis should these services be available? The four allocative principles offer an orderly framework for conceptualizing alternatives. As indicated in Table 3–1, eligibility at one extreme might be extended to all families with young children, based on a community-felt need for an institutional arrangement to allow fathers and mothers greater freedom during the early years of childrearing. However, such a diminution of child-rearing responsibilities is unlikely to receive normative sanction in a child- and achievement-oriented society. A more plausible condition of eligibility might require casting attributed need, not into the mold of untrammeled freedom, but rather in the image of freedom to achieve commonly valued objectives such as a career or an education. In this case, eligibility would be limited to working parents

TABLE 3–1 Alternative Bases for Allocations of Day-Care Services

CONDITIONS OF ELIGIBILITY	EXAMPLES OF ALTERNATIVE BASES FOR ALLOCATIONS
Attributed need	All families
	Single-parent families
	Families with working parents
	Families with student parents
Compensation	Minority families
	Families of servicemen and servicewomen
	Families of workers in specified occupational groups
Diagnostic differentiation	Families with physically or emotionally handicapped children
	Families in short-term crises
Means-tested need	Families whose earnings and resources fall beneath a designated standard of economic need

and/or students. Other options might involve day-care entitlements on compensatory and diagnostic bases. Finally, there is the means test, which could be used independently or in combination with any of the other principles.

WHO WANTS TO BENEFIT?

So far we have focused on a question that receives much attention in the design of social welfare policies: Who is to be eligible for benefits? But there is another side to this issue that is often ignored or misinterpreted by social welfare policymakers. To conclude this chapter it seems fitting to address this question: Who *wants* to benefit?

In selecting the basis of social allocations there is a strong tendency to proceed on the assumption of receptivity. That is, those who qualify as recipients are expected to accept readily the provisions offered. Eligible clients or consumers who do not are labeled hard to reach or resistant, and attention is then directed toward developing specially responsive service structures that take account of the ethnic or linguistic or other differences that impede program participation.[51] However, these are not problems of eligibility determination but rather of service delivery, a subject covered in Chapter Five.

Still, the assumption of receptivity, even with special delivery efforts, bears closer scrutiny than it is usually given. For a variety of reasons, those eligible for benefits may be uninterested in becoming recipients. They are hard to reach because they do not want to be reached. The costs of program participation may be perceived as outweighing the benefits. For instance, although it meant a considerable loss of federal funds, citizens in one city refused to have their neighborhood designated part of a CAP target area, in part because they believed that CAP was a scheme for racial integration.[52] Religious or political or cultural convictions may also inhibit involvement.

Often the issue of eligibility is not so much who wants to benefit but rather who is able to benefit. Individuals with severe emotional problems, addictive behaviors, or antisocial attitudes, whatever their desires or needs, may be "bad" candidates for assistance because they are not likely to make good use of whatever help is offered. Counseling programs offered in a mental health agency, for example, may simply not be able to meet the severe needs of the mentally disabled. Similarly, job training may not work for disturbed or hostile members of the underclass.

Service-providing organizations, seeking to make the most efficient use of their own limited resources, frequently avoid clients who are less than likely to benefit from their programs. This avoidance of the hard to serve is widespread in several social service sectors. For years, for example, critics have charged vocational rehabilitation and job-training organizations with "creaming" their prospective clientele—focusing their efforts on those most likely to succeed while disregarding the least skilled and the least able. The Job Training Partnership Act, for example, legislated in 1982 to assist the economic have-nots, has served mainly to help those who are very close to being "job ready" rather than the hard-core poor.[53]

Of course, not everyone who needs help can be served, and human service organizations must determine how best to employ their scarce resources. It may not make good sense, for example, to assign one of very few units of transitional housing to homeless individuals who have little potential for permanent independence and self-sufficiency. In fact, providers of transitional housing generally screen for candidates who are likely ultimately to succeed on their own—motivated people who will meet with social workers, attend training classes, save money, and seek out jobs and permanent accommodations. The hard-core homeless, those with drug, alcohol, and mental health problems, are not likely to be selected even when they have the interest and motivation to apply for transitional housing. This policy creates a discouraging irony. The creaming phenomenon means benefits for those most likely to benefit—even if this group is likely to succeed without help—and no benefits for those least likely to succeed—even if these are the ones with the greatest objective needs.

CONCLUSION: EQUITY BETWEEN YOUNG AND OLD

Issues of social allocation—whether described in racial, ethnic, gender, disability, income, or other terms—are persistent concerns of social policy practitioners and analysts. To a significant degree, the method that determines allocations at the broad society-wide scale is arbitrary and political. Each generation defines allocation issues in its own way, reflecting its own unique history, economic circumstances, and needs and perspectives.

As we approach the third millennium, much of the social allocation debate has come to focus on the results of past social policies and the inequities they seem to have produced. In examining welfare state outcomes as a whole, for example, we see that the various principles underlying social allocations have certainly resulted in clear winners and losers. One of the most resounding successes has been the dramatic decline in poverty among the elderly. One of the most distressing failures has been the deteriorating well-being of children and adolescents.

The contradictory results of the American welfare state for young and old largely reflect the fundamental bifurcation of income-support policy into universal and means-tested components. The elderly, covered by universal old-age insurance plus universal medical insurance through Medicare, have had their material circumstances substantially bettered. In 1983,

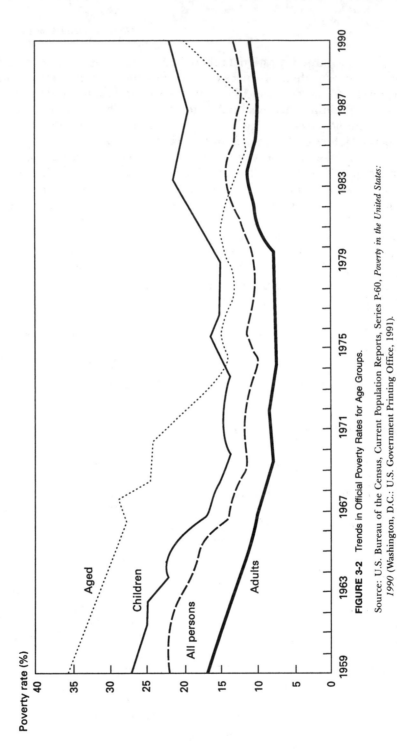

FIGURE 3-2 Trends in Official Poverty Rates for Age Groups.

Source: U.S. Bureau of the Census, Current Population Reports, Series P-60, *Poverty in the United States: 1990* (Washington, D.C.: U.S. Government Printing Office, 1991).

Note: Children = age 17 and under; adults = ages 18–64; aged = ages 65 and over.

for example, as Figure 3–2 indicates, poverty rates for the elderly in the United States for the first time dropped below those for the overall population. Indeed, counting the value of in-kind benefits, the poverty rate for those over 65 dropped to below 6 percent by 1990. For children, however, the scope of poverty has been increasing over the past decade, with young children the worst off. The 1990 poverty rate for children age 17 and under was 20.6 percent; for those under 6 it was 23.5 percent. Even when adjusted for in-kind benefits, the rate for all children remained over 17 percent.[54]

Although not all of the dire circumstances facing children today reflect public policy choices—divorce and unwed parenthood and unemployment are certainly independent factors—choices concerning social allocations and social eligibility have been of critical importance. Means-tested benefits—highly vulnerable to swings in ideological currents and political alignments as well as constrained federal and state budgets—have shrunk in terms of both coverage and benefit levels. Critical programs such as preventive health and legal services have been restricted, and the real (spendable) value of AFDC payments has dropped in almost all states.

Whereas most means-tested programs have been slashed as a result of the cutbacks of the 1980s, universal programs have proven resistant. Thus most of the major ideas recently advanced for generational equity, for improving the life chances of children, have focused on broad and comprehensive programs,[55] such as education reform, an expanded EITC, or universal child support.

The issue of how benefits are allocated cannot be carried much further without some reference to substance, to what it actually is that clients receive. In the next chapter we turn to this issue and examine the nature of social provisions.

NOTES

1. Edward Bellamy, *Looking Backward* (New York: New American Library, Signet Classic, 1960), p. 75. Notice how this notion of entitlement parallels the quotation cited earlier concerning Marx's view on equality of human labor.

2. Ibid., p. 95.

3. Alvin Schorr, *Common Decency*, (New Haven: Yale University Press, 1986), 31.

4. Sheila B. Kamerman and Alfred J. Kahn, "Universalism and Income Testing in Family Policy," *Social Work*, July–August 1987, pp. 277–280.

5. For a representative sample of the voluminous literature in this area, see James C. Vadakin, "A Critique of the Guaranteed Annual Income," *Public Interest*, Vol. 11 (Spring 1968), 53–66; Edward Schwartz, "A Way to End the Means Test," *Social Work*, Vol. 9, no. 3 (July 1964), 3–12; James Tobin, "The Case for an Income Guarantee," *Public Interest*, Vol. 4 (Summer 1966), 31–41; Alvin Schorr, "Against a Negative Income Tax," *Public Interest*, Vol. 5 (Fall 1966), 110–117; Scott Briar, "Why Children's Allowances?" *Social Work*, Vol. 14, no. 1 (January 1969), 5–12; Irwin Garfinkel, "Negative Income Tax and Children's Allowance Programs: A Comparison," *Social Work*, Vol. 13,

no. 4 (October 1968), 33–39; Helen O. Nicol, "Guaranteed Income Maintenance: Another Look at the Debate," *Welfare in Review*, Vol. 5, no. 6 (June/July 1967), 1–13; Alvin Schorr, "To End the 'Women and Children Last' Policy," *The Journal of the Institute for Socioeconomic Studies*, Vol. 9, no. 2 (Summer 1984), 58–78.

6. Eveline M. Burns, "Where Welfare Falls Short," *Public Interest*, no. 1 (Fall 1965), 88.

7. Actually, not all children's allowance programs are universal in the sense that they cover all families in the country. In some countries, such as France, eligibility for the children's allowance is employment related. In France the program is financed through payroll taxes imposed on the employer rather than out of general funds. Eligibility is extended to employees, although some provisions are made for coverage of the unemployed. For a more detailed description of the French scheme, see Wallace Peterson, *The Welfare State in France* (Omaha: University of Nebraska Press, 1960), pp. 19–39.

8. For a description and analysis of these experiments, see Mordecai Kurz and Robert Spiegelman, *The Design of the Seattle and Denver Income Maintenance Experiments*, Center for the Study of Welfare Policy Research Memorandum no. 28 (Menlo Park, CA: Stanford Research Institute, 1972); and Martin Anderson, *Welfare: The Political Economy of Welfare Reform* (Stanford, CA: Hoover Institution Press, 1978).

9. For several proposals, see Alvin Schorr, *Poor Kids* (New York: Basic Books, 1966).

10. Mike Reddin, "Universality Versus Selectivity," *The Political Quarterly*, January/March 1969, p. 14.

11. James Cutt, "Income Support Programmes for Families with Children—Alternatives for Canada," *International Social Security Review*, Vol. 23, no. 1 (1970), 104–105.

12. George Break, "The Effects of Taxation on Work Incentives," in *Private Wants and Public Needs*, ed. Edmund Phelps (New York: W. W. Norton, 1965), p. 65.

13. Fred Cook, "When You Just Give Money to the Poor," *New York Times Magazine*, May 3, 1970, pp. 23, 109–112. A more detailed breakdown of these findings is presented by David N. Kershaw, "A Negative Income Tax Experiment," *Scientific American*, Vol. 227, no. 4 (October 1972), 19–25. For a description of the research design used in this study, see Harold W. Watts, "Graduated Work Incentives: An Experiment in Negative Taxation," *The American Economic Review*, Vol. 59, no. 2 (May 1969).

14. Michael Keelye et al., "The Labor-Supply Effects and Costs of Alternative Negative Income Tax Programs," *Journal of Human Resources*, Vol. 13, no. 6 (Winter 1978), 3–26. See also Henry J. Aaron, "Six Welfare Questions Searching for Answers," *Brookings Review*, Vol. 3 (Fall 1984), 13.

15. A description of the Hawthorne effect can be found in almost any textbook on social research methods. This phenomenon derives its name from the study of the Hawthorne Plant of the Western Electric Company, in which the effect was first identified. See F. J. Roethlisberger and W. J. Dickson, *Management and the Worker* (Cambridge, MA: Harvard University Press, 1939).

16. Anderson, *Welfare*, pp. 104–127.

17. Mildred Rein, "Determinants of the Work-Welfare Choice in AFDC," *Social Service Review*, Vol. 46, no. 4 (December 1972), 563–564. For a more detailed analysis see Leonard Hausman, "The Impact of Welfare on the Work Effort of AFDC Mothers," *Technical Analysis* (Washington, DC: U.S. Government Printing Office, 1970), pp. 83–100. See also Sheldon Danziger and Robert Plotnik, "Poverty and Policy: Lessons of the Last Two Decades," *Social Service Review*, March 1986, pp. 36–50.

18. Eveline M. Burns, "Childhood Poverty and the Children's Allowance," in *Children's Allowances and the Economic Welfare of Children*, ed. Eveline M. Burns (New York: Citizen's Committee for Children of New York, 1968), p. 12.

19. Walter Friedlander, *Individualism and Social Welfare* (New York: Free Press, 1962), p. 161. Peterson, *The Welfare State in France*, notes that the rise in population is in part accounted for by a decline in the death rate from 15.3 per thousand in 1939 to 12.2 per thousand in 1955.

20. Alvin Schorr, "Income Maintenance and the Birth Rate," *Social Security Bulletin*, Vol. 28, no. 12 (December 1965), 2–10.

21. Ibid., p. 4. Additional evidence on this issue is presented by Vincent Whitney, "Fertility Trends and Children's Allowance Programs," in *Children's Allowances, and the Economic Welfare of Children*, ed. Eveline Burns (New York: Citizen's Committee for Children of New York, 1958), pp. 123–139.

22. Richard Tomlinson, "The French Population Debate," *The Public Interest*, 76 (Summer 1984), 111–120.

23. Daniel Moynihan, "The Case for a Family Allowance," *New York Times Magazine*, February 5, 1967, p. 71.

24. David T. Ellwood, *Poor Support* (New York: Basic Books, 1988), p. 117.

25. Phillips Cutright, "Income and Family Events: Marital Stability," *Journal of Marriage and the Family*, 33 (May 1971), 291–306.

26. William J. Goode, "Marital Satisfaction and Instability: A Cross Cultural Analysis of Divorce Rates," *International Social Science Journal*, Vol. 5 (1982), 507–526.

27. Michael Hannan, Nancy Tuma, and Lyle Groeneveld, "Income and Marital Events: Evidence from an Income Maintenance Experiment," *American Journal of Sociology*, Vol. 82 (May 1977), 186–211.

28. Ibid. For additional discussion of the implications of these findings, see Maurice MacDonald and Isabel V. Sawhill, "Welfare Policy and the Family," *Public Policy*, Vol. 26 (Winter 1978), 107–119.

29. The short-term versus long-term effects of SIME/DIME on marital stability are analyzed in James W. Albrecht, "Negative Income Taxation and Divorce in SIME/DIME," *Journal of the Institute of Socioeconomic Studies*, Vol. 4 (Autumn 1979), 75–82.

30. Richard Titmuss, *Commitment to Welfare*, p. 122.

31. Alfred Kahn, *Theory and Practice of Social Planning* (New York: Russell Sage, 1969), p. 203.

32. For example, in 1970 students at the School of Social Welfare, University of California, Berkeley, strongly requested that the means test be the main criterion for determining the award of fellowships and other financial aid.

33. See, for example, Joe Handler and Ellen Hollingsworth, "How Obnoxious Is the 'Obnoxious Means Test?' The View of AFDC Recipients," Institute for Research on Poverty Discussion Paper (Madison: University of Wisconsin, January 1969); Richard Pomeroy and Harold Yahr, in collaboration with Lawrence Podell, *Studies in Public Welfare: Effects of Eligibility Investigation on Welfare Clients* (New York: Center for the Study of Urban Problems, City University of New York, 1968); and Martha Ozawa, "Impact of SSI on the Aged and Disabled Poor," *Social Work Research and Abstracts*, Vol. 14 (Fall 1978), 3–10.

34. A penetrating description of how administrative practices are used to intimidate and deter public assistance applicants is presented by Frances Fox Piven and Richard Cloward, *Regulating the Poor: The Functions of Public Welfare* (New York: Pantheon Books, 1971), pp. 147–182. Also see Betty Mandell, "Welfare and Totalitarianism: Part I. Theoretical Issues," *Social Work*, Vol. 16, no. 1 (January 1971), 17–25.

35. For a discussion of income testing, see Sheila Kamerman and Alfred Kahn, "Universalism and Income Testing in Family Policy: New Perspectives on an Old Debate," *Social Work*, Vol. 32, no. 4 (July-August 1987), 279.

36. For example, see George Hoshino, "Can the Means Test Be Simplified?" *Social Work*, Vol. 10, no. 3 (July 1965), 98–104.

37. Ellwood, *Poor Support*, p. 115.

38. Titmuss, *Commitment to Welfare*, pp. 114–115.

39. Vera Shlakman, "The Safety-Net Function in Public Assistance: A Cross-National Exploration," *Social Service Review*, Vol. 46, no. 2 (June 1972), 207.

40. For further discussion of some of the complexities in the application of this principle, see Joseph Eaton and Neil Gilbert, "Racial Discrimination and Diagnostic Differentiation," in *Race, Research and Reason*, ed. Roger Miller (New York: National Association of Social Workers, 1970), pp. 79–88.

41. Different strategies and implications of compensation are examined in Neil Gilbert and

Joseph Eaton, "Favoritism as a Strategy in Race Relations," *Social Problems*, Vol. 18, no. 1 (Summer 1970), 38–51.

42. The iron law of specificity is based on our experiences participating in and observing the behavior of numerous planning and policy-making bodies. To see it operate in a microcosm (for those who doubt its power), we would suggest that at the next meeting you attend in which a policy decision is pending on a fairly abstract issue around which there is some floundering, deliberately make a proposal that is simply plausible and contains some specification of the issue in concrete units, such as amount of dollars, units of service, numbers of people to be served, and the like. Then mark the time it takes for the discussion to shift from philosophy to considerations of whether the decision should involve a little more or a little less of the concrete units in your proposal.

43. Martin Rein observes, "The SSA procedure for defining and measuring poverty is especially vulnerable to the criticism that when a choice among alternative estimating procedures was necessary the rationale for selection was arbitrary, but not necessarily unreasoned," in *Social Policy* (New York: Random House, 1970), p. 452. For further discussion of this index, see Mollie Orshansky, "Measuring Poverty: A Debate," *Public Welfare*, Vol. 33 (Spring 1975), 46–55. For an approach to the measurement and policy implications of poverty defined in existential terms, see Morton S. Baratz and William G. Grigsby, "Thoughts on Poverty and Its Elimination," *Journal of Social Policy*, Vol. 1, no. 2 (April 1972), 110–134; and Peter Townsend, *Poverty in the United Kingdom: A Survey of Household Resources and Standards of Living* (Berkeley: University of California Press, 1979).

44. Robert Hunter, *Poverty*, ed. Peter d'A. Jones (New York: Harper & Row, 1965; originally published 1904), p. 2.

45. "If Your Spouse Must Enter a Nursing Home" (San Francisco: Bay Area Advocates for Nursing Home Reform, 1986).

46. Patricia Ruggles, *Drawing the Line: Alternative Poverty Measures and Their Implications for Public Policy* (Washington, DC: Urban Institute Press, 1990), pp. 141–142.

47. See, for example, Richard Titmuss, "Equity, Adequacy, and Innovation in Social Security," *International Social Security Review*, Vol. 23, no. 2 (1970), 259–268.

48. Richard Hohaus, "Equity, Adequacy, and Related Factors in Old-Age Security," in *Social Security: Programs, Problems, and Policies*, eds. William Haber and Wilbur Cohen (Homewood, IL: Richard Irwin, 1960), p. 61.

49. Drawing boundaries is a recurrent problem with this method of allocation. Exactly where any given central-city, low-income neighborhood begins and ends is a matter that even carefully designed empirical research rarely settles to everyone's satisfaction. For a technical analysis of this issue, see Avery Guest and James Zuiches, "Another Look at Residential Turnover in Urban Neighborhoods: A Note on 'Racial Change in a Stable Community' by Harvey Molotch," *American Journal of Sociology*, Vol. 77, no. 3 (November 1971), 457–471. We should add that methodological efforts at boundary definition in most CAPs were superficial.

50. Sar Levitan, *The Great Society's Poor Law* (Baltimore: Johns Hopkins University Press, 1970).

51. For example, see Oliver Moles, Robert Hess, and Daniel Fascione, "Who Knows Where to Get Public Assistance?" *Welfare in Review*, Vol. 6, no. 5 (September/October 1968).

52. Neil Gilbert, *Clients or Constituents* (San Francisco: Jossey-Bass, 1970), p. 75.

53. Kirk Victor, "Helping the Haves," *National Journal*, April 14, 1990, pp. 898–901.

54. "Figures Show Poverty Is Up," *New York Times*, September 27, 1991, pp. A1, A14.

55. Ibid., p. 16.

Chapter Four
THE NATURE OF SOCIAL PROVISIONS

The only crucial question becomes one of waste or economy. The two alternatives for redistributional reforms, in-cash or in-kind, therefore have to be compared as to their effectiveness in relation to financial outlays. Just because both systems are costly, they must be scrutinized as choices. It would be an illusion to pretend that both lines could be followed. No budget could expand widely in two different directions.

Alva Myrdal
Nation and Family

The strain between collectivist and individualist tendencies is nowhere more readily apparent than in the dimension of choice that concerns the forms of social provision. Two forms of social provision mark the traditional demarcation of thought and debate in this area of social welfare policy decision: benefits in cash versus benefits in kind. For example, should clients in need of shelter be provided with a subsidized public housing apartment or with cash to seek shelter through the private housing market? The issue is fairly simple to comprehend, but the resolution is quite another matter. Equally reasoned arguments have been made for the primacy of both cash and in-kind provisions. To begin we will examine the opposing views concerning the special advantages and failings of these two basic forms of social provision.

BASIC FORMS: IN CASH OR IN KIND

One of the earliest arguments in favor of in-kind benefits was advanced in the 1930s by Swedish economist Alva Myrdal in the context of that country's debate over the nature of child welfare provisions. For Myrdal, benefits in kind were superior to in-cash children's allowances because of economies of scale. That is, public enterprise, presumably efficient in the manufacture and distribution of mass-produced goods and services, would provide shoes or clothing or similar products at low cost. The alternative— cash grants that could be used to purchase privately produced goods—was viewed as far more expensive. In the state planning perspective of the period, a standard benefit, mass-produced and centrally distributed by government, was seen as eliminating many of the supposedly wasteful aspects of competition in the open marketplace.[1]

Myrdal also suggested that assistance in kind was more effective than cash subsidies because benefits landed squarely on their targets. If the purpose of policy, for example, is to enhance child welfare, the question of effectiveness becomes this: How much of the benefit directly serves this objective?[2] Using this criterion, the drawback of cash subsidies was clear— they simply could not be controlled at the point of consumption. There is no way to guarantee that a children's allowance (or a cash subsidy for any designated purpose) will not be incorporated into the general family budget and used to purchase a variety of items, only a portion of which apply directly to the intended purpose.

Many economists favor cash provisions because they view welfare maximization as the highest plan of satisfaction or "happiness" an individual can achieve for a given outlay of public funds. Theoretically at least, it can be demonstrated that the rational person, given $50 to spend as he or she pleases, will invariably achieve a higher level of satisfaction than one given $50 worth of government-specified goods and services. However, this position assumes that our consumer is indeed rational and capable of judging precisely what is in his or her best interest, and that the judgment of "best interest" is the same for the individual as it is for the community. This position further assumes that policy is motivated primarily for the good of the designated beneficiary as the beneficiary defines it rather than according to the preferences of the larger collectivity,[3] and that the choices made by consumers to maximize their happiness will also enhance the common welfare so that the larger collectivity does not suffer for the satisfaction of its members.[4]

The case for the superior effectiveness of in-kind benefits hinges on the fact that they ensure state control of public spending. Thus, food, medical care, and school lunches can be distributed so that their full impact is focused on the needs of the target population. Benefits in cash, by promoting consumer decision making, permit a wide range of choices, some of which may not correspond with the intent of policymakers. With the free-choice approach, quite clearly, recipients of welfare benefits can buy liquor, cable television, or $100 sneakers. Benefits in kind restrict such "bad" choices, ensuring that public intentions are fulfilled.

Some of the hazards of cash benefits are apparent from the results of the Experimental Housing Allowance Program (EHAP) initiated by the Department of Housing and Urban Development in 1970. An elaborate social experiment executed over an 11-year period at a cost of $160 million, EHAP covered 30,000 households in 12 sites across the country. The impact of unrestricted housing allowances on patterns of housing consumption was one of several questions analyzed in this experiment. In Pittsburgh and Phoenix, the sites chosen to explore the issue, 1,800 low-income households received housing allowance grants of $38 to $95 per month for 3 years. Findings revealed that only very small amounts of these allowances were actually spent on housing. Just 10 percent of the grants in Pittsburgh and 25 percent in Phoenix were applied to housing consumption;[5] for most, the allowances principally served as a general income supplement.

To ensure that social provisions serve the purposes for which they are designated by the community, Myrdal called for

> increasing control from the consumption side, which is a comparatively easy task for competent social engineering. . . . Cooperation, finally, may be the key word for this social policy in a deeper sense because it rests fundamentally on social solidarity, on pooling of resources for common aims, wider in their loyalty than just insurance of individual interest.[6]

Hence, we arrive at the core of the argument supporting benefits in kind, the imposition of social controls that harness individual interests to the collective good. As Holden puts it, "Only through in-kind assistance is society able to exercise a measure of control over the final utilization of the tax dollar. . . ."[7]

The term *social control,* of course, has a distinctly negative connotation, and critics of social welfare have always charged that the welfare state is nothing but a device for regulating the conduct of the poor and underprivileged, a repressive mechanism that "keeps people in their place," maintaining conformity to an unjust order. The frequency with which this indictment is made does not constitute proof of guilt. Yet, to be sure, the charge is not without substance, neither today nor 100 years ago. As Briggs notes,

Many of Bismarck's critics accused him, not without justification, of seeking through his legislation to make German workers "depend" upon the state. The same charges have been made against the initiators of all "welfare" (and earlier, of poor law) policy. Yet it was Bismarck himself who drew a revealing distinction between the degrees of obedience (or subservience) of private servants and servants at court. The latter would "put up with much more" than the former because they had pensions to look forward to. "Welfare" soothed the spirit, or perhaps tamed it.[8]

In general, social welfare professionals find social control a disagreeable element of policy. We mention this tendency because the objectionable functions associated with and the resistive feelings aroused by the term should not paralyze our faculty to weigh the case for provisions in kind. Social controls are required to regulate a complex and highly interdependent society. Regulation that replaces the power of the individual by the power of the community, Freud observed, "constitutes the decisive step of civilization."[9] The issue is not whether we will have controls but whether they will be deliberately designed to realize our ideals of human dignity and justice or to serve pernicious ends—to soothe or to tame the spirit.

Clearly, Myrdal proposes social controls for estimable purposes. Yet the dilemma of social control exercised through the provision of in-kind benefits is that although it may facilitate the realization of collective aims, it also restricts the freedom of the consumer, rich or poor. Myrdal recognizes these objections. However, she suggests that at least in regard to provisions for children, in-kind benefits pose no constraints on consumer sovereignty because "children rarely have much voice in decisions about the use of the family income."[10] This defense is not completely persuasive, even when applied only to children's benefits. As Friedman points out, "The belief in freedom is for 'responsible' units, among whom we include neither children nor insane people. In general, this problem is avoided by regarding the family unit as the basic unit and therefore parents as responsible for their children."[11]

Although advocating benefits in-kind, Myrdal's position is less than doctrinaire, and even she is not completely persuaded by her own argument that such benefits do not limit freedom of choice. Hence her counsel to exercise caution when applying the in-kind principle, especially for inexpensive items that often are imbued with personal meaning:

> Clothing falls in that category and it thus seems to be difficult to subsidize in-kind. Here personal taste is delicate and social prestige has become involved. Even if some class equalization in clothing, especially for children, is judged desirable, it would probably be extremely unwise to force any uniformity on families. . . . It would be cheaper, perhaps extremely rational but still a bit inhuman, to provide layettes, bedding, and baby carriages for all newborn children. All these cost items, invested with so much tender care, are certainly not appropriate for communalization.[12]

As a final qualification, Myrdal advises that a serious preference for benefits in kind rather than cash subsidies can be entertained only when an adequate family income already exists. When it does not, she considers cash assistance for children to be an "appropriate deviation" from the in-kind principle.

Turning now to the other position, we see that two pervasive themes advance the case for benefits in cash as the preferred form of social provision. First, the alleged cost savings of benefits in kind is challenged. Although economies of scale may apply to certain forms of technology, it is certainly questionable in the case of social services such as casework and vocational counseling[13] because they tend to draw on what Thompson describes as "intensive technology"—a variety of techniques used to change and aid the client, with the precise treatment based on constant feedback.[14] This type of technology is tailored to individual cases, which hinders standardization.

With social provisions that are more amenable to standardization, such as clothing, the sacrifice of freedom of choice in favor of a regimented universal product is bound to be discomforting. Moreover, although these benefits in kind may theoretically eliminate some of the "wasteful" attributes of competition, it is likely that the market competition associated with cash benefits will generate innovations resulting in significant cost reductions over the long haul.

Where economies of scale are not clearly operative, the issue turns on the question of whether cash subsidies that stimulate competition in the private marketplace are really less expensive than provisions in kind, which foster the growth of publicly run or publicly controlled bureaucracy. Examining this choice in the context of education, Friedman opts for grant subsidies rather than in-kind provisions because

> [grants] would bring a healthy increase in the variety of educational institutions available and in competition among them. Private initiative and enterprise would quicken the pace of progress in this area as it has in so many others. Government would serve its proper function of improving the operation of the invisible hand without substituting the dead hand of bureaucracy.[15]

A more potent argument for benefits in cash is the appeal to consumer sovereignty and freedom of choice. Frequently, arguments concerning the apparent costs of cash versus in-kind benefits are employed as "neutral" justifications for underlying currents of individualistic and collectivist thought. There is a compelling quality to the argument for consumer sovereignty. In essence it posits the right to self-determination, the right to squander one's resources on luxurious and frivolous items for whatever the psychological or material benefits derived, and conversely, the right to husband one's resources toward whatever future is desired. It is the right of individuals to exercise self-indulgence as well as self-denial.

This viewpoint relies heavily on the faith that the market works according to principle and is in fact responsive to consumer demands. On this point, those who favor collective interventions are not convinced. Galbraith, for example, argues that the consumer "is subject to forces of advertising and emulation by which production creates its own demand." According to this proposition, which he labels the "dependence effect," consumer wants are not determined independently. Rather, the producers who create goods and services also manufacture desires for them among consumers.[16] The counterargument is that producers cannot determine consumer wants; they merely provide information about what is available and endeavor to convince the consumer of the worth and value of their product.[17] Whether or not the dependence effect is as consequential as Galbraith would have, his proposition discloses one of the hidden perils of unqualified acceptance of the market mechanism: Namely, consumer ignorance must be taken into account when considering voluntary exchanges in pursuit of rational self-interest. Rational choices require objective information about the items to be consumed. Such knowledge is expensive and difficult to obtain. The predicament is more intense if one is poor and ill educated to begin with. As Rivlin explains,

> Unless he knows what he is buying, a consumer cannot chose rationally. Yet, in the social action [i.e., welfare] area, it is very difficult for him to find out anything about the quality of service before he uses it. Moreover, the costs of shopping around or sampling the merchandise of a hospital or a school may be prohibitive.[18]

Another argument in favor of cash is that income transfers provide a far more efficient means of reducing poverty. According to Gary Burtless of the Brookings Institution, distributing all public assistance to the poor in the form of cash would "completely eradicate poverty as officially measured and do so at less cost" than the current mix of programs because in-kind programs today cost far more than income supports. The value of in-kind health, housing, and nutrition public aid programs in 1988, for example, totaled approximately $95 billion compared to just $38 billion for SSI and AFDC.

This efficiency argument, of course, is somewhat misleading because "welfare" is more than simply an income above the poverty line. If all antipoverty programs were "cashed-out" (i.e., converted to their dollar equivalents) and then distributed on the basis of need, we might eliminate "official poverty" but we would certainly aggravate the problems that in-kind benefits address—poor health, malnutrition, and inadequate housing, partly because cash means consumer choice, and consumer choice means that people may spend their dollars frivolously. But it also reflects the fact that cash assistance, even at levels near the poverty line, would not provide coverage anywhere close to that which in-kind programs—especially medical programs—currently provide. Elderly people in nursing homes, for example, often receive Medicaid benefits at levels two to three times the poverty line. The acutely ill often receive Medicaid benefits worth even more.

Benefits in kind, then, can promote a more genuine concept of welfare than cash alone. At the very least, the social control of consumption, which is ensured by the in-kind approach, offers a degree of protection to the unwary and the ignorant. From this perspective it might be said that it is not so much freedom to choose that is reduced by in-kind help as freedom to err or to choose poorly on the basis of limited knowledge. The response to this statement might be that without freedom to err, self-determination is a hollow construct. What the collectivist sees as the desirability for social protection, the individualist views as a paternalistic infringement on individual responsibility.

The cash versus kind issue pitches the discussion of social provisions at a fairly high level of generality. From this level we can observe contending arguments, but no general solution is visible. To draw a general conclusion about the primacy of either cash or in-kind benefits would involve imposing an absolute standard in a realm of policy choice where relativity is the more appropriate stance. Much depends on the esteem in which individual freedom and consumer choice are held compared to social control and the collective good. But even the most ardent supporters of consumer choice bow to the necessity of collective interventions under certain circumstances, such as for the mentally incompetent or when the market mechanism is inoperative because of technical conditions.[19] And those who prescribe benefits in kind are sensitive to both the need for adequate cash support and the social and psychological benefits of self-expression and autonomy derived from consumer choice. For them, as Mencher suggests, "The problem is not the potential conflict between individual rights and social controls but the maintenance of maximum opportunity for individual choice as an integral part of the system of government responsibility."[20] To achieve this balance, a mixture of different forms of social provision that offer varying degrees of consumer sovereignty and social control must be considered.

ALTERNATIVE FORMS: AN EXTENSION OF CHOICE

We have discussed the nature of social provisions in terms of two basic benefit forms, cash and kind. The forensic utility of this classification affords reasonably firm lines for debate. Yet to think of social provisions in these terms alone oversimplifies the realities that policymakers face in practice. Finer distinctions are possible and desirable for analytic precision.

Social provisions may come in a variety of forms, from those that enhance individual power to concrete goods. Embedded in these varied forms is a dimension of transferability—the extent to which the provision allows for consumer choice. For example, public housing units, home repair services, cash supplements for housing, and rent vouchers offer varying degrees of freedom of choice to the consumer. Conversely, they ensure to varying degrees that the provision will not be used for other than its intended purposes. In terms of form and transferability, social provisions may be classified broadly into six categories: opportunities, services, goods, vouchers and tax credits, cash, and power.

Opportunities are incentives and sanctions employed to achieve desired ends. Although this is the vaguest type of direct provision, it is not unimportant; much social welfare policy is concerned with the creation and distribution of opportunities. Unlike goods and services, benefits in this category involve the provision of civil rights or an "extra chance." Sometimes the extra chance is built into the basis of social allocations, as in the additional points for veterans on civil service exams and special efforts of schools to recruit underrepresented students. In these cases the nature of the provision considerably overlaps the basis of social allocations. Opportunities ultimately lead to the acquisition of other benefits. However, opportunities have no immediate transfer value inasmuch as they must be utilized within the context that they are offered. A recipient of opportunity X cannot trade it for the opportunity Y or for goods, services, or other social provisions.

Services are activities performed on the client's behalf, such as in-home care, counseling, planning, and training. These provisions are nontransferable in terms of their immediate market value to recipients.

Goods are concrete commodities such as food, clothing, and housing. These benefits have limited transfer value, generally confined to marginal channels of exchange such as pawnshops, flea markets, and informal barter.

Vouchers and tax credits are benefits that have a structured exchange value and may be transferred for a choice among resources within a delineated sector. Tax credits, for example, can be used to offset day-care expenses; food stamps can be exchanged for a variety of edible goods. Such provisions offer greater degrees of freedom of choice than goods or services. As a form of social provision, vouchers have special appeal because they preserve a modicum of consumer sovereignty (within a sector) while allowing for the exercise of social control (between sectors). Thus, they attract a range of proponents with both collectivist and individualist predilections.[21]

Cash benefits are provided through programs like public assistance, children's allowances, and social insurance. Any tax arrangements that let individuals and families keep more of their own income also qualify as cash benefits. These forms of provision, of course, have universal exchange value, offering the most latitude for consumer choice.

Power involves the redistribution of influence over the control of goods and resources. It can be achieved through policies that require representation of the poor, clients, and other disadvantaged people on the boards of agencies that dispense social welfare benefits, such as Area Agencies on Aging. Here, the social provision is incorporated into policy decisions about the structure of the delivery system (which we will examine in Chapter 5). Although power cannot be "spent" in the same way as cash or credits, it offers a higher degree of control over social and economic choices than goods, services, or opportunities. In this sense, power has a fluid exchange value.[22]

In addition to these forms of provisions, there are social interventions that indirectly assist individuals and groups. A good deal of important social welfare policy, rather than providing tangible benefits to specific individuals in need, establish programs that are instrumental in the development and implementation of benefit programs. *Instrumental provisions* are those that encourage more efficient and effective arrangements among agencies that supply direct social welfare benefits.

To illustrate, let us consider the provisions under Title III of the 1973 amendments to the Older Americans Act, which established more than 600 Area Agencies on Aging (AAAs) throughout the United States. These agencies are responsible for planning, pooling, and coordinating local resources to produce a comprehensive service system for the elderly. The AAAs also are expected to function as advocates for the elderly, monitoring and evaluating policies and programs that might affect this group. In this fashion, AAAs furnish indirect forms of aid in their jurisdictions. Whereas instrumental provisions influence the distribution of social benefits through planning and coordination, there appears to be a tendency among indirect service agencies, such as AAAs, to move into the provision of direct services. There are several reasons for this sort of functional drift, not the least of which is that it strengthens the agencies' ties to the elderly constituents who receive immediate and concrete benefits from the direct services offered.[23]

Instrumental provisions are important in molding the process through which policy choices concerning tangible social welfare benefits are made. Because they are most pertinent to the process of social welfare planning, we will engage in a more detailed discussion of instrumental provisions in Chapter 8, where policy choices concerning the question "Who plans?" are examined. For the remainder of this chapter we will discuss the nature of social provisions that offer direct forms of aid to individuals and groups.

VOUCHERS: BALANCING SOCIAL CONTROL
AND CONSUMER CHOICE

Recently there has been an increasing interest in the use of vouchers. Compared to government provisions in cash or in kind, social welfare benefits in the form of vouchers hold a special attraction. They preserve consumer choice while allowing for a degree of social control over consumption patterns. This arrangement ensures that benefits will serve a socially defined purpose, be it the provision of food, shelter, education, health care, or some other vital service.

The food stamp program is the largest and best-known voucher scheme in the United States. Public assistance recipients and other low-income persons are eligible for food stamp coupons with a designated cash value that may be used to purchase food at supermarkets. Starting as a pilot project in 1961, serving fewer than 400,000 persons, this program grew at a phenomenal pace after it was enacted nationally under the Food Stamp Act of 1964. Between 1967 and 1975, the number of participants soared from 1.5 million to 19.3 million, at which time the program came to be known in Congress as the "food stampede."[24] From 1975 to 1980 the program continued to expand as costs doubled from $4.4 to $9.1 billion.[25] By 1992, costs had risen to $22.3 billion.

On a smaller scale, the voucher experiment conducted between 1972 and 1977 at the Alum Rock Union Elementary School District in California sought to demonstrate the advantages of competition and consumer choice in education. One of the first educational voucher schemes was devised by Milton Friedman in 1955.[26] Instead of financing public schools, he proposed that the government should distribute money directly to parents in the form of vouchers that could be used to purchase education at the schools of their choice. By introducing the competition of the economic market, school programs presumably would become more innovative and the overall quality of education would improve. Of course, it is also possible that some schools might deny access to the poor by charging more than the cash value of vouchers, employ admissions tests that reject weak students, discriminate against ethnic and racial groups, and mislead the unsophisticated consumer about the pedagogical quality of their programs. To guard against such discrimination and deception, a plan for educational vouchers developed by Jencks and his associates in 1970 included a series of regulations governing admissions policies and requiring that precise information on educational programs be made available to aid parents in the intelligent exercise of choice.[27]

When the Alum Rock demonstration was launched in 1972, the design was closer to the restrictive scheme proposed by Jencks than to Friedman's laissez-faire approach. In Alum Rock the voucher concept was modified in a number of ways: Choice was limited to the 13 of the district's 24 public schools that elected to participate; enrollment ceilings were used to maintain a degree of balance between demand and supply; and teachers were assured they would not lose their jobs if their school did not attract enough pupils. Despite these modifications the Alum Rock demonstration did enhance consumer choice and promoted a degree of competition beyond that normally operating in the school district.[28]

The findings from Alum Rock reveal that although the range of educational alternatives increased, in the final analysis geographical proximity was the predominant consideration for most parents. More than 80 percent of the participants selected the schools nearest their homes. Choices made among different miniprograms within schools favored the traditional curricula over new, more experimental modes of education.[29] On the matter of educational quality, data from several studies found no significant differences between test scores on academic achievement of students from voucher and nonvoucher schools.[30] Despite these generally unpersuasive results, educational voucher schemes continue to draw interest. In 1979 the Coons and Sugarman proposal to replace public education in California with a state voucher gained considerable support. Although this proposal failed to qualify for the 1980 California ballot, public opinion polls suggest that if it had qualified the vote would have been close.[31] In 1991, President George Bush made "choice" a key portion of his own legislative proposals for educational reform.

In the housing field, conservatives have long argued for vouchers that would allow people to find their own housing in the private market. Indeed, in the Reagan years a demonstration voucher program provided 80,000 low-income families with such assistance. These families paid 30 percent of their income for housing; a Housing and Urban Development (HUD) voucher paid the rest. Eligible families could rent any apartment they wanted, but they received a voucher only for the difference between their 30 percent and the fair market rent in their locale. If their actual rent exceeded this amount, families had to pay the increment; if the rent was below the market level, the family could keep the difference.

This kind of program has many appealing features. One commentator remarked that it turned "low income renters into an army of deputies who monitor government spending. Their collective, self-interested discretion amounts to an invisible hand that decides whether the housing needs of the poor are most cheaply met through new construction, existing units, moderate rehabilitation," or some other alternative.[32]

The idea of housing vouchers has a special appeal given the disappointing record of federal housing policy over the past 40 years. Government public housing strategies—especially inner-city "meta-projects"—have often been fiascos, and HUD bureaucracy has been prone to inefficiency and scandal. Nevertheless, housing vouchers have not caught on in any appreciable way for one important reason: cost. A universal voucher system covering a major portion of the population in poor housing would be enormously expensive.

SUBSTANCE OF THE SOCIAL PROVISION

Our elementary categorization of six types of benefits in terms of their form and transferability is useful in permitting insights into the nature of social provisions, particularly for cash, credits, and goods that are fairly concrete. A tremendous variety is possible within each of these categories. For example, the provision of goods may include numerous commodities in food, clothing, and shelter; cash may be provided in amounts ranging from small sums to thousands of dollars; and credits may be designed to cover part or all of the costs of different goods and services. Despite the many alternatives, there is a palpable quality to these types of provisions that makes them readily comprehensible. The substance of these provisions is evident; most of the relevant qualities of the benefit become known as soon as the amount of cash, type of good, and credit or voucher sector are specified.

Consider the educational voucher. We can specify a cash value that can be exchanged only for designated educational programs. Different programs might be housed in a single local public school, spread out among a few local public and private schools, or encompass all accredited schools in the country. The point is that once the value of the voucher and the sector in which it can be exchanged are identified, the nature of the provision is substantially clear. It should be noted that with both cash and vouchers, our analysis of social provisions ends at the point at which recipients obtain either of these benefits. Subsequent choices concerning how these benefits are utilized involve individual transactions. What is purchased on the open marketplace becomes a matter of individual choice much like any other, whether it is how to spend one's weekly paycheck, a tax refund from the government, or a credit at a local department store.

For the other benefits categories—opportunities, services, and power —the substance of the social provision is more abstruse. To understand what is provided requires some probing. Consider a proposal to provide family counseling services. The type of service has been designated— counseling—but the substance of the provision remains virtually unknown. It may emphasize information giving, insight therapy, behavior modification, or the alteration of environmental contingencies; it may center on individuals, family units, or groups; it may be short term or long range; and it may be conducted by personnel with a variety of backgrounds and training who base their practice on alternative theories of change.[33]

Likewise, "day care" may involve a range of services, from custodial care to comprehensive child development, depending on staff-child ratios, staff qualifications, program content, equipment, and related characteristics.[34] Opportunity benefits in employment may range from equal access to preferential treatment to discrimination in reverse through the use of federal subsidies, legal sanctions, and political pressure. In education there is considerable debate regarding the substance of affirmative action provisions, running the gamut from special recruitment efforts to the modification of admission standards.[35] The redistribution of power in various settings may cover a spectrum of influence, from that exercised by a citizens' advisory committee to community control of local institutions.[36] Without clarifying the substantive aspects of services, opportunities, and power, we are severely limited in understanding precisely what it is that social programs provide.

Expediency of Abstraction

To prescribe that policy analysts should strive for precision in defining the nature of social provisions is not to deny the political function of abstraction. Although our major concern is with comprehending social welfare policy by dissecting the various dimensions of choice, we allow ourselves a momentary detour because in the real world of policy choice, ambiguity in the design of social provisions serves an important purpose. This is critical to note, if for no other reason than to balance the wanton analytic impulse to dissect social choices endlessly with the wisdom of practical experience. The advantage of leaving the nature of the social provision vague when there are strong contending views concerning the specifics of solutions to social problems is not a secret. The advantage is that it allows those who formulate policies to secure broader support. When social provisions are defined at a high level of abstraction, different parties may read into them what they please, and agreement is easier to reach. Also, upon implementation there is greater flexibility and potential for experimentation. Once such vague provisions are operationally transformed, of course, former advocates may find themselves startled at the substance of their creation, and perhaps may even end up seeking its undoing. Hence, there is a fragile quality to the political expedience of abstraction; it can smooth the way for passage of legislation without necessarily developing the commitments required to support a program over the long haul.

The classic example, the Community Action Program (CAP), Title II-A of the Economic Opportunity Act of 1964, spearheaded the War on Poverty under President Johnson. It took approximately six months for this program to move from the drawing board to enactment. John Donovan indicates that few single pieces of domestic welfare legislation of comparable importance had ever moved through Congress with such ease and rapidity. He also observes, "There were only a few people in Washington early in 1964 who had any very clear notion of what community action in fact was."[37]

According to the bill presented to Congress, community action was defined as a program that

1. mobilizes and utilizes, in an attack on poverty, public and private resources of any urban or rural, or combined urban and rural geographical area . . . including but not limited to a state, metropolitan area, county, city, town, multicity unit, or multicounty unit;

2. provides services, assistance, and other activities of variety, scope, and size to give promise of progress toward elimination of poverty through developing employment opportunities, improving human performance, motivation, and productivity, and bettering the condition under which people live, learn, and work;

3. is developed, conducted, and administered with the maximum feasible participation of residents of the areas and members of the groups [served] . . . ; and

4. is conducted, administered, or coordinated by a public or private non-profit agency . . . which is broadly representative of the community.[38]

This statement is seemingly innocuous, in part because of the legal syntax but also because its deft phrasing is general enough to allow different minds to draw different conclusions about its intent. The task force responsible for drafting the antipoverty bill viewed community action as a mechanism for increasing the participation and power of the poor in the political life of the community. Moynihan notes, "The occasionally-to-be-encountered observation that Community Action Programs are a federal effort to recreate the urban ethnic political machines that federal welfare legislation helped dismantle, would not misrepresent the attitudes of the task force."[39]

During the congressional hearings on the antipoverty bill there was little explication of the idea that community action was intended to transfer power to the poor. One notable exception was Attorney General Robert Kennedy, who pointed out that the poor were powerless to affect the institutions that served them and that community action could change this pattern.[40] Another, New York City Mayor Robert F. Wagner, opposed the provision giving decision-making power to the poor: "The sovereign government of each locality in which a Community Action Program is proposed should have the power of approval over the makeup of the planning group, the structure of the planning group, and over the plan."[41]

What emerged from the hearings was a number of interpretations, many of which implied that community action would provide primarily instrumental, opportunity, or service benefits.[42] Stressing the instrumental provision, Marion Crank, Speaker of the Arkansas House of Representatives, told the subcommittee, "The important new feature of Title II is that it will encourage a coordinated effort toward solving some of the serious problems in our area."[43] Emphasizing service provision, Robert C. Weaver noted, "The Community Action Programs will focus upon the needs of low-income families and persons. They will provide expanded and improved services and facilities where necessary in such fields as education, job training and counseling, health, and housing and home improvement."[44] But the nebulous quality of the provision was typified by the comments of Representative Perkins, who referred to Title II as the "community facilities provision."[45] Under the circumstances, it is not surprising that the requirement for "maximum feasible participation" in Section 202(a)(3), which was to become for politicians the bête noire of community action, slipped through the congressional hearings virtually unquestioned.

Thus, depending largely on the different viewpoints and preferences of those assessing the policy, it was assumed that the major social provision of community action would take one of three forms: an instrument to coordinate the planning and delivery of services, an increase in the level of services for the poor, or an increase in the decision-making powers of the poor to formulate and administer their own local programs.

The Community Action legislation was defined broadly enough to encompass all of these interpretations. But two things were left unclear. The first was the order of priority. The possibility that the provisions might be mutually inconsistent was largely overlooked; for example, no one dealt with the possibility that the transfer of power to the poor might require tactics militating against the increase of goods and services and impeding efforts at coordination. No guidelines were offered for trade-offs among different objectives. Second, and more significant, there was little probing of the substance of these various social provisions. What types of services did the poor need and want? How much power and influence did "maximum feasible participation" imply? Did "participation" mean that the poor were to be advisors or to have a controlling vote? Serious consideration of these choices would, no doubt, have delayed passage of the legislation. Instead, it sailed through Congress in a haze of abstraction.

When it came to implementation, and efforts were made to specify and operationalize the phrase "maximum feasible participation," the program encountered heavy resistance. By 1965, when the first guidelines for involvement of the poor were issued, local mayors were already expressing considerable displeasure with the program and were demanding that local governments be given greater control.[46] The Bureau of the Budget also reacted by suggesting that the poor should be involved less as policymakers and more as community action personnel.

In 1966, Congress imposed its own restrictions on the use of community action funds, and by 1967 the Economic Opportunity Act was amended to clarify the substance of "maximum feasible participation." These amendments gave states, counties, and cities the power to incorporate local CAP agencies within their own government structures or to designate other groups to fill this role. Although very few local governments chose to exercise this option, the amendments symbolized and reaffirmed the fundamental authority and control of local governments. In addition, these amendments limited the composition of CAP agency boards to no more than one-third poor, with the remaining membership divided equally between public officials and representatives from the private sector. When the dust had settled, the definition of "maximum feasible participation" as power allocated to the poor had been carefully limited.

In 1974 the scale tipped even further toward conservatism. The Office of Economic Opportunity (OEO), which financed and coordinated the local CAP agencies, was dismantled. With its removal, control of the program was transferred to a new Community Services Administration (CSA), and its financial base experienced a precipitous decline, from $1.1 billion in 1977 to $527 million in 1981.[47] By 1984 the Republican administration was recommending that CSA's functions be incorporated under the Social Services Block Grant.[48]

Although the Community Action Program did not achieve the empowerment of the poor hoped for by many of its supporters, it did pave the way for significant increases in citizen participation in social welfare programs. Indeed, since the mid-1960s, citizen participation has become an institutionalized feature of community planning and decision making.[49]

SOCIAL PROVISIONS AS REFLECTIONS OF POLICY OBJECTIVES

Choices concerning the form of social provision can be understood in reference to underlying values reflecting individualist and collectivist orientations toward social control and consumer sovereignty. Whereas this perspective affords a general level of explanation, particular choices concerning social provisions are more complicated.

Social provisions also directly reflect policy objectives. To comprehend fully why a policy design contains specific provisions requires insight into the assumptions that underlie policy objectives. To gain such insight we must understand policy objectives not simply as ends but also as means-ends relationships. That is, objectives articulate how the cause-and-effect relationships of social problems are perceived and therefore represent statements of the theoretical outlooks of those involved in policy formulation.

In practice, of course, policy objectives are rarely stated in theoretical terms since that would tend to make decision makers appear tentative and unsure. The notion that objectives are only theories does find its way into many research and demonstration programs. But on the whole, program objectives are put forth with emphatic assurances that the suggested provisions are valid solutions to clearly understood problems. To do otherwise—to assess proposals candidly and skeptically—is to invite the wrath of advocates and to undermine the confidence of potential allies. On the one hand, if policymakers are too critical and pessimistic about a program, the public is not likely to be supportive. On the other hand, if their optimistic confidence is misplaced, they can lose credibility and may suffer at the polls.

Although planners, administrators, and policy analysts may sympathize with the plight of elected officials, it is not their own. To be effective in what they do, they need a clear grasp of the theoretical and tentative quality of policy objectives. Moynihan's charge that the failure of professionals in the development of the War on Poverty "lay in not accepting—not insisting upon—the theoretical nature of their propositions" may be somewhat inflated but it underscores the point.[50] That is, professional obligation entails the critical examination of the theories and assumptions that support the choice of different social provisions. As Suchman explains,

> The process of seeking to understand the underlying assumptions of an objective is akin to that of questioning the validity of one's hypothesis. Involved is a concern with the theoretical basis of one's belief that "activity A will produce effect B." Such concerns are the earmark of professional growth. So long as one proceeds on faith in accepted procedures without questioning the basis for this faith, one is functioning as a technician rather than a professional. The future development of the various fields of public service as science as well as art will depend to a large extent upon their willingness to challenge the underlying assumptions of their program objectives.[51]

With this in mind let us take a final look at the Community Action Program. We have noted that its major thrust was posited in the form of instrumental, service, and power provisions, depending on the different viewpoints and preferences of those promoting the policy. These different viewpoints and preferences did not derive from whim; in most cases they reflected certain theories and assumptions about the causes of and remedies for poverty.

There are many intricate theories of poverty, but the purpose of this discussion is to illustrate how theory applies to the analysis of social provisions. Rather than present the details of these theories, we will consider three independent variables around which many are organized: resource deficiency, individual deficiency, and institutional deficiency.[52]

From the viewpoint of *resource deficiency*, lack of resources such as health care and adequate housing is a primary characteristic of poverty and also a factor contributing to its development and perpetuation.[53] Simply put, this is a formal expression of the conventional assumption that "to get, you must first have." To the extent that CAP provisions were concentrated on special kinds of services, such as neighborhood health centers and home improvement, program objectives were based on the proposition that poverty could be reduced by changing the circumstances under which people live.

The theory of *individual deficiency* is based, in its most primitive form, on Social Darwinism: Poverty is attributed to personal defects, which make some less fit to prosper than others. A less invidious version of the theme focuses on the "culture of poverty"; poverty is explained in terms of a debilitating cultural and environmental milieu that incapacitates the poor. The defect is not biological; rather the values, norms, and behaviors of the poor are at fault. In either case, this perspective leads to the conclusion that poor people must be changed.[54] To the extent that CAP provisions were concentrated on counseling, training, and educational services, program objectives were based on the proposition that reducing poverty required changing skills, values, and behaviors.

Poverty may be explained also in terms of *institutional deficiency.* The basic assumption here is that social welfare institutions not only fail to function properly but also operate in ways that sustain poverty.[55] This perspective found expression in two provisions of the Community Action Program. The objective of the instrumental provision, with CAP agencies serving a coordinating and planning function, was to improve institutional performance by increasing rationality, efficiency, and comprehensiveness. The institutional deficiency, here interpreted as a technical problem, was addressed through administrative channels. The provision of power, in contrast, views institutional deficiency as a political problem. The objective, then, is to make social welfare institutions more responsive to the poor, not through technical rationality but by increasing the poor's political capacity to influence these institutions. To the extent that community action was interpreted in these terms, program objectives were based on the proposition that reducing poverty requires change in the institutional structures that contribute to its maintenance.

Which are the best or the preferred interpretations of the Community Action Program? On this question the analysis sheds little light. An explication of the theories and assumptions that underlie the choice of different social provisions does not create the rules for choosing. It does help to clarify what we are choosing, which is useful in two respects. First, it offers a basis for making judgments about the coherence of policy design in terms of the complementarity of social provisions. Many social welfare policies have multiple objectives, requiring the delivery of more than one type of provision. In some cases, these objectives are incompatible because of their underlying assumptions. For instance, it has been suggested that community action's service and power objectives were contradictory because of the different assumptions underlying each. To put it bluntly, if the poor suffer mainly from individual deficiencies (e.g., their need for services), increasing their power vis-à-vis service-giving agencies is placing the healer in the arms of the lame. However, if institutional deficiency is seen as the major problem, offering increased services only buffers and protects the status quo.

The second function of this analysis is to specify the major independent variables on which we are putting our money, so to speak. Clarification of this point provides guidelines to assemble empirical data that bear on the validity of the assumptions and also furnishes referents for policy evaluation once it is implemented. Social welfare policy is rarely based on evidence that is so overwhelmingly weighted in one direction as to be determinate. Nevertheless, it is pertinent to inquire about whether there is evidence that a given provision will produce a specified outcome. Faith may be a potent sedative for uncertainty, but for the thoughtful design of social provisions it is insufficient.

However, the influence of sheer faith in underlying theories and assumptions cannot be ignored; although we emphasize empirical grounding, choices regarding social provisions are, often as not, light on evidence.[56] A prominent example is cited by Connery and others in discussing the major assumptions supporting the development of community mental health programs:

> In 1963, when the basic legislation was being considered, it was noted that there were no American studies demonstrating that, when the quality of care was held constant, community-based treatment facilities functioned any better than those located in large hospitals. If this is valid, it would appear that the nature of mental health services and the investment of hundreds of millions of dollars throughout the country was substantially shaped on the basis of firmly held and persuasively argued beliefs that lacked a substantial empirical base.[57]

We introduced this section by suggesting that understanding specific choices concerning social provisions required a grasp of the theories and assumptions underlying policy objectives. At this point we advise that a distinction be drawn between theories and assumptions (along the lines noted in Chapter Two), theories being considered as deriving largely from empirical insights and assumptions being based on articles of faith and ideology. Obviously, this distinction will often be difficult to make, and it will always be relative. Yet heightened sensitivity to the *why* of social choice is enhanced by considering not only the proposed cause-and-effect relationships that underlie policy objectives but also the degree to which these relationships are informed by theory or assumption—by the tenets of evidence or faith.

WHAT IS NOT PROVIDED?

In analyzing the nature of social provisions, we have focused on delineating the form and substance of social welfare benefits. We have sought also to understand the reasons for social choices among alternatives with reference to broad value orientations as well as theories and assumptions underlying specific policy objectives. Overall, we have focused on what is provided. Therefore, it may seem odd to conclude this chapter with the question "What is not provided?" This question requires another class of latent assumptions to be recognized and brought into the analysis of choice. These assumptions do not bear directly on the cause-and-effect relationships relating to specific policy objectives; rather they are integral to the design of social provisions in general. They have to do with assumptions about what exists in the external system and can be counted on to accompany the provision of social welfare benefits. One need not look very hard to find that the social provisions of welfare policies frequently require human resources and supportive services that are nonexistent and unlikely to develop within a reasonable period of time. Indeed, it is almost embarrassingly simple to provide examples. Consider, for instance, some brief observations on the following four programs.

Public Assistance

In 1965 it was estimated that to obtain the full advantage of services under the 1962 Social Security Act amendments, 31,000 graduate social workers would be needed by 1970. At the time of this estimate, public assistance agencies employed fewer than 2,500 graduate social workers, and fewer than 3,000 graduate social workers were being educated annually for all public and private programs, most of whom were predisposed to work for private agencies.[58] Although the legislation contained provisions to increase the supply of qualified workers, they were severely inadequate for the task. Examining the record, Steiner notes,

> In some ways the services emphasis did not have a real test, but the disturbing factor is that it was always obvious that personnel to do the job were not available. . . . No one had ever claimed that just anybody could provide services. This is the way it worked out, however, and what the House Ways and Means Committee saw in 1967 was the big picture: five years of service, no results. Of course, there was no point in offering as an explanation the absence of trained personnel because there was no more likelihood that trained personnel could be provided in subsequent years than had been the case in previous years.[59]

Community Mental Health

Conservative estimates of the personnel requirements for staffing the nationwide network of centers proposed in the 1965 amendments to the Community Mental Health Centers Act showed a need for 30,000 professionals from the four basic mental health disciplines of psychiatry, psychology, social work, and mental health nursing. As reported during the congressional hearings, this figure equaled almost half the total supply of such professional personnel at that time. Although federal grants were made available to train additional mental health professionals, the expansion of human resources in these fields is clearly subject to the strictures of prolonged training, especially for psychiatrists. This fact led one team of investigators to conclude, "Even with money available to pay them, it seems highly questionable whether these professionals will be available in sufficient numbers to make the program a reality."[60]

Social Services

In the 1970s there was a surge of planning for the delivery of social services. One of the first large-scale planning efforts was introduced by the 1973 amendments to the Older Americans Act, which established a network of more than 600 Area Agencies on Aging responsible for developing annual plans for services to the elderly. An even more significant planning effort was set in motion through the 1974 Title XX Amendments to the Social Security Act. Under Title XX, the states were required to engage in a tremendous amount of work each year to produce a Comprehensive Annual Service Plan (CASP). In 1978, for example, Massachusetts had 40 area planning teams, which performed county needs assessments, conducted public hearings, and submitted 149 program proposals. This vast planning activity, annually involving hundreds of citizens, professionals, and elected officials in each state, placed a heavy burden on human resources in the social welfare system. A nationwide study of Title XX plans reveals little evidence, however, that annual planning generated much in the way of program change, reallocation of resources, or fine tuning of policies from one year to the next. The annual plan appeared to be a ritualistic activity justified more by tradition than by principles of prudent forecasting.[61] Recognizing this fact, federal officials in 1980 permitted states to shift from a one-year to a two- or three-year planning cycle. Also in 1980, federal regulations for the Older Americans Act jettisoned the requirement of annual planning by AAAs in favor of a three-year planning cycle.

Employment

An expanded role for job-training programs has been a goal of numerous federal and state policy initiatives since the 1960s. From the WIN (Work Incentive) program of 1965 (discussed in Chapter Two) to the Welfare Reform Act of 1988, public assistance and employment and training policies have sought to increase broadly the ability, the "human resources," of disadvantaged youths and adults to enter the labor market and support themselves and their families. Commenting on this trend, Levitan and

Taggart have pointed out major obstacles to program success that are often overlooked, not the least of which is the availability of training personnel.

> One constraint is the lack of trained manpower to administer projects. Too often it is assumed that demand will create supply. As proof, many point to the fact that while there were only a handful of manpower "experts" ten years ago there are now many thousands. No doubt there has been an increase in competent personnel, but the administrative difficulties of the programs suggest that many of the instant experts are lacking adequate preparation. If the programs are continuously expanded, it is doubtful that personnel can be supplied to take care of needs.[62]

This obstacle is not easily overcome. A study by Mary Sanger in 1984 revealed several major deficiencies in the WIN program, including "poor administrative structure, inadequate funding for supportive services, and lack of staff training."[63]

In more recent years, it has been the lack of available support services that has received the most attention. Job-training efforts, no matter how competent the staff, may be of limited utility if recipients are unable to obtain basic education, medical aid, child care, family planning and life skills assistance, transportation, and counseling.

Dubinsky describes one training program that was forged in a cauldron of heated rhetoric and arduous negotiations between indigenous black groups from Pittsburgh's poverty neighborhoods and local construction unions. Out of a hard-won struggle, the basic provision of on-the-job training slots was finally secured. But when the program was implemented, the trainees often did not show up for work. At the point of success, major difficulties were encountered because a support service that received casual attention in the policy design failed to materialize. That is, many job sites were out of reach of public transportation and few trainees owned automobiles. Only as an afterthought, following a period of confusion and hardship for trainees and program officials, was this necessary support service created through a special contract for transportation with the city bus company.[64]

In the recent debate over welfare reform, the importance of support services has been endorsed by most analysts, although there is considerable disagreement concerning the mix and quantity of the services necessary to promote self-sufficiency. One of the most obvious needs, however, is child care. If women with preschool-age children are to participate conscientiously in work training efforts, they need to have care for their children. About 82 percent of AFDC (Aid to Families with Dependent Children) recipients have children under six, and most of these parents report needing reasonably priced child care in order to work. It is safe to conclude that a broad expansion in the availability of care is necessary if job-training programs are to succeed.[65]

CONCLUSION

Social provisions often depend for implementation on a complex system of interrelated services and human resources. In examining the design of social provisions we must be attentive to what exists in the larger context, in the field or system in which the benefit is being offered. Thus, through the analytic lens applied to this dimension of choice, we view the form and substance of social provisions not only in terms of values, theories, and assumptions regarding what is explicitly proposed but also with an eye toward what is taken for granted as available in the external system. Accordingly, we may begin to discern what is intended and what is possible in the choice of policy benefits.

Once these benefits have been decided on, it is necessary that some organizational structure be created to connect the social provision with relevant support services and the recipient population, which leads us to the next chapter and an analysis of the systematic arrangements for the delivery of social provisions.

NOTES

1. Alva Myrdal, *Nation and Family* (Cambridge, MA: MIT Press, 1968), pp. 133–153. A similar position is offered in Charlotte Whitton, *Dawn of Ampler Life* (Toronto: Macmillan of Canada, 1943). And for a utopian proposal where benefits in kind are employed more generally as the foundation of a guaranteed standard of living, see Paul Goodman and Percival Goodman, *Communitas,* 2nd ed., rev. (New York: Vintage Books, 1960), pp. 188–217.

2. The question of how directly the objective is served can be asked quite apart from the issue of how well the objective is served. The former involves effectiveness in terms of impact, the latter in terms of performance or ultimate outcome.

3. For further discussion of this assumption, see James Buchanan, "What Kind of Redistribution Do We Want?" *Economia,* Vol. 35 (May 1968); and Martin Rein, "Social Policy Analysis as the Interpretation of Beliefs," *Journal of the American Institute of Planners,* Vol. 37, no. 5 (September 1971).

4. This assumption, drawing on the interrelated notions of the "common welfare" and the "harmony of human interests," is examined by Gunnar Myrdal, who observes, "We want to believe that what we hold to be desirable for society is desirable for all its members." See Gunnar Myrdal, *Value in Social Theory,* ed. Paul Streeten (London: Routledge & Kegan Paul, 1958), p. 137.

5. Raymond J. Struyk and Marc Bendick, Jr., eds., *Housing Vouchers for the Poor* (Washington, DC: Urban Institute Press, 1981).

6. Alva Myrdal, *Nation and Family,* p. 151.

7. Gerald M. Holden, "A Consideration of Benefits In-Kind for Children," in *Children's Allowances and the Economic Welfare of Children,* ed. Eveline M. Burns (New York: Citizen's Committee for Children of New York, 1968), p. 151.

8. Asa Briggs, "The Welfare State in Historical Perspective," in *Social Welfare Institutions,* ed. Mayer Zald (New York: Wiley, 1965), p. 62.

9. Sigmund Freud, *Civilization and Its Discontents,* ed. and trans. James Strachey (New York: W. W. Norton, 1962), p. 42.

10. Alva Myrdal, *Nation and Family*, p. 150.

11. Milton Friedman, "The Role of Government in Education," in *Economics and the Public Interest*, ed. Robert Solo (New Brunswick, NJ: Rutgers University Press, 1955), p. 124.

12. Alva Myrdal, *Nation and Family*, p. 150.

13. See, for example, Shirley Buttrick, "On Choice and Services," *Social Service Review*, Vol. 44, no. 4 (December 1970), 427–433; and Anthony Pascal, "New Departures in Social Services," *Social Welfare Forum* (New York: Columbia University Press, 1969), pp. 75–85.

14. James Thompson, *Organizations in Action* (New York: McGraw-Hill, 1976), pp. 17–18.

15. Friedman, "Role of Government in Education," p. 144.

16. John K. Galbraith, *The Affluent Society* (New York: Mentor Books, 1958), p. 205.

17. See Friedrick Hayek, "The *Non Sequitur* of the 'Dependence Effect,'" in *Private Wants and Public Needs*, ed. Edmund S. Phelps (New York: W. W. Norton, 1962), pp. 37–42.

18. Alice M. Rivlin, *Systematic Thinking for Social Action* (Washington, DC: Brookings Institution, 1971), pp. 137–138.

19. A more detailed discussion of these conditions is presented by Milton Friedman, "The Role of Government in a Free Society," in *Private Wants and Public Needs*, ed. Edmund S. Phelps (New York: W. W. Norton, 1962), pp. 104–117.

20. Samuel Mencher, *Poor Law to Poverty Program* (Pittsburgh: University of Pittsburgh Press, 1967), p. 336.

21. For example, see Friedman, "Role of Government in Education"; Buttrick, "On Choice and Services"; and Christopher Jencks, "Private Schools for Black Children," *New York Times Magazine*, November 3, 1968.

22. At some point in the utopian future, status/prestige as a distinct category may be appended to this list of social provisions. In Bellamy's society in *Looking Backward* (see Chapter Three), the distribution of opportunities as well as goods and resources was more or less equal among the population. But here the link between status/prestige and wealth/power was broken. Status positions and symbols that conferred honor and esteem with neither direct nor indirect material benefits (i.e., they had no market value) became the major form of social provision to compensate those who made special contributions to society.

23. Neil Gilbert and Harry Specht, "Title XX Planning by Area Agencies on Aging: Efforts, Outcome, and Policy Implications," *The Gerontologist*, Vol. 19, no. 3 (June 1979), 264–274; Stephanie Fall Creek and Neil Gilbert, "Aging Network in Transition: Problems and Prospects," *Social Work*, Vol. 26, no. 3 (May 1981), 210–216.

24. American Public Welfare Association, "The Fiscal Year 1980 Food Stamps Budget," *W-Memo*, April 5, 1979.

25. U.S. Department of Commerce, Bureau of the Census, *Statistical Abstract of the United States, 1981* (Washington, DC: U.S. Government Printing Office, 1981), p. 322.

26. Friedman, "Role of Government in Education."

27. Christopher Jencks et al., *Education Vouchers: A Report on Financing Elementary Education by Grants to Parents* (Cambridge, MA: Center for the Study of Public Policy, 1970).

28. Paul Wortman and Robert St. Pierre, "The Educational Voucher Demonstration: A Secondary Analysis," *Education and Urban Society*, Vol. 9 (August 1977), 471–491.

29. David Cohen and Eleanor Farrar, "Power to Parents? The Story of Education Vouchers," *Public Interest*, Vol. 48 (Summer 1977), 72–97.

30. See, for example, D. Weiler, ed. *A Public School Voucher Demonstration: The First Year at Alum Rock* (Santa Monica, CA: Rand Corporation, 1974); Wortman and St. Pierre, "Educational Voucher Demonstration"; and R. Crain, *Analysis of the Achievement Test Outcomes in the Alum Rock Voucher Demonstration, 1974–75* (Santa Monica, CA: Rand Corporation, 1976).

31. E. G. West, "Choice or Monopoly in Education," *Policy Review*, Vol. 15 (Winter 1981), 103–117.

32. *National Journal*, August 21, 1990, p. 38.

33. For a review of the various perspectives that might be included under this type of provision, see Scott Briar and Henry Miller, *Problems and Issues in Social Casework* (New York: Columbia University Press, 1972).

34. See, for example, Pamela Roby, "How to Look at Day-Care Programs," *Social Policy*, Vol. 3, no. 2 (July/August 1972), 220–226; and Angela Browne, "The Mixed Economy of Day Care," *Journal of Social Policy*, Vol. 13, no. 3 (July 1984), 321–331.

35. Neil Gilbert and Harry Specht, "Institutional Racism and Educational Policy," *Journal of Social Policy*, Winter 1973, pp. 27–39.

36. Further discussion of these alternatives is presented in the next chapter.

37. John C. Donovan, *The Politics of Poverty* (New York: Pegasus, 1967), p. 40.

38. U.S. House of Representatives, *A Bill to Mobilize the Human and Financial Resources of the Nation to Combat Poverty in the United States*, 88th Cong., 2nd sess., March 1964, H.R. 10443, pp. 17–18.

39. Daniel Moynihan, "What Is 'Community Action'?" *The Public Interest*, no. 5 (Fall 1966), 7.

40. U.S. House of Representatives, Economic Opportunity Act of 1964, *Hearing Before the Subcommittee on the War on Poverty Program* (Washington, DC: U.S. Government Printing Office, 1964), Part I, p. 305.

41. Statement of Robert F. Wagner before the Ad Hoc Subcommittee on the Poverty Program of the House Education and Labor Committee, April 16, 1964, pp. 3–4 (mimeographed).

42. For a more thorough discussion of these various interpretations, see Moynihan, "What Is 'Community Action'?"

43. Statement by the Honorable Marion H. Crank, speaker of the Arkansas House of Representatives, before the Ad Hoc Subcommittee on the Poverty Program of the House Education and Labor Committee, April 10, 1964, p. 3 (mimeographed).

44. Statement of Robert C. Weaver before the Ad Hoc Subcommittee on the Poverty Program of the House Education and Labor Committee, April 16, 1964, p. 12 (mimeographed).

45. Quoted in Elinor Graham, "Poverty and the Legislative Process," *Poverty as a Public Issue*, ed. Ben B. Seligman (New York: Free Press, 1965), pp. 251–271.

46. For example, see Advisory Commission on Intergovernmental Relations, *Intergovernmental Relations in the Poverty Program* (Washington, DC: U.S. Government Printing Office, 1966); and William F. Haddad, "Mr. Shriver and the Savage Politics of Poverty," *Harpers*, December 1965, pp. 43–50.

47. Michael Gutowski and Jeffrey Koshel, "Social Services," in *The Reagan Experiment*, eds. John Palmer and Isabel Sawhill (Washington, DC: Urban Institute Press, 1982), p. 311.

48. Social Legislation Information Services, "The FY 1985 Reagan Budget Social Program Proposals," *Washington Social Legislation Bulletin*, Vol. 28, no. 27 (February 13, 1984), 108.

49. For a detailed analysis of this trend, see Harry Specht, "The Grass Roots and Government in Social Planning and Community Organization," *Administration in Social Work*, Vol. 2 (Fall 1978), 319–334.

50. Daniel Moynihan, *Maximum Feasible Misunderstanding* (New York: Free Press, 1969), pp. 188–189.

51. Edward A. Suchman, *Evaluative Research* (New York: Russell Sage, 1967), p. 41.

52. For a concise review of the literature and an elaboration of these perspectives on poverty, see Martin Rein, *Social Policy* (New York: Random House, 1970), pp. 417–445.

53. For an excellent example along this line of study, see Alvin Schorr, *Slums and Social Insecurity* (Washington, DC: U.S. Government Printing Office, 1963).

54. See Michael B. Katz, *The Undeserving Poor* (New York: Pantheon Books, 1989), esp. pp. 9–36.

55. See, for example, Frances Piven and Richard Cloward, *Regulating the Poor* (New York: Random House, 1971); and Ian Gough, *The Political Economy of the Welfare State* (London: Macmillan, 1979).

56. Joel F. Handler & Jane Hollingsworth, *The Deserving Poor* (Chicago: Markham Publishing, 1971), p. 127.

57. Robert H. Connery et al., *The Politics of Mental Health* (New York: Columbia University Press, 1968), p. 478.

58. Advisory Council on Public Welfare, *Having the Power We Have the Duty*, Report to the Secretary of Health, Education, and Welfare (Washington, DC: U.S. Government Printing Office, 1966), p. 79.

59. Gilbert Steiner, *The State of Welfare* (Washington, DC: Brookings Institution, 1971), p. 39.

60. Connery et al., *Politics of Mental Health,* p. 530.

61. Neil Gilbert, Harry Specht, and David Lindeman, "Social Service Planning Cycles: Ritualism or Rationalism?" *Social Service Review,* Vol. 55, no. 3 (September 1981), 419–433.

62. Sar A. Levitan and Robert Taggart, II, *Social Experimentation and Manpower Policy: The Rhetoric and the Reality* (Baltimore: Johns Hopkins University Press, 1971), p. 85.

63. Mary Bryna Sanger, "Generating Employment for AFDC Mothers," *Social Service Review,* Vol. 58, no. 1 (March 1984), 32.

64. Irwin Dubinsky, "Operation Dig: A Black Militant Program to Train Trade Union Craftsmen," Ph.D. dissertation, Graduate School of Public and International Affairs, University of Pittsburgh, 1971.

65. Denise F. Polit and Joseph J. O'Hara, "Support Services," in *Welfare Policy for the 1990's,* eds. Phoebe H. Cottingham and David T. Ellwood (Cambridge, Mass: Harvard University Press, 1989), pp. 173–182.

Chapter Five
THE STRUCTURE OF THE DELIVERY SYSTEM

"You're very strict," said the Mayor, "but multiply your strictness a thousand times and it would still be nothing compared with the strictness that the Authority imposes on itself. Only a total stranger could ask a question like yours. Is there a Control Authority? There are only Control Authorities. Frankly, it isn't their function to hunt out errors in the vulgar sense, for errors don't happen, and even when once in a while an error does happen, as in your case, who can say finally that it's an error?"

Franz Kafka
The Castle

When Kafka's hero wanders through a bureaucratic maze, continually confounded in his attempts to make sense of the system, his fictional world is not far removed from the real-life experiences encountered by many applicants for social welfare benefits. The system for delivering these benefits is closed to certain applicants; others enter it only to find themselves shuffled from one agency to another without receiving appropriate assistance. And many will ask in despair for a "control authority" through which to seek redress for their grievances. At times the answer they receive closely approximates the preceding quotation.

This situation does not necessarily arise out of authoritarian mentalities or bad intentions. Indeed, there is no way to avoid some measure of bureaucracy in structuring services. Organization, to a considerable degree, requires bureaucracy. But there are important choices to consider in designing organizational forms, choices that give policymakers and planners opportunities to avoid some of the more Kafkaesque aspects of service delivery. In this chapter we will examine some of these choices and explore areas of uncertainty in the design of social welfare delivery systems. Although much of the analysis is applicable to the various forms of social provision discussed in the previous chapter, our emphasis will be on the delivery of social services.

The delivery system, as noted in Chapter Two, refers to the organizational arrangements that exist among service providers and between service providers and consumers in the context of the local community. We focus on the local community because this is where providers and consumers usually come together.[1] Service providers may be individual professionals, self-help associations, professional groups, or public and private agencies acting separately or in concert to provide services in private homes and offices, community centers, welfare or mental health departments, hospitals, and so forth.

The number of choices involved in designing delivery systems is large. Consider, for example, the following six options (which by no means exhaust the possibilities). Providers may:

Be administratively centralized	or Be decentralized
Combine services (e.g., health, probation, and income support)	or Offer single services
Be located under one roof	or Maintain separate facilities
Coordinate efforts	or Never communicate
Rely on professional employees	or Employ consumers or "paraprofessionals"
Concentrate authority in the hands of "experts"	or Give major authority to service users

If we were to consider only these six choices and treat each as dichotomous (which they are not), we would end up with 64 possible delivery system combinations. Obviously, we must find some means to make the selection manageable. Before presenting the analytic concepts that can help do so, however, let us outline certain basic problems facing those whose job it is to design local service arrangements.

SERVICE DELIVERY: PROBLEMS OF EXPANSION AND CONTRACTION

Since the rapid expansion of the 1960s and early 1970s, the magnitude and scope of social services have contracted. As noted in Chapter Two, public expenditures for social welfare nearly doubled, from 10 percent to 19 percent of the gross national product, between 1960 and 1975, stimulated by national legislation helping communities deal with poverty, mental health, unemployment, delinquency, education, and the general quality of urban life. The development and growth of local services were accomplished with a good deal of haste and no small amount of confusion.

The subsequent contraction of services funding was abrupt. Between 1978 and 1981 federal support for major social service programs decreased by almost 20 percent. At the end of fiscal year 1982 another 20 percent was cut from these programs.[2] Through the Reagan years, inflation combined with political resistance to social spending tightly squeezed service budgets.

Expansion and contraction present different kinds of problems for the design of service delivery systems. As funding increases, interests naturally turn to devising effective means for delivering increasing levels of service; the problem is how to make a comprehensive range of services readily available to all possible beneficiaries. In periods of contraction, when demands for services far exceed available resources, the focus of concern shifts to methods of rationing; the critical issue is how to restrict the distribution of services so that demand and supply are brought into balance.

Reflecting circumstances in the field, most of the literature over the last three decades has dealt with strategies to improve the effectiveness of service delivery. By the late 1970s, however, as service funding declined, new issues came to the fore and a literature on rationing began to emerge. Although this literature is still in its formative stages, its importance is sufficient to warrant attention in any assessment of service delivery choices. Thus, the concluding section of this chapter addresses the alternatives posed by rationing strategies, as well as other emerging issues in service delivery. First, however, we analyze choices among effectiveness strategies, efforts to promote the coherence and accessibility of services.

Broadly speaking, issues of effectiveness relate to three kinds of service delivery questions: (1) Where will authority and control for decision making be located? (2) Who will carry out the different service tasks to be performed? (3) What will be the composition (the number and types of units) of the delivery system?

Attempts to answer these questions often stir controversy as they respond to the tug and pull of conflicting social values. In addressing questions about where authority should be vested, for example, the value of consumer participation may be emphasized regardless of its impact on the efficiency of service delivery. Issues having to do with efficiency compete with other values that may be equally important to society, such as providing jobs for low-income people or ensuring equity in the geographic distribution of services.

In the heat of controversy, criticisms of service delivery intensify. Such criticism tends to focus on the characteristic failings of local service delivery systems, particularly fragmentation, discontinuity, unaccountability, and inaccessibility. These problematic facets of service delivery have been amply documented and analyzed.[3] Plans to reform the organization and delivery of social services usually concern one or more of them.

For a description of these problems, consider the following hypothetical circumstances: A man injured in an automobile accident is rushed by ambulance to ward A, where he is examined; he is next taken to ward B for medical treatment and then moved to ward C for rest and observation. If wards A, B, and C are in different parts of town, operate on different schedules, and provide overlapping services, that is *fragmentation*. If the ambulance disappears after dropping the patient at ward A, that is *discontinuity*. If the distance between the accident and ward A is too far; if there is no ambulance; if the patient is not admitted to the ward because of his place of residence, lack of medical insurance, or the like; or if he is taken to a ward for mental patients, that is *inaccessibility*. When any or all of these circumstances exist and our patient has no viable means of redressing his grievances, the delivery system suffers from *unaccountability*.

These problems have many facets, are interconnected at some points, and span a broader range of issues than we have just described. Problems of fragmentation concern organizational characteristics and relationships, especially coordination, location, specialization, and duplication of services. (For example, are services available in one place? Do agencies try to mesh their activities?) Problems of inaccessibility concern obstacles to a person's entering the network of local social services. (For example, does bureaucratic selectivity based on income, age, success potential, or other characteristics exclude certain persons from service?) Problems of discontinuity concern obstacles to a person's movement through the network of services and the gaps that appear as an agency tries to match resources to needs. (For example, are there adequate channels of communication and referral?) Problems of unaccountability concern relationships between persons served and the decision makers in service organizations. (For example, are those needing help able to influence decisions that affect their circumstances? Are the decision makers insensitive and unresponsive to clients' needs and interests?)

Phrased as policy issues, these problems confront policy planners and administrators with choices that although conceptually distinct, become confounded with one another in practice. That is, the ideal service delivery system is one in which services are integrated, continuous, accessible, and accountable. Taken separately, however, each of these elements strains against one or more of the others. We may summarize some of the choices as follows:

1. Reduce fragmentation and discontinuity by increasing coordination, opening new channels of communication and referral, and eliminating duplication of services (possibly increasing unaccountability and inaccessibility).

2. Reduce inaccessibility by creating new means of access to services and duplicating existing service efforts (possibly increasing fragmentation).
3. Reduce unaccountability by creating a means for clients and consumers to have input into, and increased decision-making authority over, the system (possibly increasing fragmentation and discontinuity).

Problems in service delivery do not exist because there is a shortage of ideas about how to improve the situation. On the contrary, the technical repertoire of social planners and public managers includes a wide range of strategies for effecting the delivery of local services. It is matters of choice and uncertainty that need to be resolved. We approach this task in the following sections by identifying the choices among service delivery strategies, analyzing the types of systemic changes related to different strategies, suggesting what needs to be known about the effects of these strategies, and explicating alternative theoretical paradigms that influence the selection of different strategies.

SERVICE DELIVERY STRATEGIES

Proposals for reform invariably accompany critical analyses of service delivery. Although specific proposals for reform contain considerable variation, most correspond to one or another of six general strategies, each of which addresses at least one of the service delivery questions mentioned earlier:

A. Strategies to restructure policy-making authority and control
   1. Coordination
   2. Citizen participation
B. Strategies to reorganize the allocation of tasks
   3. Role attachments
   4. Professional disengagement
C. Strategies to alter the composition (i.e., number and types of units) of the delivery system
   5. Specialized access structures
   6. Purposive duplication

Each of these strategies seeks to restructure local service systems to enhance service delivery. Coordination and citizen participation each impinge on the bureaucratic hierarchy of the system. Role attachments and professional disengagement alter the roles and status of actors in the systems. Specialized access structures and purposive duplication change the substantive composition of the elements in the system.

Strategies to Restructure Authority:
Coordination and Citizen Participation

Coordination. Social workers and other professionals are quick to declare their faith in the generic, the whole person, and the comprehensive approach to service. They recognize the complexity of social causation and the interdependency among the mental, physical, and environmental factors that influence clients' functioning and life chances. At the same time, the thrust of practice among professionals is toward specialization and the development of technical skills within narrowly defined areas of expertise. In one sense, service coordination helps to mitigate the strains created by the juxtaposition of specialization and the comprehensive approach in the professional value structure.

Coordination is a strategy aimed at developing an integrated and comprehensive social service system. Whereas innumerable arrangements have been suggested and tested for bringing some coherence to the natural fragmentation of services, three approaches capture most of the possibilities —centralization, federation, and collaboration. These models are exemplified in different approaches to the organization of local social services in England and the United States.

The current structure of the British system is a product of the 1970 Local Authority and Social Services Act, which prescribed a major reorganization of local service agencies. The staffs and functions of children's and welfare departments, community development services, home-help services, and other local agencies were centralized under the auspices of newly created Local Authority Social Services Departments (LASSD). In turning to the LASSD as a mechanism for centralization, the British utilized what Simon recommends as being among the most powerful of coordinative procedures.[4]

At the same time that increased coordination through administrative unification offers a remedy for service fragmentation, it also gives rise to potentially dysfunctional consequences. For instance, service centralization tends to increase the organizational distance between clients and decision-making authorities. Centralization may lead to an internalization and perhaps heightening of what were previously *inter*organizational strains. The potential for *intra*organizational conflict is especially sharpened when a variety of heretofore autonomous agencies with different aims, technologies, and perceptions are cast into a unitary organizational mold, as in LASSD.[5]

In addition, the consolidation of services under one administrative structure limits service accessibility. The "single door" may in fact be at a number of centers dispersed throughout a community. It is a single door only in the sense that it functions according to the rules and regulations of one administrative authority, with intake into the service network concentrated in the hands of a relatively few gatekeepers. Such a single door can serve as a mechanism to rationalize service delivery from the standpoint of case referral and continuity, or it can act as a barrier to service for those who, inadvertently or by design, do not fit the administrative criteria for eligibility.

The second major approach to the coordination of services is through federation, which often involves the geographic centralization of different agency resources but not their administrative unification. In the 1960s and 1970s, continuous efforts along these lines were made under federal sponsorship through neighborhood service centers sponsored by the Community Action Program of the War on Poverty, City Demonstration Agencies organized by the Model Cities Program, and focal-point agencies authorized in the 1978 amendments to the Older Americans Act.[6]

Federative structures encompass a variety of more or less formal and binding arrangements. This variability is usually expressed by reference to the degree of time, resources, and decision-making authority invested by member organizations in the joint enterprise.[7] Warren distinguishes between a federation and a coalition in this way: The former is an ongoing collaboration with a formal staff structure that has some decision-making authority generally subject to ratification by component agencies; the latter is more ad hoc, with no sharing or modifications of component agency decision-making authority.[8]

Federative arrangements require organizations to pool their skills, resources, knowledge, and staff in a cooperative venture. The costs to member agencies of such an undertaking frequently are less than the benefits of coordination.[9] By and large the goals and policies of local service agencies are not like interlocking pieces of a big jigsaw puzzle, which given time, patience, and a constructive mentality, can be fit neatly into the frame of a common cause. The fit, of course, can be accomplished but with costs to autonomy that many organizations are disinclined to pay. Thus, federative efforts often result in loosely knit coalitions that fall considerably short of the cooperative ideal.

In comparing centralization and federation strategies, the crucial distinction resides in the different control mechanisms employed in each. Federative structures involve voluntary collaboration of autonomous agencies: Cooperation is based primarily on reciprocity, and units are not bound to a formal hierarchy of positions, as they are under a centralized administration such as Britain's LASSD. Compared to bureaucratic authority, of course, reciprocity is a tenuous mechanism of control. It is operative, as Dahl and Lindblom note, "provided that the people have the same norms and conceptions of reality."[10] The federative model frequently takes the form of bilateral agreements among agencies serving overlapping clienteles. Because most agencies have a single function, individuals with multiple problems (e.g., alcoholism and mental illness; mental and physical disability; homelessness, poverty, and drug abuse) will find it difficult to deal with several separate and independent service systems. To tie these networks together, agencies frequently enter into cooperative arrangements specifying their respective roles and responsibilities for helping people in need.

During the 1980s, interagency agreements in the child and family field were frequently executed to coordinate services for multiproblem clients.[11] Collaboration among child welfare and mental health agencies became increasingly important because large numbers of troubled children and adolescents were being placed in foster care and other types of out-of-home arrangements. Working together, mental health and child welfare officials have formulated agreements identifying their joint responsibilities, creating cross-system program models, pooling funds for common clients, and requiring cross-training of personnel.[12]

Another variety of federative coordination is based on the purchase of service. This form of program integration, known as contracting, refers to arrangements promoted by state and local governments in which public funds are used to establish and implement interrelated program networks with private agencies. Although contracting is only infrequently used as a device for comprehensive planning and coordination, it does give states and localities a tool for arranging services in ways that reflect locally determined priorities. Establishing community service plans, issuing RFPs (requests for proposals), and funding service activities that connect to the public services network provides a framework for ensuring that services follow common goals and common ground rules.

Contracting systems are frequently touted as arrangements that permit governments to get out of the service-provision business altogether. Rather than overhauling public services in the comprehensive and centralized fashion of Great Britain, the contracting model can facilitate the development and coordination of private services in specific program areas. For example, by employing the leverage of federal block grants for community development, social services, and job training, state and local governments have at least the theoretical potential to bring together community agencies in ways that fit an overall, publicly determined scheme of service provision.[13]

Case-level collaboration, the third coordinative model, comprises decentralized interactions among service agencies and personnel rather than formal, structured patterns of service unification or federation. Lacking a system of coordination from above, it is often the ground-level service worker who must connect the diverse components of the helping network. Such coordination from below is nothing new, of course. Service workers have traditionally had to ensure that clients with multiple problems receive the various services they need, but the complexity of today's service delivery system increasingly demands caseworkers who have the sophistication and knowledge, and the mandate, to link clients to services in a timely and efficient manner.

Case management is one method for planning and delivering services to people who require assistance from several different sources. The case manager, a designated agency representative with cross-organizational responsibilities, works with clients in an ongoing relationship to develop a suitable service plan, to facilitate access to services, to monitor service delivery, and to evaluate service outcomes and client progress. Although "linkage" is clearly the key component, case managers must often serve as advocates and resource developers as well in order to ensure appropriate services. The model is particularly suitable for vulnerable clients who, on their own, are unable to maneuver in the service network.[14]

Case management is a primary element in the new welfare reform legislation.[15] It is also employed in complex agency systems like child welfare, where children are subject to fragmented services provided by schools, mental health services, juvenile courts, departments of social services, and other child- and youth-serving organizations. Such organizational fragmentation is often aggravated by the differing orientations of service workers, health personnel, and judges, each of whom may deal with problems like abuse and neglect by using their own theories and solutions. Pediatricians, for example, are mainly interested in the physical health of the abused child, whereas the emphasis of the caseworker is on adjudicating the child's dependency status. Similarly, the child welfare worker may find that the reluctance of some physicians to report findings of abuse obtained during physical exams undercuts their ability to investigate and prosecute the abuse.

As a coordinating mechanism, case management facilitates access to services. Although it often raises costs, especially if the case manager is effective in lobbying on behalf of clients, it can be viewed as cost effective because it leads to early identification of problems when they are, presumably, easier to treat. Moreover, case management can ensure greater efficiency in the use of services by eliminating duplication. In several welfare reform demonstrations, case managers serve a gatekeeping function, helping to focus limited services, such as child care, on those participants in greatest need.[16]

Citizen participation.   Unlike coordination strategies, in which new relationships are forged among agencies, the strategy of citizen participation is aimed at redistributing decision-making power between agencies and clients. The rationale for citizen participation is that clients will be guaranteed responsive and effective services only if they are in positions of influence. Neither the good will of professionals nor bureaucratic rationality is considered sufficient to ensure that recipients' needs are met because both professionals and organizations have multiple objectives, their own survival in the system being foremost.

The redistribution of authority through citizen participation is distinguished according to different levels and types of participation. For example, Arnstein identifies nine levels of participation, ranging from manipulation to citizen control.[17] Spiegel discusses types of citizen participation from the point of view of the level of government involved, the functional area in which decisions are made, and the degree of technicism involved in the decision.[18] Kramer approaches the analysis of this strategy by focusing on the functions and purposes of different types of citizen participation, which he describes as ranging along a continuum from receiving information to advising to planning jointly to having complete control.[19]

Ignoring the various nuances, three modal types tend to emerge. First, there is *nondistributive participation* or pseudoparticipation, which may involve therapy, education, or plain deception; in any case, there is no perceptible change in the established pattern of authority. The second is *normal participation* (tokenism to critics), in which citizen influence on decision-making authority is clear and present but to a degree that makes only modest differences in final outcomes. The third type is *redistributive participation*; here the shift in authority is such that citizen participants are able to exert substantive influence on decisions affecting the service delivery system.

Citizen participation is a strategy wherein the means represent a value in their own right, that value being democracy. The basic assumption is that democratic services will be more responsive than a system in which decision making is the prerogative solely of professionals. However, it is possible that a system can be democratized and at the same time suffer a deterioration in the quality of service delivery. In such a case the strategy might be valid for broader political reasons but not for the objectives being considered here.

Although participatory democracy connotes the idealized New England town meeting, where everybody had a right to vote (except, of course, women, slaves, and those too poor to own land), in practice citizen participation invariably requires the election or appointment of representatives. People simply do not have the time or the inclination to participate in every decision that affects them. The point is that rhetoric notwithstanding, this strategy must come to grips with the notion of representativeness and the concomitant issues of which citizens will participate, on whose behalf, and how they will be chosen.

Participation was a prominent service delivery theme during the 1960s, when the involvement of poor people became an intrinsic element of varied radical movements to organize the disadvantaged for social change (i.e., "power to the people"). Its legislative equivalent—maximum feasible participation—became not only a standard for the organization of community action boards under the War on Poverty but also the ethos for redistribution of bureaucratic and political power in society. The participation ethos joined neighborhood activists, civil rights advocates, and cultural radicals in a short-lived movement for change that sought to bring the disenfranchised into positions of genuine inclusion in society.

At the level of service delivery, the goal of maximum feasible participation sought to decenter decision making by requiring elections in low-income neighborhoods to select the boards of directors of community action agencies. The resulting experiences, however, suggest some of the problems of using this strategy. Neighborhood elections were conducted in several communities around the country, but turnouts were always disappointing—and always far below voter participation in regular municipal, state, and federal elections. In Pittsburgh, for example, less than 2 percent, and in Philadelphia, less than 3 percent, of eligible residents participated in such elections.[20] Kramer reports that "the numerous neighborhood elections in San Francisco and Santa Clara can best be described as pseudo-political processes."[21] In addition, it was not uncommon for citizen representatives to be appointed by social service agencies or to be self-selected rather than chosen through some type of electoral process.[22]

What continues to be lacking in many endeavors to select citizen representatives are mechanisms of accountability to ensure that the opinions and objectives of participants are valid expressions of local sentiment. In the absence of such accountability, the strategy of citizen participation has the potential for reproducing, on a different plane, the very difficulties it seeks to ameliorate. As Weissman observes, "Community control tends to become control of the community by some elements to the exclusion of others and does not necessarily lead to more effective services."[23] Under these circumstances, "welfare colonialism" may be replaced by an approach to local planning and decision making in which an elite group of citizen activists monopolizes the role of neighborhood spokesperson. In extreme cases, citizen activists may even become a new generation of political bosses, snatching much of the power and many of the prerogatives of the previous elites.[24]

In the post-War on Poverty era, participation models took on more conventional forms. Many of the block grants enacted in the 1970s and 1980s promoted civic mechanisms to encourage the involvement of the poor in service programs affecting their communities. The Community Development Bloc Grant, for example, provides for advertised public hearings, and many communities have established elaborate procedures involving advisory boards, need surveys, and service evaluations to ensure client participation.[25] In addition, several pieces of major legislation have incorporated provisions to stimulate the involvement of service users. Federal child welfare legislation, for example, emphasizes opportunities for the participation of natural parents in deliberations concerning the legal status of their children. More recently, federal housing policies have been reformulated to involve tenants more fully in the management of public housing. Harking back to earlier community action models, HUD (Housing and

Urban Development) has established alliances with nonprofit tenant activist groups, bypassing the traditional power centers of municipal housing professionals.

Strategies to Reorganize the Allocation of Tasks: Role Attachments and Professional Disengagement

Role attachments. Social services, in the main, are performed by middle-class professionals. Although services are offered to the entire community, a disproportionate segment of the population in need comes from the lower socioeconomic classes. The class chasm between the servers and the served is viewed, according to role attachment strategy, as an impasse to movement into and through local delivery systems. On the one hand, the middle-class professional may not understand the lower-class client's outlook on life, behavioral patterns, or cultural values. Inarticulate by middle-class standards, clients may be perceived as recalcitrant or even threatening. The norms of professional objectivity and impersonal treatment, on the other hand, prescribe behavior that may be perceived by clients as unfriendly or officious. Given these mixed perspectives, problems of access and discontinuity occur because of social stratification rather than organizational structure.[26] The case is stated succinctly by Miller and Riessman:

> The agencies must take upon themselves the responsibility for seeing that the individual patient gets to the service, or gets from one service to another. Without the assumption of this responsibility, the concept of continuity of care or services will become a meaningless programmatic shibboleth. Nor can these problems be resolved through administrative improvements alone. *A human link is needed.*[27] [Emphasis added.]

This human link, it has been argued, should be indigenous nonprofessional aides, persons who, by virtue of their lifestyles and special skills, can bridge the gap between professional agencies and poverty clientele, serving what Brager describes as a social-class-mediating function.[28] Certainly, other general economic and political values support the employment of indigenous nonprofessionals, but it is as expediters of service that such employment is relevant to a discussion of delivery system strategies.

At least three potential problems may undermine this strategy. First, the employment of nonprofessionals may mean that clients receive services that are amateurish or of a lesser quality than those offered by professionals. Second, efforts to integrate aides into the delivery structure may engender stiff resistance from professionals. Pruger and Specht comment on the inevitability and the source of this resistance:

> It is inevitable because it is rooted in the virtually irresistible structural forces that shape organizational behavior. . . . In the case of the organizationally-

based professions, the forces that insure organizational discipline comple-
ment the pressures that induce professional reliability. And because much of
the professional's self-image rests on this perception of his dearly bought
competence, competitors arriving on the scene through nontraditional routes
must almost certainly be considered impudent upstarts if not conscious
usurpers.[29]

Finally, even when nonprofessionals are effective in linkage roles and are
integrated into the service delivery structure, the latter may vitiate the
former. The effectiveness of the nonprofessionals will wane under pressures to resolve the strains between bureaucratic conformity and the freewheeling style of the indigenous worker. Examining the integration of
nonprofessionals into agency structures, Hardcastle concludes, "The diminution of the non-professional's indigenous qualities—the emphasis on
primary role skills, extemporaneousness, and lower-class behavior and
communication patterns—appears inevitable because of the essentially bureaucratic nature of the organization."[30] In addition, it is not surprising to
find that once they are on the job, many nonprofessionals bend their efforts toward becoming professionals. They seek the financial and status
rewards accruing to those who achieve higher degrees of usable knowledge
and skill.[31]

The literature on cultural factors in service delivery, it should be
noted, continues to emphasize the need for service personnel to be ethnically and culturally sensitive. This condition, however, does not require
personnel to be of the same socioeconomic class, race, or culture as the
client in order to be effective. A recent review of the literature by Snowden
and Derezotes, for example, points out that the utilization of minority staff
is associated with an increased number of minority clients. They caution,
however, against concluding that majority staff cannot work effectively with
minority clients: "Cross-race pairings can be, and often are, effective. Indeed in certain cases they may be preferable to same-race pairings. When
they go wrong for reasons related to race, this usually occurs in the early
phases of the relationship."[32]

Professional disengagement. Although the imperative of bureaucratic
conformity may cramp the style of nonprofessionals, forcing them to adopt
a professional or quasi-professional modus operandi, it has been observed
that the same imperative operates to inhibit professional functioning. For
example, Levy describes a public welfare setting where the discrepancy
between the needs of administration and those of clients posed an acute
moral dilemma for many workers.[33] He suggests that the high turnover
rate of workers in this setting was related to difficulties in reconciling their
inner feelings with the stringent logic of welfare administration. Piliavin
states the case more generally:

Social work has acquired many of the earmarks of a profession, including a professional association that has developed and promulgated standards, goals, and an ethical code for those providing social services. The members of this association and other social workers guided by its framework of values encounter a dilemma unknown to their early predecessors; they find agency policies and practices frequently in conflict with avowed professional norms.[34]

To enhance service delivery, then, it would seem to be more effective to disengage from the bureaucracy rather than try to reform it. That is, professionals are advised to undertake private practice on a fee-for-service basis to circumvent the constraints to service delivery posed by agency policies; they are to change roles, from bureaucrat to entrepreneur. Because many people who use social services cannot afford to support a fee system, it is further proposed that the financial base for implementing this strategy be furnished through government grants (e.g., Medicaid) that give clients the opportunity to choose the service provider of their choice.

Assuming that government financing through such voucherlike arrangements could somehow be accomplished, we see that this strategy has certain limitations. Private practitioners may have expertise in public welfare, corrections, relationship counseling, family services, school social work, services to the aged, and the like, but they cannot possibly be specialists in all of them. In this sense the private practitioner is subject to the same professional myopia as the agency-based worker, except that agencies may incorporate a variety of specialists. Just as in the case of the bureaucratic delivery of services, there is little to prevent private practitioners from imposing their particular brand of service—be it education, insight therapy, behavior modification, or some other technology—rather than dealing with the recipient's unique needs. And even for the least avaricious, the tendency to interpret clients' problems in terms of one's own expertise is reinforced under a fee-for-service arrangement. As a means of increasing accessibility to and coherence of the delivery system, the entrepreneurial model may prove less effective than agency-based practice.

Although there is little empirical evidence to support the presumed virtues of the entrepreneurial model, the move toward private practice has been gaining in popularity among professional social workers. According to a 1982 survey of 56,000 members of the National Association of Social Workers, 12 percent were employed under profit-making auspices, mainly private practice. This figure represents close to a fourfold increase over the 3.3 percent reporting similar employment in a 1972 survey.[35] There is some indication, in addition, that the proportion of professionals engaged in private practice increases along with experience and formal qualifications. A 1984 study in Massachusetts, for example, revealed that 45 percent of the state's 4,400 licensed independent clinical social workers—the highest of four levels of licensed social workers in that state—were employed in private practice on a full-time (19 percent) or part-time (26 percent) basis.[36]

The major assumption underlying this strategy is open to question. Although some professionals may function poorly in organizational settings, it is not necessary to conclude that organizational demands inherently limit professional functioning. Reasoned arguments can be made that there is much greater latitude for individual discretion to negotiate the constraints and opportunities of organizational life than many professionals exercise, mainly because they lack the expertise required to be effective in their roles as bureaucrats. Most professionals prefer to identify themselves as helpers and service-givers; and training is consciously sought to prepare for these roles. They tend to ignore or reject the bureaucratic role that they must carry.[37]

Furthermore, it is possible to design agency-based practice in ways that tap the energies and resources associated with entrepreneurial activity. In the Kent Community Care Project, for example, British social workers are given a budget they may spend according to the needs and circumstances of each frail elderly client. The objective is to create a local network of support services that will allow the frail elderly to remain living in the community rather than being institutionalized, and at a lower cost to the public than would result from an institutional placement.[38]

Strategies to Alter the Composition of the Delivery System: Specialized Access Structures and Purposive Duplication

Specialized access structures.   The objective of this strategy is neither to change the combination of roles in the service delivery system nor to change authority relationships through centralization or federation. Its advocates believe that specialized, professional, bureaucratic services perform important functions despite their weaknesses as delivery mechanisms. Instead of changing roles and the like, they want to change the composition of the delivery system by adding a new element, one that acts on other service agencies, to pry open their entry points and to ensure that proper connections are made by clients. In a word, access is to be provided as a social service.

Traditionally, the provision of access was considered a marginal function carried out by agency staff rather than a separate function around which to organize a distinct set of services. As a marginal function, access is unduly restricted by the narrow perspectives of agency specializations, perspectives relating primarily to an agency's core function instead of the particular problems brought by clients. This phenomenon is a byproduct of neither incompetence or malice. It is a normal structural reality of specialized service organizations.

To facilitate client access to service while maintaining a relatively high degree of specialization, it has been proposed that a new structure be added to the delivery system, one characterized as a "professionally un-biased doorway."[39] This doorway is a special agency that offers case-advocacy, advice, information, and referral services to help clients negotiate the bureaucratic maze.

Although it is in many respects a persuasive strategy, the conse-quences of access agencies may be more wished for than assured. From the client's perspective, one effect of this strategy may be increased service fragmentation and complexity. Further, whereas access services are increas-ingly important in urban societies, they are among the least tangible of services. Thus the access agency may be perceived by clients as merely another bureaucracy to negotiate, another base to be touched before the proper resources are matched to their needs.

Access strategy is also likely to influence other service agencies in the delivery system. The addition of an access agency can cause other service-providing agencies to diminish their own access services. For instance, there is likely to be reduced pressures on these agencies to perform outreach or to make referrals to clients they are unable to serve. The extent to which the creation of the access agency lessens traveling time, expense, or confu-sion in the client's search for service is presently unclear. Moreover, the separation of assessment and diagnosis (access) from treatment (services) that results from this strategy may prove rather clumsy in practice.

Purposive duplication.   Purposive duplication entails re-creating in a new agency any or all of the services available in the existing system. Purpo-sive duplication is advanced in two forms that have a surface resemblance but are dissimilar enough to warrant distinction—competition and separa-tism.

Competition involves the creation of duplicate agencies within the exist-ing delivery system to compete with established agencies for clients and resources. This strategy increases choice. More important, competition is expected to have an invigorating effect on agencies and professionals, sensitizing them to clients' needs and producing greater enterprise and creativity. The consequences of this strategy, however, are not always com-patible with its motives. Instead of a healthy competition for clients and resources, internecine conflict may ensue between powerfully entrenched agencies and new agencies scraping for a foothold in the system. The outcome of such conflict is reasonably predictable.[40]

The duplication of services to stimulate competition may be achieved through direct or indirect methods. The direct approach involves the re-structuring of the delivery system with the creation of new agencies. Com-munity action funds, for example, were often provided to develop new agencies that offered day-care, counseling, and community organization services to a community rather than to old agencies to expand service offerings already functioning. The indirect approach involves changing the form of the social provision. That is, social provisions are distributed to consumers in the form of vouchers for services.[41]

Separatism differs from competition in both the systemic location of new structures and their purposes. In the separatist design, new agencies are created and organized outside the established delivery system, which they do not seek to enter. Competition is likely to be an inadvertent and unplanned byproduct of separatism, more so for resources than for clients. The intention is to form an alternative network that will serve certain disadvantaged groups who, because of their race, ethnicity, gender, sexual orientation, or socioeconomic status, are served poorly or not at all by the existing system.

While offering direct aid to clients neglected by the existing network of services, alternative agencies also perform other functions. As Miller and Philipp point out, they engage in unorthodox activities that help to clarify legal issues; offer a theoretical critique of conventional service paradigms; and provide a community of interest for new, often unpopular, client groups.[42] In recent years, for example, independent, community-based service networks have developed for battered women, gays and lesbians, persons with AIDS, and newly arrived immigrant groups. Proponents of separatism emphasize that this strategy contains social and political values for disadvantaged groups that transcend the enhancement of service delivery.[43]

Duplicatory strategies, in either form, are enormously expensive. The money may be well spent if the new agencies become a dynamic force for desired changes in the delivery system and reach those who are excluded from services. Weighing against these benefits are the risks of expending scarce resources to produce fruitless conflict and to create even greater program fragmentation.

UNSETTLED QUESTIONS

We have identified six major strategies for improving the delivery of social services: changing patterns of authority by coordination and citizen participation, altering roles and status by role attachments and professional disengagement, and changing substantive composition by development of specialized access structures and purposive duplication. We have analyzed each for their expected benefits as well as how they may exacerbate difficulties in other directions. All of these strategies are plausible ways to develop more effective service delivery; yet each has limitations and latent dysfunctions. And although some strategies may be complementary, others are just as clearly contradictory.

Before we can accurately judge the efficacy of any of the reform strategies, certain empirical questions must be answered. We will not attempt to discuss all of these questions but rather to identify several key issues requiring more intense investigation.

Coordination

Within what range and mix of services does coordination operate most effectively? At issue here are the criteria for selecting the number and types of services to be incorporated in a coordinating structure to produce minimum strain and maximum productive collaboration. There is substantial evidence, for instance, that certain service functions (such as social action and direct services) create disharmony and strain when joined.[44] We have little evidence, however, of what the optimal mix of services is and whether coordination is more likely to improve service integration when organized around a geographic base (all services in a designated neighborhood), a clientele with special demographic characteristics (such as the aged, adolescents, lone parents, and ethnic groups), functional areas (such as health and employment), or combinations thereof.

In addition, it is difficult to gauge what, if any, cost savings are achieved through coordination. Again, the evidence is sparse and tentative. The following conclusions drawn from a study of 30 service integration projects illustrate some of the variables that enter into the measurements.

> It may not be possible to justify services integration strictly in terms of total dollar savings. Centralized/consolidated operation of core services, record-keeping, joint programming, joint funding, joint training and/or central purchase of service arrangements on behalf of a number of service providers promote economies of scale, and coordinated staff utilization, funding, planning and programming, and evaluation help reduce duplication.
>
> Although there are some cost savings resulting from economies of scale and reduction of duplication, they do not appear (at least in the short-run) to equal the input costs of administrative and core service staff required to support integrative efforts. However, if one includes protection of public investment in services as a measure of efficiency, then a stronger case can be made for service integration on grounds of efficiency,. If the public investment in one service (job training, for example) is to have lasting benefit only if another service (a job placement service, for example) is also provided, the cost involved in assuring that the client get the job placement services as well as job training may be justified in terms of protecting the investment in job training.[45]

Purposive Duplication

Under what circumstances do the savings that accrue to a large-scale organization make the duplication of services practical? The research required to answer this question involves cost-benefit analyses of social service programs. A major argument against purposive duplication and in favor of coordination is the increased efficiency attributed to the latter. However, the gain in efficiency may vary from one type of service to another.[46] At the same time, coordination or administrative unification is usually achieved at the expense of diversity. Ultimately, value judgments will be made concerning the relative desirability of efficiency versus diversity in the delivery of social services. The more information available regarding the economic costs and social benefits of duplication, the better informed these value judgments will be.

Access Agencies

To what extent does the creation of an access agency facilitate entry into social services? One issue already suggested is that the addition of an access agency to the local service system may have the unanticipated effect of decreasing the net amount of information and referral provided within that system (because other agencies may diminish similar services they previously offered). This question remains open to direct empirical investigation. Another line of study involves an analysis of the percentage of persons in need and searching for help who actually receive services. It would be useful to know how many bases these persons touch before they receive services and how this varies in the presence and absence of access agencies.

Role Attachments

What types of local nonprofessional workers are best suited to withstand the strains inherent in the performance of linkage functions between professional workers and the community serviced? At issue here is the fact that the term *indigenous nonprofessional* is applied to a variety of people with diverse values, commitments, aspirations, and reference groups. Workers in this category are likely to possess different capacities for coping with pressures toward bureaucratic conformity and professionalism. Accordingly, a useful line of investigation suggested in an exploratory study develops a typology based on the differences among nonprofessional workers.[47] It was found that certain types of nonprofessional staff members appear better suited than others to perform tasks such as outreach. Further investigation is needed to extend and substantiate these tentative findings.

Professional Disengagement

How does the move from agency-based to private practice affect access to and continuity of services offered? Although the disengagement strategy assumes that the delivery of social services will improve when the professional worker is freed from bureaucratic restriction, little evidence exists either way. A line of inquiry might involve the effects of similar services offered in a few cities by private practitioners and agency-based practitioners with regard to the characteristics of the persons served, the percentage of referrals made, the percentage of follow-ups, and the like.

Citizen Participation

To what degree does substantive citizen participation in agency decision making increase accountability to those being served? As indicated, election and selection procedures for citizen participants are frequently such that those who actually participate are not accountable to the service users they ostensibly represent. We lack careful comparisons of the decision-making behavior of citizen participants and the expressed wishes and interests of the people they serve as well as delineation of selection procedures that produce participants with a high degree of accountability. One issue for further investigation involves the extent to which elected representatives (on a block, neighborhood, and citywide basis), appointed representatives, and volunteer (or self-selected) representatives differ in their accountability.

Each of these unsettled questions contributes to the uncertainty that surrounds policymakers who are concerned with selecting the right strategy to improve the delivery of social services. To conclude that more research is needed (which it is) is the unblemished mark of academicians (which we are). To this advice practitioners may nod abstractly in agreement while they continue to design and implement the policies that govern service delivery. Thus, policy choices regarding service delivery may eventually benefit from future investigation, but they will not wait the results; choices will be based on the knowledge we possess, imperfect as is.

SELECTING STRATEGIES

All the strategies discussed are plausible approaches to improving the delivery of services. All contain different limitations, and there is considerable uncertainty surrounding the consequences of each. Given these circumstances, how do administrators and planners choose? From a policy-planning perspective, the answer depends on the operational context in which choices are made; the values to be maximized; empirical evidence about the consequences of different strategies; and in the absence of compelling evidence, theories and assumptions about how delivery systems function. It is the last aspect of choice—theories and assumptions—to which our analysis now turns.

Social service staff and organizations are the two major elements in the delivery system that can be manipulated to build coherent and effective connections between services and clients. Orientations that program planners bring to bear in considering service delivery, therefore, may be perceived as the result of the interplay of theories and assumptions regarding staff and organizations. Our purpose is to explain the ways in which these two major perspectives influence the selection of delivery strategies.

Social Service Staff: Perspectives on the Function of Professionalism

Broadly speaking, there are two perspectives on the function of social service professionalism: status enhancement and service. From the perspective of *status enhancement,* professionalism serves to protect and enlarge professional prerogatives and status. In contrast, the perspective of *service* views professionalism as a means to aiding those in need.

The service perspective corresponds to the model of a profession described by Greenwood in terms of five distinguishing attributes: (1) knowledge based on a systematic body of theory; (2) authority derived from and functionally specific to professional expertise; (3) sanction of the community to perform special services over which the profession has a monopoly; (4) a regulative code of ethics that compels moral behavior and prevents the abuse of the powers and privileges granted by the community; and (5) a professional culture consisting of values, norms, and symbols.[48] For Greenwood, the ethical code offers the clearest expression of the service perspective, requiring the "highest caliber service, irrespective of the identity and finance of the recipient," and the subordination of the practitioner's personal needs and interests to client welfare.[49]

These virtues notwithstanding, professionalization even at its best is frequently perceived as incompatible with a spirit of social reform. As stated by Wilensky and Lebeaux,

> The notion that professionalism is corrupting because it brings economic rewards and social recognition, making its adherents fat, comfortable, and lazy, is much too simple . . . more impressive is the argument that a professional absorbed in the technical side of his work aiming mainly at full use of his skills and training, preoccupied with that competent, efficient performance of which his professional colleagues would approve . . . does not have the time, energy or inclination necessary for social reform, for dedicated attention to the broader social purpose.[50]

Others adopting the status-enhancement perspective see professionals driven less by service ideals than by self-interest. For Dumont, for example, the "personal dread of poverty, the insatiable appetite for wealth, the fascination with esoteric skills and complicated machinery, and the yearning for status and command of others" constitute the true motivations of professionals.[51]

In a less polemic vein, professional knowledge and expertise may be cast in the mold of credentialism,[52] especially in the social services, where results and achievements are difficult to evaluate and a professional credential is often presumed to be synonymous with ability.[53] Professional authority is perceived as a mechanism of client control flowing from the practitioners' monopoly over service rather than their presumed technical competence.[54] Community sanction of the professional's service monopoly is viewed as bestowed by established elites to whom the professionals are accountable, not by clients. The self-regulative code of ethics may be interpreted as a device to protect professionals from outside meddling and to reaffirm their claim to esoteric knowledge; they prevent "outside interference" by asserting that only professionals are competent to judge professional work.[55] And finally, the good intentions and altruistic motives emphasized by the professional culture are questioned.[56] It has been shown, for instance, that the difference between professionals and businesspersons lies in the different paths to achievement and recognition afforded by their occupational situations rather than in their motives.

These perspectives on professional functioning are rarely applied in their extreme forms. Most planners recognize that social service staffs are motivated by mixed sets of inducements. It is not implausible, however, to presume that the extent to which this mixture is weighted in favor of one or another perspective is likely to influence strategy choices. This view suggests two broad propositions. First, to the degree that staff functioning is directed by a desire for status enhancement, efforts to improve or develop service delivery will rely on strategies that constrain, modify, or otherwise limit the prerogatives of professional staffs by (a) redistributing authority from agencies to clients, affording them some direct control over professionals (i.e., citizen participation); (b) changing roles so that staffs include indigenous nonprofessionals who are better equipped for certain functions (i.e., role attachments); and (c) adding elements to the system that create competition among professionals, stimulating them to greater effort and eventually eliminating the less competent (i.e., purposive duplication). Second, to the degree that the service perspective informs the behavior of professionals, the choice of delivery strategies will be inclined toward giving professionals greater latitude by (a) redistributing authority in ways that consolidate and strengthen the hierarchy of professional control (i.e., coordination); (b) changing the professional role from bureaucrat to entrepreneur, thereby allowing professionals to ply their trade unencumbered by the prerequisites of organizational life (i.e., professional disengagement);

TABLE 5–1 Perspectives on Professionalism and Responses to Service Delivery Questions

	PERSPECTIVES ON PROFESSIONALISM	
SERVICE DELIVERY QUESTIONS	STATUS ENHANCEMENT	SERVICE
Where shall authority and control rest?	Citizen participation	Coordination
Who carries out different tasks?	Role attachments	Professional disengagement
What will be the composition of the delivery system?	Purposive duplication	Specialized access structures

and (c) introducing new access structures that support specialization and produce further refinement in the division of labor among professionals (i.e., specialized access structures).

In Table 5–1 we summarize the propositions that are derived from the application of these perspectives to the service delivery questions identified at the beginning of this chapter.

ORGANIZATIONS: PERSPECTIVES ON THE STRUCTURE OF THE SERVICE NETWORK

Theoretical perspectives on the structure of the service network (which comprises the agencies in the delivery system) are another variable that may inspire different strategy choices. Here the concern is with the impersonal forces of organizational behavior in a systemic context rather than with the forces generated by professional behavior per se, although these phenomena are separable only in the abstract.

Two fundamental perspectives tend to direct perceptions of the organizational structure of services: the *rational* model and the *natural-system* model. According to Gouldner,

> In the rational model, the organization is conceived as an "instrument"—that is, as a rationally conceived means to the realization of expressly announced group goals. . . . Fundamentally, the rational model implies a "mechanical" model, in that it views the organization as a structure of manipulable parts, each of which is separately modifiable with a view to enhancing the efficiency of the whole. Individual organizational elements are seen as subject to successful and planned modification, enactable by deliberate decision.
>
> The natural-system model regards the organization as a "natural whole," or system. The realization of the goals of the system as a whole is but one of several important needs to which the organization is oriented. . . . The organization, according to this model, strives to survive and to maintain its equilibrium, and this striving may persist even after its explicitly held goals have been successfully attained. This strain towards survival may even on occasion lead to the neglect or distortion of the organization's goals.[57]

Thompson refined this formulation with the notion that the rational model involves a closed-system perception, whereas the natural system views organizations as open systems.[58] Each of these perspectives draws attention to certain aspects of organizational functioning and tends to neglect others. Needless to say, most planners and administrators know that organizations behave in accordance with both perspectives, although they are not always taken into account equally. There appears to be a strong susceptibility, reflected in the organizational literature, toward envisioning organizations as either closed or open systems rather than as systems that are partially closed, or half rational, and that sustain otherwise contradictory tendencies. This susceptibility occurs, Thompson suggests, because there is no convenient conceptual means of thinking simultaneously of a system as half open and half closed.[59]

The open-system perspective explains organizational behavior in terms of the organizational "task environment"—clients, funders, staff, equipment, competitors, and regulatory groups.[60] In applying this perspective, the elements originating outside the subsystem of existing service agencies can be viewed as key leverage points for change. To the extent that the professional looks at the service network with an open-system perspective, delivery system strategies will follow along lines that (1) organize clients to demand a share of authority and control over services (citizen participation); (2) utilize more essential organizational resources (professional staff) outside of the service network hierarchy, making them elements of the task environment (professional disengagement); and (3) add new elements to the task environment that will compete with the service network for clients and resources or that will operate independently as mediators between the service network and clients (purposive duplication and specialized access structures).

However, if the professional views the service network more in terms of a closed system, attention, as Gouldner implies, will be directed to strategies that enhance the efficiency of the "instrument" by manipulating organizational components to place them in better balance or welding on additional parts to make the instrument more functional. That is, the tendency will be to select strategies that (1) redistribute authority either by centralization or federation but with authority always remaining within the closed service network (i.e., coordination) and (2) incorporate roles to improve network functioning over which service organizations exercise authority (i.e., role attachments).

In Table 5–2, propositions that may be derived from the application of these perspectives are summarized for the three kinds of service delivery questions.

TABLE 5–2 **Perspectives on the Structure of the Service Delivery Network and Responses to Service Delivery Questions**

| | PERSPECTIVES ON PROFESSIONALISM | |
SERVICE DELIVERY QUESTIONS	CLOSED SYSTEM	OPEN SYSTEM
Where shall authority and control rest?	Coordination	Citizen participation
Who carries out different tasks?	Role attachments	Professional disengagement
What will be the composition of the delivery system?	Existing mix of units in the service network remains unchanged	Purposive duplication and specialized access structures

TABLE 5–3   Orientations to Service Delivery as a Function of Theoretical Perspectives

PERSPECTIVES ON STRUCTURE OF THE SERVICE DELIVERY NETWORK	PERSPECTIVES ON THE FUNCTIONS OF PROFESSIONALISM	
	SERVICE	SELF-ENHANCEMENT
Closed system	Professional/bureaucratic (coordination)	Egalitarian/bureaucratic (role attachments)
Open system	Professional/activist (professional disengagement; special access structures)	Egalitarian/activist (citizen participation; purposive duplication)

Orientations to Service Delivery

The interplay of theoretical perspectives regarding the structure of the service network and the functions of professionalism generates four types of orientations toward service delivery: professional/bureaucratic, egalitarian/bureaucratic, professional/activist, and egalitarian/activist. The relationship between the structure of the service network and the functions of professionalism is illustrated in Table 5–3.

The reader should remember that these orientations are ideal types. In reality, there are innumerable variations on each of these orientations, often with cloudy distinctions.

Professional/bureaucratic.   Professional/bureaucratic is the orientation of the administrator who "runs a tight ship," who ensures that lines of authority within the system are clear and hierarchical. A high degree of reliance is placed on professional expertise, as demonstrated by both credentials and performance, and on the rationality of bureaucratic organization. At the extreme, this orientation seeks to maximize the discretion of professionals and enhance the relationships of professionals within and between agencies. The organization and the professional are viewed as mutually supporting entities. When each is committed to the values of the other, they constitute a formidable system of institutional control.

Egalitarian/bureaucratic.   In the egalitarian/bureaucratic orientation, the importance and the power of the principles of organization are valued, as in the previous orientation. Solutions are based on a belief that whatever is done should be rationalized and brought under organizational control. Professionals, however, are not viewed as especially well equipped for service delivery—linking clients to resources. Rather, they are perceived as concerned primarily with self-enhancement. Thus, the attachment of non-professional role functions is likely to be advocated.

Professional/activist.   This orientation relies heavily on outreach strategies, sometimes referred to as aggressive casework, case-finding, or health education, depending on the area of service. In our schema such approaches support special access and professional disengagement strategies. Here the belief in professionals is strong; it is the organization that is believed to be confining. With this orientation the proper role for administrators and professionals is "enabling"; professionals can provide good services, and the function of the organization is to develop the most effective means to help consumers use them, even at the cost of organizational power and control.

Egalitarian/activist.   The egalitarian/activist orientation, the polar opposite of the professional/bureaucratic model, rejects professionalism and embraces an open-system perspective of organization. Neither the organization nor professionals are to be relied on; one must turn to different sources of legitimacy, wisdom, and policy. These sources may be alternative institutions, such as free clinics and cooperative schools, that duplicate existing agencies, or they may be the recipients of services—the people, the community, the poor. These constituencies may be defined ethnically, geographically, or any other way that suits the ideological tastes of the planner. In the extreme, this orientation is similar to Rousseau's doctrine of the general will, with its implied reduction of government to a mere agent of the community's corporate personality.[61] This orientation's answer to all service delivery questions is "Ask the people what they want and help them get it."

Is there an orientation of choice? As we have indicated, each of the strategies may mitigate some service delivery problems and exacerbate others. There is no calculus for computing all of the social costs and benefits. Any service network, whether it is "establishment" or "people-run," may operate as a system that is too closed and unable to deal efficiently with elements in its task environment or one that is too open and unable to deal efficiently with internal functioning. Any service network, whether it is highly centralized with firm boundaries or diffuse, loosely structured, and community-run may be too weighed down by the methods and doctrine of professional personnel or may lack sufficiently clear professional standards of behavior and conduct.

No orientation is ipso facto superior to another. In selecting service delivery strategies, policy planners are influenced by a combination of circumstantial factors, social values, empirical evidence, and theoretical viewpoints. At best, their choices are infused with much uncertainty.

In articulating how orientations toward strategy choices are informed by perspectives on the structure of service networks and the functions of professionalism, we sought to illuminate the contributions made by competing theoretical viewpoints. To fixate on any one strategy as a panacea for service delivery problems is to foreclose prematurely on other options, which are untested and which may have untapped potential.

CONCLUSION: RATIONING AND PROFIT IN THE 1990s

The service delivery strategies we have described were formulated in the 1960s and 1970s, an era of notable expansion in social services. The presumption of growth, as Glennerster puts it, was deeply imbedded in the intellects of social welfare planners.[62] When social services expenditures declined in the late 1970s and political support arose for meeting service needs through the market economy (discussed in Chapter Two), new issues of choice surfaced. Foremost among them are questions concerning rationing and the delivery of social services for profit.

Rationing

When social service budgets are reduced through legislative cutbacks, the burden of implementation falls on the organizations and professionals responsible for service delivery. At the juncture where clients' needs intersect with social service resources the issue is how to make do with less. The ways that service delivery systems respond affect the fundamental design of social welfare policy.

To some extent, agencies have always engaged in service rationing— the distribution of limited resources to meet social needs of greater proportions. However, during periods of expansion there is less pressure for careful thought about and stringent application of rationing methods. It is in periods of fiscal retrenchment that choices among these methods become pivotal.

Rationing may be accomplished through several processes. Ellie Scrivens analyzes the dynamics of service rationing methods by dividing them into two broad categories: demand inhibitors and supply inhibitors. Strategies that act to reduce demand erect physical, temporal, and social barriers to service. On the deterrence of physical barriers, Scrivens cites a report on the British social services in which it is observed that some of the buildings they occupy are "forbidding and the reception arrangements are often not such as to encourage anyone, let alone anyone in distress, to approach them."[63] Temporal barriers can be raised in the form of waiting lists, time-consuming application procedures, remote service locations, and inconvenient office hours. Clients also may be put off by social barriers that involve embarrassing eligibility requirements. The failure to communicate relevant information to clients about available services is another effective deterrent.

On the other side of the ledger, strategies to reduce the supply of services include restriction and dilution. With a restrictive strategy, eligibility criteria are tightened so that fewer clients needing a service actually qualify for it. This goal is accomplished by narrowing the rules governing eligibility and more stringently applying professional discretion in interpreting these rules. Strategies for diluting services decrease the amount and quality of provisions by cutting time spent with clients, prematurely terminating cases, lowering the qualifications of professional staff, and substituting volunteers for professionals.[64]

As long as demand exceeds supply, there will be some form of rationing in service delivery. Thus we must ask, "On what grounds might one choose among the various strategies outlined in this chapter?" Some of these strategies are objectionable because of their furtive character. They amount to what Lipsky calls "bureaucratic disentitlement," where service delivery is curtailed not by open and formalized policy choices but rather by "low-level marginal decisions or non-decisions of low visibility."[65] The problem, as Lipsky sees it, is that through obscure actions and inactions social service agencies may devise allocative policies that are not open to public inspection. In choosing among rationing strategies, those based on explicit procedures open to public scrutiny, such as tightening formal eligibility requirements, offer greater protection to the public than veiled activities designed to discourage consumption and dilute services.

Service for Profit

Before the 1960s, social services were delivered almost exclusively by public and voluntary nonprofit organizations. When they were addressed, questions of auspice involved the relationship between public and voluntary nonprofit providers.[66] With the increasing involvement of commercial, profit-making agencies in the delivery of social services after the mid-1960s, new questions emerged concerning how well social welfare objectives are served by profit- versus non-profit-oriented providers.

Social welfare advocates view the emergence of profit-oriented agencies in the social service arena with a jaundiced eye.[67] There is a strong suspicion that the profit motive is not morally compatible with the delivery of social welfare provisions. Yet moral objections would be difficult to sustain if it could be shown that profit-oriented agencies are the most effective and efficient means for delivering social services. In contrast, if it could be shown that profit-oriented agencies are less efficient and effective than nonprofit providers, moral objections would be unnecessary to deter the privatization of services. Assessing the efficiency and effectiveness of social services, however, is a complex business. Service objectives are often multiple and vague. They are no less important for these qualities, but they frequently defy precise measurement.[68]

Despite the difficulties of empirical measurements, there is a body of research comparing the relative effectiveness of profit versus nonprofit providers.[69] Some of these studies reveal that nonprofit providers are more sensitive to clients' needs; others show areas of care in which profit-oriented agencies do the best job; still others find no significant differences between profit and nonprofit agencies. On the whole, findings in this area are indeterminate.

In the absence of decisive empirical evidence, theoretical analyses of the distinguishing features of profit- and non-profit-oriented organizations offer several guidelines for choosing between service providers. Theoretically, nonprofit organizations have a higher degree of public accountability than profit-oriented organizations. That is, the structure of governance in nonprofit agencies typically involves boards of directors made up of people who are expected to promote the broad interests of the community. In contrast, the directors of profit-making agencies are expected to protect the financial interests of owners. In a nonprofit agency there is less temptation to exploit vulnerable service consumers for personal gain because of the legal prohibition against the distribution of net earnings among the agency's staff. Finally, there is a charitable ethos associated with nonprofit agencies that is at variance with the capitalist spirit of profit-making enterprises. There are, of course, exceptions to and degrees of these distinguishing characteristics.[70]

These differences suggest several practical conditions that bear on the choice between profit-making and nonprofit providers of social services:[71]

1. Standardization of service: Services that involve uniform procedures and standard products, such as public health vaccinations, readily lend themselves to the economic planning skills and business initiative of profit-making organizations. At the same time, the uniform character of these services allows the purchaser to monitor their delivery for potential abuses more easily than services that require a technology that is custom tailored to each case (such as therapeutic services).

2. Client competence: Many social services deal with client groups that are highly vulnerable to exploitation. Children, the mentally retarded, and confused and emotionally upset people do not have the ability to hold service providers accountable for the quality of their services. To the extent that public accountability and the charitable ethos influence the behavior of non-profit agencies more than that of profit-making agencies, the nonprofit form is preferable for delivering services.

3. Coerciveness of service: Services invested with coercive powers, such as protective services for children and work with parolees, pose a significant threat to personal liberty. In these cases, the service provider's degree of public accountability is of foremost importance. With the clients' freedom at stake, the lack of public accountability of profit-making organizations would not seem to offer the most adequate form of protection.[72]

4. Potency of the regulatory environment: Profit-oriented and nonprofit providers would seem equally preferable in delivering services that are under sufficient public regulation to ensure the maintenance of standards and client protection. We should note, however, that the scope and potency of regulatory activity in the social services are limited.

Although these conditions tend to favor nonprofit agencies as the optimal social service providers, there are clearly service areas where this general proposition does not hold, such as transportation for the handicapped and elderly. In choosing between profit and nonprofit providers, the essential issue is not to seek the universally superior form of organization but to determine the particular conditions under which profit- or nonprofit-oriented agencies may best serve social welfare clients. In assessing these conditions we must consider not only the points noted but also the nature of the purchase-of-service arrangement, especially the extent to which funding agencies can design grant requirements to ensure compliance with their objectives—an issue that brings us to the mode of finance.

NOTES

1. Although most services are designed for delivery (i.e., policy implementation) at the local level, designing and planning activities may or may not occur at the local level. Frequently, program designers and planners may be several steps removed from the local community, located as far away as the state house or the White House. The location of the program planners is a factor of major significance in policy development.

2. Michael Gutowski and Jeffrey Koshel, "Social Services," in *The Reagan Experiment*, eds. John Palmer and Isabel Sawhill (Washington, DC: Urban Institute Press, 1982), pp. 310–315.

3. Harry G. Bredemeir, "The Socially Handicapped and the Agencies: A Market Analysis," in *Mental Health of the Poor*, eds. Frank Riessman, Jerome Cohen, and Arthur Pearl (New York: Free Press, 1964); Richard Cloward and Frances F. Piven, "The Professional Bureaucracies Benefit Systems as Influence Systems," in *The Role of Government in Promoting Social Change*, ed. Murray Silberman (New York: Columbia University, School of Social Work, 1966); Alfred J. Kahn, "Do Social Services Have a Future in New York?" *City Almanac*, Vol. 5, no. 5 (February 1971), 1–11; Irving Piliavin, "Restructuring the Provision of Social Service," *Social Work*, Vol. 13, no. 1 (January 1968); William Reid, "Interagency Coordination in Delinquency Prevention and Control," *Social Service Review*, Vol. 38, no. 4 (December 1964); Martin Rein, *Social Policy: Issues of Choices and Change* (New York: Random House, 1970); Gideon Sjoberg, Richard Brymer, and Buford Farris, "Bureaucracy and the Lower Class," *Sociology and Social Research*, Vol. 50, no. 3 (April 1966), 325–337.

4. Herbert H. Simon, *Administrative Behavior*, 2nd ed. (New York: Free Press, 1965), p. 238.

5. Peter Townsend et al., *The Fifth Social Service: A Critical Analysis of the Seebohm Report* (London: Fabian Society, 1970).

6. See, for example, Neil Gilbert and Harry Specht, *Coordinating Social Services* (New York: Praeger, 1977); and Stephanie Fall Creek and Neil Gilbert, "Aging Network in Transition: Problems and Prospects," *Social Work*, Vol. 26, no. 3 (May 1981), 210–215.

7. James D. Thompson, *Organizations in Action* (New York: McGraw-Hill, 1967); and Reid, "Interagency Coordination in Delinquency Prevention and Control."

8. Roland L. Warren, "The Interorganizational Field as a Focus for Investigation," *Administrative Science Quarterly*, Vol. 12, no. 3 (December 1967), 396–419.

9. Reid, "Interagency Coordination in Delinquency Prevention and Control."

10. Robert A. Dahl and Charles E. Lindblom, *Politics, Economics, and Welfare* (New York: Harper & Row, 1953), p. 238.

11. Mary Richardson et al., "Coordinating Services by Design," *Public Welfare*, Summer 1989, pp. 31–36.

12. Jane Knitzer and Susan Yelton, "Collaboration Between Child Welfare and Mental Health," *Public Welfare*, Spring 1990, pp. 24–33.

13. For the views of public administrators on both the pros and cons of contracting, see Ralph Kramer and Paul Terrell, *Social Services Contracting in the Bay Area* (Berkeley: University of California Press, Institute of Governmental Studies, 1984).

14. Karen Orloff Kaplan, "Recent Trends in Case Management," in *Encyclopedia of Social Work*, 18th ed., 1990 Supplement (Silver Spring, MD: National Association of Social Workers, 1990), pp. 60–77.

15. Denise Polit and Joseph O'Hara, "Support Services," in *Welfare Policy for the 1990s*, eds. Phoebe Cottingham and David Ellwood (Cambridge, Mass.: Harvard University Press, 1989), pp. 191–192.

16. Ibid., p. 193.

17. Sherry Arnstein, "A Ladder of Citizen Participation," *Journal of the American Institute of Planners*, Vol. 35, no. 4 (July 1969).

18. Hans B. C. Spiegel et al., *Neighborhood Power and Control: Implications for Urban Planning* (New York: Columbia University, Institute of Urban Environment, 1968), p. 157.

19. Ralph M. Kramer, *Community Development in Israel and the Netherlands* (Berkeley: University of California Press, Institute of International Studies, 1970), p. 127.

20. Neil Gilbert, *Clients or Constituents* (San Francisco: Jossey-Bass, 1970), p. 145; and Arthur B. Shostak, "Promoting Participation of the Poor: Philadelphia's Antipoverty Program," *Social Work*, Vol. 11, no. 1 (January 1966).

21. Ralph M. Kramer, *Participation of the Poor* (Englewood Cliffs, NJ: Prentice Hall, 1969), p. 127.

22. There is some evidence that local citizen elections may improve over time. Brager and Specht indicate that voter turnouts in Model Cities elections, although usually low, tended to be higher than turnouts for earlier elections sponsored by the Economic Opportunity Program. For example, nearly 30 percent of eligible voters participated in Trenton's Model Cities election in 1968. George Brager and Harry Specht, *Community Organizing* (New York: Columbia University Press, 1973).

23. Harold Weissman, *Community Councils and Community Control* (Pittsburgh: University of Pittsburgh Press, 1970).

24. Neil Gilbert and Joseph Eaton, "Who Speaks for the Poor?" *Journal of the American Institute of Planners*, Vol. 36, no. 6 (November 1970).

25. George Peterson et al., *The Reagan Block Grants: What Have We Learned?* (Washington D.C.: Urban Institute Press, 1986).

26. Sjoberg, Brymer, and Farris, "Bureaucracy and the Lower Class."

27. S. M. Miller and Frank Riessman, *Social Class and Social Policy* (New York: Basic Books, 1968), p. 207.

28. George Brager, "The Indigenous Worker: A New Approach to the Social Work Technician," *Social Work*, Vol. 10, no. 2 (April 1965).

29. Robert Pruger and Harry Specht, "Establishing New Careers Programs: Organizational Barriers and Strategies," *Social Work*, Vol. 13, no. 4 (October 1968), 23–24.

30. David A. Hardcastle, "The Indigenous Non-professional in the Social Service Bureaucracy: A Critical Examination," *Social Work*, Vol. 16, no. 2 (April 1971), 63.

31. Charles Grosser, "Manpower Development Programs," in *Non-professionals in the Human Services*, eds. Charles Grosser, William E. Henry, and James G. Kelly (San Francisco: Jossey-Bass, 1969), pp. 136–137.

32. Lonnie Snowden and David Derezotes, "Cultural Factors in the Intervention of Child Maltreatment," *Child and Adolescent Social Work*, Vol. 7, no. 2 (April 1990).

33. Gerald Levy, "Acute Workers in a Welfare Bureaucracy," in *Social Problems and Social Policy*, eds. Deborah Offenbacher and Constance Poster (New York: Appleton-Century-Crofts, 1970); see also Harry Wasserman, "The Professional Social Worker in a Bureaucracy," *Social Work*, Vol. 16, no. 1 (January 1971), 89–95.

34. Piliavin, "Restructuring the Provision of Social Service," p. 35.

35. "Membership Survey Shows Practice Shifts," *NASW News*, Vol. 28, no. 10 (November 1983).

36. Thomas McGuire et al., "Vendorship and Social Work in Massachusetts," *Social Service Review*, Vol. 58, no. 3 (September 1984), 372–383.

37. Robert Pruger, "The Good Bureaucrat," *Social Work*, Vol. 18, no. 4 (July 1973), 27.

38. Interim results of the project are reported by Bleddyn Davies and David Challis, "Experimenting with New Roles in Domiciliary Service: The Kent Community Care Project," *Gerontologist*, Vol. 20 (June 1980), 288–299.

39. Alfred J. Kahn, "Perspectives on Access to Social Service," *Social Work*, Vol. 15, no. 2 (March 1970), 99.

40. Rein, *Social Policy.*

41. For a description of this method, see P. Nelson Reid, "Reforming the Social Services Monopoly," *Social Work*, Vol. 17, no. 6 (November 1972), 44–54.

42. Henry Miller and Connie Philipp, "The Alternative Service Agency," in *Handbook of Clinical Social Work*, eds. Aaron Rosenblatt and Diana Waldfogel (San Francisco: Jossey-Bass, 1983), pp. 779–791.

43. Richard Cloward and Frances Piven, "The Case Against Urban Desegregation," *Social Work*, Vol. 12, no. 1 (January 1967).

44. Edward J. O'Donnel and Marilyn M. Sullivan, "Service Delivery and Social Action Through the Neighborhood Center: A Review of Research," *Welfare in Review*, Vol. 7, no. 6 (November/December 1969), 95–102; and Gilbert and Specht, *Coordinating Social Services.*

45. Marshall Kaplan, Gans, and Kahn, and The Research Group, Inc., "Integration of Human Services in HEW: An Evaluation of Services Integration Projects," An Executive Summary of a Study for the Social and Rehabilitation Service of the Department of Health, Education, and Welfare, 1972, p. 11.

46. For an insightful analysis of the vital functions that may be served by duplication within systems, see Martin Landau, "Redundancy, Rationality, and the Problem of Duplication and Overlap," *Public Administration Review*, Vol. 29, no. 4 (July/August 1969), 346–358.

47. Philip Kramer, "The Indigenous Worker: Hometowner, Striver, or Activist," *Social Work* Vol. 17, No. 1 (January 1972).

48. Ernest Greenwood, "Attributes of a Profession," *Social Work*, Vol. 2, no. 3 (July 1975).

49. Ernest Greenwood, "'Attributes of a Profession' Revisited," in *The Emergence of Social Welfare and Social Work*, eds. Neil Gilbert and Harry Specht (Itasca, IL: Peacock Publishers, 1981), p. 264.

50. Harold Wilensky and Charles Lebeaux, *Industrial Society and Social Welfare* (New York: Russell Sage, 1958), p. 330.

51. Matthew Dumont, "The Changing Face of Professionalism," *Social Policy*, May/June 1972, p. 32.

52. Marie R. Haug and Marvin B. Sussman, "Professional Autonomy and the Revolt of the Client," *Social Problems*, Vol. 17, no. 2 (Fall 1969), 153–161; and Miller and Riessman, *Social Class and Social Policy.*

53. As Eaton found in a study of professional employees in two treatment-oriented organizations, one of the difficulties of service evaluation stems from the reluctance of professionals to make interpretations of evaluative research data and their disinclination to communicate the findings of evaluative research. Joseph Eaton, "Symbolic and Substantive Evaluative Research," *Administrative Science Quarterly*, Vol. 6 (March 1962), 421–442.

54. Haug and Sussman, "Professional Autonomy and the Revolt of the Client."

55. Everett C. Hughes, "Professions," *Daedalus*, Vol. 92, no. 4 (Fall 1963).

56. Richard Cloward and Irwin Epstein, "Private Social Welfare's Disengagement from the Poor: The Case of Family Adjustment Agencies," in *Social Welfare Institutions*, ed. Mayer Zald (New York: Wiley, 1965), pp. 628–629.

57. Alvin W. Gouldner, "Organizational Analysis," in *Sociology Today*, eds. Robert K. Merton, Leonard Broom, and Leonard S. Cottrell, Jr. (New York: Harper & Row, 1959), pp. 404–405.

58. Thompson, *Organization in Action*.

59. Thompson (ibid., p. 10) offers a creative synthesis of these two models by suggesting that organizations be viewed dynamically as open systems striving for the rationality, control, and certainty of a closed system.

60. Ibid., pp. 27–28.

61. Harry Specht, "The Deprofessionalization of Social Work," *Social Work*, Vol. 17, no. 2 (April 1972).

62. Howard Glennerster, "Prime Cuts: Public Expenditure and Social Services Planning in a Hostile Environment," *Policy and Politics*, Vol. 8, no. 4 (1980), 367–382.

63. Ellie Scrivens, "Towards a Theory of Rationing," *Social Policy and Administration*, Vol. 13, no. 1 (Spring 1979), 53–84.

64. For more detailed discussions of these strategies, see Abraham Deron, "The Welfare State: Issues of Rationing and Allocation of Resources," in Shimon Spiro & Ephraim Yuchtman-Yaar (eds.) *Evaluating the Welfare State: Social & Political Perspectives* (New York: Academic Press, 1983), 149–159; and R. A. Parker, "Social Administration and Scarcity," *Social Work Today*, Vol. 12 (April 1967), 9–14.

65. Michael Lipsky, "Bureaucratic Disentitlement in Social Welfare Programs," *Social Service Review*, Vol. 58, no. 1 (March 1984), 20.

66. See, for example, Ralph Kramer, "Public Fiscal Policy and Voluntary Agencies in Welfare States," *Social Service Review*, Vol. 53 (March 1979), 1–14; and Alfred Kahn, "A Framework for Public-Voluntary Collaboration in the Social Services," in *Social Welfare Forum 1976* (New York: Columbia University Press, 1976), pp. 47–62.

67. Kurt Reichert, "The Drift Toward Entrepreneurialism in Health and Social Welfare: Implications for Social Work Education," *Administration in Social Work*, Vol. 1 (Summer 1977), 129. See also Mimi Abramovitz, "The Privatization of the Welfare State: A Review," *Social Work*, July/August 1986, pp. 257–264.

68. For further discussion of problems in this area, see R. M. Kanter, "The Measurement of Organizational Effectiveness, Productivity, Performance, and Success: Issues and Dilemmas in Service and Non-profit Organizations," *Program on Non-profit Organization*, Working Paper 8 (New Haven, CT: Institution for Social Policy Studies, Yale University, 1979).

69. Richard Titmuss, *The Gift Relationship* (New York: Pantheon Books, 1971); Cynthia Barnett, "Profit and Non-profit Distinctions in Theory and in Fact: The Lack of Fit Between Theory and Empirical Research in Health Care Organizations," 1982 (mimeographed); Lenard Kaye, Abraham Monk, and Howard Litwin, "Community Monitoring of Nursing Home Care: Proprietary and Non-Profit Association Perspectives," *Journal of Social Service Research*, Vol. 7, no. 3 (Spring 1984), 5–19; Catherine Born, "Proprietary Terms and Child Welfare Services: Patterns and Implications," *Child Welfare*, Vol. 62, no. 2 (March/April 1983), 109–118; Stephen Shortell, "Hospital Ownership and Nontraditional Services," *Health Affairs*, Winter 1986.

70. For elaboration on this point, see Neil Gilbert, *Capitalism and the Welfare State* (New Haven, CT: Yale University Press, 1983), pp. 17–19.

71. Ibid.; see also Neil Gilbert, "Welfare for Profit: Moral, Empirical, and Theoretical Perspectives," *Journal of Social Policy,* Vol. 13, no. 1 (January, 1984), 63–74.

72. This concern, it appears, is not always decisive. For example, in recent years federal and state agencies have contracted with profit-making corporations to run prisons. See Harry Hatry et al., "Comparison of Privately and Publicly Operated Corrections Facilities in Kentucky and Massachusetts," Urban Institute, August 1989.

Chapter Six
MODE OF FINANCE: SOURCES OF FUNDS

Taxes are a changing product of earnest efforts to have others pay them.

Eisenstein
The Ideologies of Taxation

Let me tell you how it will be; there's one for you nineteen for me. 'Cause I'm the taxman. . . .
the Beatles (George Harrison)
"Taxman"

As these quotations indicate, people do not much care for paying taxes; this makes the process of raising revenue for social purposes difficult and controversial. Our objective in this chapter and the next, then, is to examine this process analytically, to explore some of the basic policy choices involved in financing welfare state programs, and to sensitize students to the implications of different funding sources and different systems of funding transfers. In social welfare, the things that money can do are substantially influenced by how that money is obtained.

In describing our framework for analysis, we stated that policy choices involve the different origins of welfare funding and the conditions placed on the flow of funding to the point at which it reaches providers. Essentially, these choices specify the varied relationships that exist among those who finance and those who deliver social welfare services.

Questions about the mode of finance interest administrators and planners more than they do direct-service practitioners. Administrators and planners are concerned with securing resources to sustain their programs. They need to understand the kinds of programs funders will support. Funders, whether they are legislators, foundation trustees, or executives of agency federations, are concerned with making choices among competing interests and programs to achieve their goals. In negotiations for program support, both funders and fund seekers address the questions of the previous chapters: Who is eligible for help? What will they receive? How will service delivery be organized?

The direct-service practitioner is usually less attentive to questions of finance than to other dimensions of policy choice because financing choices are often remote from the exigencies of day-to-day practice, and their effects on client welfare are more difficult to comprehend. Funding decisions for almost any kind of social welfare program—whether mental health, housing, or community planning—are likely to involve "big government" somewhere along the line. Because most programs of significance require the money, sanction, or surveillance of one or more levels of government, direct-service practitioners are likely to think that funding questions are not within their influence. Certainly the thought is based on a good deal of reality. Funding arrangements are complex, and final program decisions are frequently made by individuals and groups many steps removed from where services are actually applied.

Nevertheless, it is important for professionals concerned with social welfare to have a working knowledge of the major issues, concepts, and values involved in the mode of finance. Although the vast majority of professionals may not directly participate in allocation decision making, in their roles as citizens, members of professional associations, and agency employees, they often can affect how decision makers think and act. It is not unreasonable, then, to expect professionals, regardless of their specific job, to be able to respond thoughtfully to questions such as these: Should a public agency purchase services by entering into a contract with a voluntary or for-profit agency? If so, under what circumstances? Are block grants preferable to categorical funding? What are the constraints of voluntary financing? What assumptions support the use of contributory schemes and fee-charging arrangements? What are the distributional implications of different tax sources?

Two interrelated sets of choices are fundamental to the finance dimension of policy design:

1. *The source of funds*: Whether financial support is derived directly from recipients in the form of user charges and certain earmarked taxes, taxes that

make up general revenues, some form of social insurance, voluntary contributions, or some combination thereof

2. *The system of transfer*: Arrangements for the flow of money from origin to destination, the different levels of review between sources and providers, and the types of conditions placed on the transfer

We discuss in the next chapter choices that inform the design of transfer systems; here we examine alternative sources of funding and their implications.

SOURCES OF FUNDS

Funds to pay for social welfare benefits are obtained in three fundamental ways—through taxes, through contributions, and through fees. *Taxes*, compulsory and governmental, constitute public levies on citizens and businesses and are the primary source of support for public social welfare activities. *Contributions* constitute private, voluntary giving. Whether described as charity (which connotes giving for the poor) or philanthropy (which connotes giving for a broader range of health, research, civic, and religious activities), contributions represent voluntary, uncoerced donations. *Fees* constitute the cost of social welfare goods and services on the open market. The providers of these goods and services may be entrepreneurs, selling a product to make a profit, or nonprofit providers, requiring user fees to cover their expenses. In a few instances, public institutions (chiefly colleges and universities) also impose charges.

In the actual conduct of the welfare state, these three funding sources are often intermixed. That is, the actual budgets of social welfare agencies and organizations often include revenues deriving from taxes, voluntary giving, and fees and charges. Public agencies, for example, tend to be funded with tax dollars, but they may rely on user fees (e.g., tuition) or private giving (e.g., PTA fundraising). Similarly, private nonprofit agencies have become increasingly dependent on tax support, supplementing their private revenue sources with contract funding from government bodies. Also, profit-making businesses frequently rely on third-party insurers, public or private, for their income.

The pluralistic funding patterns of the welfare state—often described as the mixed economy of welfare—can create terminological confusion. To clarify the terrain a bit, the distinctive characteristics of the major social welfare auspices must be specified. In our discussion, *voluntary agencies* refer to nongovernmental, nonprofit organizations that are financed, to at least some significant extent, by voluntary contributions. These organizations devote their resources to education, science, religion, art, culture, and charity and are therefore commonly perceived as serving the public inter-

TABLE 6-1   Public and Private Social Welfare Expenditures (in Billions of Dollars)

	PUBLIC SPENDING	PRIVATE SPENDING	TOTAL
1972	$190.3	$ 93.2	$ 283.5
1980	492.0	242.7	734.7
1985	732.0	437.2	1,169.2
1988	885.8	601.2	1,487.0

Source: Wilmer Kerns and Milton Glanz, "Private Social Welfare Expenditures, 1972–88," *Social Security Bulletin,* Vol. 54, no. 2 (February 1991).

est, even though they are not publicly administered. In this sense, voluntary agencies may be conceived of as privately administered public-interest institutions.

Public agencies, for their part, are supported by government funds. Their programs are often referred to as statutory or legislative because they must be enacted in law.

For-profit organizations, a relatively new phenomenon in many sectors of the American social welfare system, are providers that operate on an entrepreneurial basis, like any commercial business. The role of these organizations remains controversial despite the strong ideological and legislative support harnessed on behalf of "privatization" since the Reagan administration.

Issues of public versus voluntary versus for-profit financing have recently been hotly debated. Although the private sector (for-profit and nonprofit combined) has always played a significant welfare role in the United States—far more so than in other welfare states—the ratio of private to public spending has grown rapidly in the past 15 years. From 1972 to 1988, as Table 6–1 indicates, social welfare outlays increased from $283 billion to $1,487 billion. But whereas public spending during this period increased 366 percent, private spending rose 545 percent. Another way of describing this gain is to note that the portion of overall social welfare spending represented by private organizations and agencies increased from 33 percent to 40 percent. Much of this increase in private spending represents the enormous growth in size and scope of private pension and health insurance plans. A major part however, also reflects the growth of nonprofit service agencies.

Much of the financial support of private agencies is not of private, charitable origin at all. It is commonly believed that nonprofit agencies rely chiefly on private donations, but donations make up only 27 percent of overall revenues—the remainder coming mainly from fees and government.[1] America's largest charity, for example, the Young Men's Christian Association (YMCA), receives just 15 percent of its income in the form of United Way or other private donations. Most of its income (almost 77 percent) derives from earnings and fees in the form of member dues. The third largest charity, the American Red Cross, relies on private donations for 29 percent of its income. The Salvation Army, the fifth largest, gets nearly half its support from donations.[2]

Private donations come mainly from the gifts of ordinary individuals, and much of it is organized through the annual fund-raising activities of federations, like the United Way and the United Jewish Appeal, that collect on behalf of member agencies. The United Way itself collects over $3 billion annually for its agency constituency, chiefly through workplace campaigns. Alternatives to the United Way—federations representing social action, environmental, ethnic, and women's causes—are growing rapidly and currently raise over $200 million annually in workplace fund-raising drives.

Overall, however, fund-raising federations tap only a small portion of philanthropic giving, which runs over $100 billion a year. Most of this giving is in the form of individual contributions, and most of it goes to religious groups. After individual giving, as Table 6–2 indicates, are corporate and foundation donations and then bequests.

Corporations gave an estimated $5 billion to philanthropy in 1989, about 4 percent of overall giving. Although corporate giving includes the spectrum of nonprofit activities, elementary and secondary school programs have been a major priority since the mid-1980s, reflecting businesses' concern about the capacity of U.S. workers to compete in the global marketplace. Education has received the largest portion of corporate giving every year since 1978, although the portion going to colleges and universities has been steadily diminishing. This trend toward corporate support of basic K–12 public education is likely to increase given President Bush's efforts to reform public schooling and increase the role of business in such reform.[3]

Private foundations are a unique creation of American capitalism. Foundations are voluntary funding agencies that exist primarily to give

TABLE 6–2   Sources of Philanthropic Contributions, 1989 (in Billions of Dollars)

Foundations	$ 6.70	5.8%
Corporations	5.00	4.4%
Individuals	96.43	84.1%
Bequests	6.57	5.7%
	$114.70	100.0%

Source: (New York: American Association of Fund-Raising Counsel, *Giving USA, 1990*, 1990), p. 6.

money to other nonprofit organizations. There are nearly 28,000 grant-making foundations in the United States, holding over $115 billion in assets and awarding approximately $7 billion annually for social welfare, scientific, and cultural activities.[4]

Despite the importance of private and voluntary welfare, the essence of today's welfare state remains one of public provision and public finance. Government is the major source of funds for health, education, income-maintenance, and welfare services, and the primacy of public financing means that social welfare policy choices are fundamentally matters of politics rather than of private consumption or voluntary philanthropy. The primacy of the public sector also means that issues of welfare policy are inextricably tied to problems of large-scale bureaucratic organizations. Finally, shifts and increases in the sources and size of social welfare expenditures reflect the emergence of the federal government as the major supporter of services.

Kramer describes the impact of the public sector on the domain and functions of voluntary service organizations:

> As the domain of government expands in financing the social services, if not directly providing them, in moving toward greater coverage and equity and toward services as a right, there has been growing pressure on voluntary agencies receiving public funds for more accountability, coordination, and cost efficiency. . . .
>
> Although the historical source of the democratic welfare state has been "voluntary action crystallized and made universal," the subsequent role of voluntary agencies in welfare states is still uncertain.[5]

The predominance of the federal role reflects the influence of extra-community systems in social welfare policy decision making. That is, policy formulation has become less a matter of the local community alone (or what Warren calls "horizontal" decision-making structures) and more a matter of the interests of several levels of government attempting to compete with or coordinate with one another (what Warren calls "vertical" decision-making structures).[6]

Historically, American individualism has undermined a reliance on government as a mechanism for meeting social welfare needs. As a result, Americans frequently tend to be suspicious and critical of the role of the state in social welfare. However, although America may still represent a "reluctant welfare state," it is unique among industrial nations in respect to the degree to which it has experienced an elaborate development of the voluntary and for-profit sectors. Furthermore, the parallel development of the voluntary and the public social welfare sectors has made the American welfare system both dynamic in its ability to change and innovate and difficult to manage and control. In this chapter, therefore, we give approximately equal emphasis to the characteristics of both sectors despite their different financial resources.

However, the discussion of systems of transfer in the following chapter is devoted largely to public programs. The practical reason for this emphasis is that once readers have grasped the nature of the relationship between the voluntary and public sectors, they must then be able to deal with the fact that transfer systems, whether for voluntary or for public programs, usually involve different levels of government.

Before examining some of the characteristics of voluntary, public, and for-profit financing, let us discuss one other source to which both voluntary and statutory programs may turn for funds—the service user.

CONTRIBUTORY SCHEMES AND FEE CHARGING

Those receiving social benefits may be asked to finance them in two ways: through "contributions" to statutory (i.e., public) social and health insurance programs and through fees paid for services rendered. Statutory insurance programs, although somewhat akin to private insurance, do not operate according to the general rules of exchange in the open marketplace. Rather, the conditions of exchange are regulated by government, the exchange reflects the recipients' need as well as their contribution, and private profit is not allowed. Fee-for-service arrangements may, of course, operate privately, as we discuss later.

The Social Security program, officially Old Age, Survivors, Disability, and Health Insurance (OASDHI), is the outstanding example of a contributory system in the United States. The basic principle is that all those who receive benefits at the time they withdraw from the labor force will have paid "insurance premiums" into the system during their working years. Like any other insurance system, their investments "earn" entitlements to benefits. However, Social Security is not like any other insurance system. First, despite the euphemism, "contributions" constitute an involuntary tax on both earnings (for employees) and payrolls (for employers); both workers and employers, therefore, are obligated to support the system. In 1990, approximately 99 percent of the American work force was covered by a combination of Social Security and other government retirement systems. Some groups of workers who are not required to participate may enter the system voluntarily.

Unlike private insurance, OASDHI benefits are not paid on the basis of a set written contract between private parties (i.e., the contributor and the insurer). Benefits, rather, are determined by Congress and change from time to time. As we shall explain, although there is an important relationship between contributions and benefits, Congress awards benefits on the basis of need as well as on the basis of contributions.

In fee-for-service systems run by public or voluntary organizations, benefits are provided on a nonprofit basis, with "user charges" covering part of the cost. Under these arrangements, fees are often calculated on sliding scales according to the user's economic circumstances; rarely covering the entire cost of services rendered, these fees subsidize poorer clients.

Fee charging can be introduced into contributory programs. Medicare, the health insurance program for the aged under Social Security, gives beneficiaries an option to participate in a Supplementary Medical Insurance Program (Part B) that covers physicians' fees. In 1992, 97 percent of all eligible beneficiaries elected Part B, paying $31.80 per month for its coverage. In addition, there is a deductible charge (approximately $1,500) for physicians' care, and one (approximately $700) for hospital insurance. This means that the recipient must pay these amounts before the program covers any costs. In some health plans (such as Britain's National Health Service) members may be required to pay a fee that covers part of the cost for each episode of care, be it a visit to a dentist, prescribed medication, or a hospital stay.

Fee charging in the social services was promoted by the 1974 Title XX amendments to the Social Security Act, which allowed states to offer social services to nonwelfare families earning between 80 and 115 percent of their state's median annual income. These services could be offered for reasonable income-related fees on a subsidized basis. In 1975, approximately 21 percent of Title XX service recipients were in the "income eligible" category.[7]

Assumptions about psychological and behavioral dynamics underlie much of the debate concerning the use of contributory and fee-charging schemes. From the psychological point of view, it is argued that recipients are less likely to feel stigma or shame when they pay their own way, even if they are still partially subsidized. At the same time, the act of contributing is believed to enhance the individual's sense of social responsibility. This has been one of the major arguments for operating Social Security on a contributory basis. The behavioral rationale for contributory schemes and fee charging, as applied to service-giving programs, is that user payments restrain overutilization. That is, even small fees for doctor or therapist visits or for prescriptions are said to discourage unnecessary or excessive care.

There is little empirical evidence to support or reject these psychological and behavioral arguments. Recipients of Social Security benefits appear to feel a greater sense of entitlement to benefits than do recipients of other programs, but what part of this feeling is due to having made contributions to the program and what part is due to general public acceptance of the program is not clear. There are other publicly accepted programs in which beneficiaries do not make direct contributions (such as unemployment insurance, public education, and veterans' services), yet they seem to develop the same sense of entitlement as OASDHI recipients.[8]

A sense of entitlement can be based on such factors as compensation or general public commitment to the program. Wolins points out that recipients of Old-Age Security in California (the federal public assistance program that preceded Supplementary Security Income) received better benefits, felt more entitled to them, and were socially perceived as being more deserving than recipients of Aid for Families with Dependent Children (AFDC).[9] Although contributory schemes may have some effect on the sense of entitlement, they are by no means determinate.

Similarly, it is not clear whether contributions and user fees affect the consumption of benefits. Although fee charging may restrain excessive use on the part of consumers, even small fees may discourage utilization by those who are so needy that even a nominal charge can be a burden. A recent study of the effect of charges in prepaid health plans, for example, found that even a modest copayment for office visits significantly reduced the use of primary care services, although they had no impact on visits to medical and surgical specialists.[10]

As Eveline Burns indicated, contributions and fee charging are likely to have a responsibility-inducing effect only in small units, where individual members can perceive the relationship between the organization's operations and the money they pay. She also noted, however, that contributions can result in greater consumer demand. The recipient's "belief that he has paid for whatever benefits he gets may . . . work in the opposite direction from that intended by those who view the contributory requirement as a brake upon unreasonable benefit increases or extensions."[11]

VOLUNTARY FINANCING: NOT ENTIRELY A PRIVATE MATTER

"Voluntary" financing of social welfare services is not quite as private or as philanthropic as we might think. Money contributed to nonprofit organizations engaged in health, education, welfare, religious, scientific, or cultural activities, for example, has been largely untaxed by the federal government since 1915, when Congress sought to promote philanthropy by making donations deductible. Philanthropy, in this sense, is a tax-saving option for many citizens. Another way of viewing philanthropic giving, of course, is as a tax expenditure—money that has "escaped" from the public treasury.[12]

It has been said that our system of private philanthropy, which costs the taxpayer "nothing," is like a painless dentist. In truth, it is hardly ever painless, and when completed, moreover, something is missing. We would have to go too deeply into the intricacies of tax law to explain these matters much further, but many studies have indicated that voluntary contributors, at least to some degree, are motivated by economic considerations as much as by charitable instincts. And under certain conditions, indeed, wealthy contributors can use the system to their net economic advantage.

In addition to questioning the charitable impulse behind philanthropic giving, one should also question how voluntary some private contributions are. Community pressures to give, whether at the office or elsewhere, may exert sufficient social coercion so that the choice not to give can be exercised only at great cost to the individual's prestige and social position. Such pressures, of course, do a disservice to the idea of voluntarism.

Tax considerations have a very powerful influence on the level of giving. In one study of the relationship between tax exemptions and giving, for example, 96 percent of donors of large sums said that they would reduce their contributions substantially if tax benefits were removed.[13] Because "tax deductions are a monetary ointment to salve the strains of charity," they provide an indispensable incentive for individuals to support the nonprofit services of their choice.[14] Little wonder that attempts to delimit the charitable deduction are always greeted with fierce denunciations by representatives of philanthropic largess—universities, art museums, and scientific research institutions, most notably.

Functions of Voluntary Services

Ideally, philanthropic incentives encourage the development of pluralism in community services and provide opportunities for the religious, ethnic, and cultural interests of individuals and groups to flourish. This, the "value guardian" function of the voluntary agency, allows for the expression of particularistic and sectarian values in social welfare.[15] In its role of value guardian, the voluntary organization is one of the major social devices for mitigating many of the strains that exist in American political life. This history of successive waves of ethnic and racial minorities who have been assimilated into American society, indeed, can be written as a biography of their organizational lives.[16]

Writing in 1895, Charles Henderson characterized voluntary organizations as social units that are less permanent and rigid than formal institutions, and thus better able to meet the needs of particular classes or social groups. Of course, many voluntary organizations evolve into large bureaucratic agencies, a phenomenon of interest in the study of social movements.[17] But Henderson's comments on the functions of voluntary associations are still quite relevant:

> [Voluntary associations] may be compared to the tenders which ply between the port and the great ships which are more at home on the deep sea than in the shallow harbor or to the skirmish lines which are thrown in advance of the main army. . . . It is said that these societies dissipate social energy, rival the home, sap the resources of the church, and multiply like a plague of locusts. Unquestionably, the objection is partly justified by facts. There are too many societies, especially too many bad ones. They overlap, duplicate, and interfere with each other. Some of them seem to be organized simply to advertise the benevolence of the executive secretary. . . . But the severest judgement of an

abuse leaves the normal use untouched. The voluntary associations require criticism and regulation but the principle of their life is legitimate.[18]

In addition to supporting diversity and pluralism in community life, voluntary services provide an important vehicle for implementing new and possibly unpopular ideas that might not find advocacy in an agency of government. The flexible and changing characteristics of some voluntary agencies make them uniquely suited to this "vanguard" function.[19] This function was exemplified in the early 1960s by the Ford Foundation's sponsorship of the Grey Areas Projects, the demonstration program that paved the way for the President's Committee on Juvenile Delinquency, the Economic Opportunity Program, and Model Cities.[20] But this is not to imply that government agencies are incapable of innovation and experimentation. On the contrary, most of the funds used for research, experimentation, and innovation in social welfare services come from public sources.[21]

Voluntary agencies also may function as "improvers" and "supplementors" of public services. They can serve as vigilant critics, ensuring the quality of public services. And finally, they can support programs to meet needs that public agencies are unable or unwilling to undertake.[22]

The case of the Family Service Association of America (FSAA) is a good illustration of the supplementary function performed by a voluntary agency.[23] The FSAA was founded in 1911 as the National Association for Organizing Charities (NAOC), an outgrowth of the Charity Organization Societies of the late 1800s. The primary function of NAOC was to coordinate the work of community agencies involved with charitable giving.[24] The organization was opposed to public relief.[25] In the first decades of the twentieth century, NAOC dropped its coordinating functions, concentrating instead on the rehabilitation of distressed families. In 1919 it became the American Association for Organizing Family Social Work, using the combined methods of relief giving and social casework.

When the Social Security Act was passed in 1935, the federal government undertook substantial relief giving for special categories of the needy. The FSAA responded by abandoning the "quantitative" job of providing income relief in favor of the "qualitative" task of providing family casework. By 1953, FSAA had developed a family-oriented casework approach for dealing with social problems, and for a while the difference between public and voluntary services seemed clear. But with the 1956 amendments to the Social Security Act, public welfare itself took on a family orientation and states were encouraged to grant assistance and "other services" to needy children, parents, and relatives "to help maintain and strengthen family life." The 1958 and 1962 amendments to the act further strengthened this orientation. By the mid-1960s, therefore, agencies such as FSAA once again began to reassess their functions vis-à-vis public services. Although, no doubt, there were many other reasons for the change, in 1971 the

Community Service Society of New York City abandoned its long tradition of family casework and took up a strategy of community organization for neighborhood self-improvement.[26] In 1973, member agencies of the FSAA in Chicago and Minneapolis also began to emphasize social advocacy.

More recently, as FSAAs have found it increasingly difficult to acquire government funds to support counseling and other community service activities, they have given greater attention to emergency and other short-term assistance, relying more heavily on fee-charging arrangements with private practitioners and developing private services such as Employee Assistance Programs focusing on corporate settings.

Problems and Issues in Voluntary Financing

Several problems arise in financing voluntary social welfare services. First, there is the question of the criteria to use in deciding which community activities should remain private and voluntary. This question partially reflects a conflict between cultural pluralism and social equality. For example, should contributions to ethnically or religiously exclusive educational, health, and social welfare agencies be tax exempt? Should governments provide direct support for exclusive agencies (such as parochial schools) if they meet community requirements and standards? Does such support violate constitutional guarantees separating church and state? These issues become even more complex when, as is generally the case, there is a mixing of voluntary and public funds.

Public support for voluntary agencies is found in a variety of forms. The tax deductibility of charitable contributions has already been noted. Public subsidies are largely unconditional lump-sum grants for voluntary agency programs. They have come to be considered poor government policy because, as an essentially agency-oriented means of financial support, they commit government to supporting all of the goals and purposes of an organization.[27] Purchase of service contracting is an arrangement whereby governments buy specific services, such as foster care, job training, or respite services. In some cases, government units may even contract with private agencies to perform managerial and oversight activities such as program development, social planning, and services evaluation.

Today, a major part of the funds expended by voluntary agencies are provided by government. In many program sectors, as much as 50 percent of the budgets of voluntary agencies come from federal funds alone, and no more than one-third of the total revenues of voluntary social service, community development, and civic organizations are accounted for by voluntary contributions.[28] It is estimated, in addition, that more than half of all Title XX social services funds (currently $2.7 billion annually) are spent on services purchased from voluntary and for-profit organizations.[29] Considering these trends, Ralph M. Kramer has stated, "It is ironic that a national coalition of non-profit organizations chose as its name 'The Independent Sector' when its constituents had become, more than ever, dependent on government."[30]

One major virtue of these government subventions to private organizations is that they provide a way to start programs quickly, avoiding the rigidities of civil service and bureaucracy. Such characteristics are especially advantageous for experiments and demonstrations. Contracting also permits public officials to tailor programs to the special circumstances of hard-to-reach or minority populations. Relying on the access and expertise of existing community-based agencies, governments can be far more responsive to special population groups than if they tried to provide services in-house.

For voluntary agencies, the obvious advantage of purchase arrangements is access to the public coffers as additional sources of income. But they pay a price. To the extent that voluntary agencies are supported by government funds, they forfeit some degree of autonomy. Consequently, their ability to function as agents for the expression of new or unpopular ideas, as critics of public services, and as the guardians of pluralistic values may be limited. Family-planning clinics funded with federal grant-in-aid funds, for example, are prohibited from providing information about abortion, a severe limitation on their ability to give their clients a comprehensive set of options. In the extreme, voluntary agencies may simply become an instrument of government policy. As Wickenden suggests, the degree to which government constraints may be imposed depends in part on the method of financing that is employed, whether indirectly through tax concessions, directly through subsidies or purchase of specified services, or through some other means of government support.[31] And in the view of some, when voluntary agencies accept funds from government, they should be treated no differently than any other agency of government. According to Glasser, for example, the private agency that accepts funds from the government should forego all of the privileges of autonomy.[32]

Accountability. The issue of government support places voluntary agencies in a paradoxical situation. On the one hand, government control and influence are seen as undesirable and dysfunctional for the special roles of voluntary agencies. On the other hand, an absence of accountability mechanisms also poses a problem. This lack of accountability, or "power without responsibility," as Marris and Rein phrase it, constitutes a dilemma for voluntary agencies: "The dilemma of philanthropy arises from its lack of a base within the political structure from which to organize reform. It must work discretely through those who have, easily finds itself at cross-purposes with its allies, and has little power to assert policy once its grants are committed."[33]

Historically, charitable trusts have been held as "in the public interest" and therefore subject to a degree of government regulation.[34] It is on this basis that voluntary funds can be restricted and some degree of control can be exercised. Tax-exempt organizations must be chartered by state governments, and the states may require various kinds of accounting procedures and impose standards of practice. One important limitation is that no substantial part of the voluntary agencies' activities may consist of efforts to influence legislation.[35] This restriction accounts, in part, for the reluctance of many voluntary welfare agencies to become engaged in political action.

Public concern regarding the accountability of voluntary organizations, particularly philanthropic foundations, found legislative expression in the Tax Reform Act of 1969. Although not as severe as many critics of voluntary organizations desired, the act imposes several important limitations on voluntary organizations. Almost one-third of the act is concerned with foundations, establishing policies regarding the investment of funds, public reporting, and the amount of income that may be received on assets. In addition, the act requires foundations to pay a 4 percent excise tax on their income and to dispose of at least 5 percent of their capital annually.[36]

The problem of establishing accountability for voluntary agencies can be understood in relation to a much older and more general notion known as charitable immunity. Originating in centuries-old English law, this concept holds that charitable trusts cannot be held responsible for derelictions of duties to clients (negligence and neglect, e.g.) because without such immunity government intervention might eventually violate the intentions of the donors and limit the functions of voluntary charity.[37] The question of charitable immunity and the extent to which bequests may be altered by the action of government is significant. In 1989 alone, $6.6 billion was bequeathed to charitable organizations;[38] more than 90 percent of all bequests of $1 million and above went to education, especially universities.[39]

For many years, charitable bequests and legacies have been protected by this concept of immunity (sometimes referred to as "the dead hand") and have been allowed to follow donors' original purposes, even when some of these appear frivolous, discriminatory, or otherwise socially harmful. Whimsical examples from recent history include a trust fund for Christmas dinners ("one bushel of oats or a half bushel of corn chops") for hungry horses in Kansas City, a trust fund establishing "marriage portions" for poor young women about to be married, and a legacy providing "a baked potato at each meal for each young lady at Bryn Mawr."[40]

A more serious illustration is the Girard College bequest. In this instance, the U.S. Supreme Court decided that the charitable bequest involved could not be tax-exempt if the activities required by the bequest conflicted with the public interest in supporting discrimination against minority groups.[41] Here, the grip of "the dead hand" was loosened by another important legal concept, the *cy pres* (i.e., "as near as may be") doctrine, which holds that courts may modify bequests to be "as near as" possible to the original intent of the giver in light of social changes that have taken place in the community.[42]

Another case of this kind, involving the Buck Trust controversy, was only recently resolved in the California courts. This case provides an interesting test of the strength of the dead hand in respect to community definitions of social need. In 1973, Mrs. Buck, following her husband's wishes, willed her estate, valued at that time at $10 million, to Marin County, California, "to be used exclusively for non-profit charitable, religious, or educational purposes in providing care for the needy." However, when Mrs. Buck died in 1979, her estate had vastly increased in value; by 1984, it was worth $360 million and was producing approximately $20 million to $25 million a year. The San Francisco Foundation, the administrators of the trust, challenged the "Marin only" provisions, arguing that the county (one of the wealthiest in the United States) was not able to make use of the funds.[43] Marin County, ultimately supported by the courts, argued for a strict construction of the will and its clear geographical limitation. Despite the fact that Marin County, by all statistical measures, had only a small amount of "need"—and a small population of the "needy"—the court decided that the definition of "need" was fundamentally subjective. Marin residents perceived of themselves as needy, the Buck instructions were clear, and the trust would not have to be shared with neighboring communities.

Who determines policy?   There is another side to the issue of accountability that concerns voluntary agency relationships, not with government, but with different socioeconomic groups. Tax-exempt funds to support nonprofit social welfare activities are distributed unequally within the population. Some people have more to contribute than others and have greater say about how funds are used. Nielsen, in his analysis of foundations, describes the fundamental contradiction of voluntary philanthropy:

> In the great jungle of American democracy and capitalism, there is no more strange or improbable creature than the private foundation. Private foundations are virtually a denial of basic premises: aristocratic institutions living on the privileges and indulgence of an egalitarian society; aggregations of private wealth which, contrary to the proclaimed instincts of Economic Man have been conveyed to public purposes. Like the giraffe, they could not possibly exist, but they do.[44]

Voluntary agencies are an important part of the policy-making system of social welfare. Like many agencies, they become organizational vehicles for their professionals, board members, and volunteers to exercise influence over community services. Consequently, voluntary social welfare agencies may be seen to reflect the interests of the economically advantaged. Elling and Halebsky argue, for example, that voluntary health services meet the needs of higher-status groups in society. In a study comparing public and voluntary hospitals, they found that the government institutions rated less favorably on several criteria, and they draw the following conclusion:

> In a democratic society, the political system, far from being the power instrument of the capitalist ruling class, as Marx maintained, has often been a major means of control and representation available to ordinary citizens. As changes in medical technology have encouraged the use of the hospital by all elements of society, "upper" elements have preserved the class structure of the community by organizing their own facilities outside of control of the masses and to some extent beyond their participation.[45]

Since the 1960s, there has been great concern about community participation in planning and decision making in all forms of social welfare services. Voluntary as well as public agencies have been criticized for their failures to provide adequate representation of low-income groups and minorities on their boards, and some have reviewed their allocation and program policies in light of these criticisms.[46]

Some writers consider United Way's substantial control over workplace access and payroll deductions to be "a kind of monopoly [that] weakens the ability of the voluntary sector to protect pluralist values."[47] In recent years, opponents of this monopoly have developed two related strategies for dealing with the United Way's presumed elitism: donor option programs and alternative funds. In donor option programs, United Way contributors may designate their gifts for any charitable organization with tax-exempt status in their area, whether a United Way member agency or not. First endorsed by the Board of Governors of United Way in 1982, donor option plans are widespread today, providing significantly broadened freedom of choice to work-site employees.

Alternative funds provide a more radical means of raising and distributing voluntary contributions for community service organizations outside of the United Way network. Organizations such as United Arts Funds, National Network of Women's Funds, Black United Funds—and at least 100 others—are currently soliciting contributions for about 2,000 non-United Way charities. Women's funds, for example, gave away nearly $13 million in 1990 to programs dealing with violence against women, pornography, health and family planning, and employment. Some of these alternative funds are quite successful in their fund-raising efforts, some less so, and many have found it difficult to survive altogether. Interestingly, however, where alternative funds have developed, the local United Ways have usually experienced an increase in revenues rather than a reduction. Perhaps the competition of the alternative fund heightens community awareness of social needs.[48]

Conservatives and voluntarism.   Conservative regimes, such as the Reagan and Bush administrations in the United States and the Thatcher government in the United Kingdom, subscribe to the view that a large part of the welfare system should be the domain of the voluntary sector. Under Reagan, it was declared policy that public sector welfare activities should be substantially privatized, absorbed by "the voluntary spirit." As Lester Salamon points out, however, the Reagan administration never converted its commitment to private giving into a serious plan of action.[49] On balance, indeed, Reagan budget and tax policy negatively affected the nonprofit sector.

To make up for the Reagan cuts in public welfare, charitable giving would have had to multiply by two to four times its very highest levels.[50] In fact, in both the United States and the United Kingdom, one of the first effects of the cutbacks in social services funding was a reduction in the capacities of voluntary agencies because one of the very first responses of local governments to budget cutbacks was to reduce their allocations to the agencies. For example, Urban Institute research reported that voluntary social services were unable to sustain their prior levels of service.[51]

Voluntarism is an enticing idea: Get government off our backs and neighbors will help neighbors, the whole family will pitch in, and the community will roll up its collective sleeves and get the job done. The only thing wrong with this idea is that it does not work. In fact, the welfare state developed because in modern society, neighbors, friends, family, and local communities—the entire "thousand points of light" celebrated by President Bush—were unable to provide for contemporary social needs. That is not to say, of course, that public agencies and social welfare professionals should disregard private support systems and community groups. There is clearly major work to be done to articulate better the functions of human service professionals and the natural helping networks and voluntary activities of communities. However, it is quite another thing to reach into the dustbin of our Victorian past for discarded ideas as solutions to contemporary social problems.

PUBLIC FINANCING: NOT ENTIRELY A PUBLIC MATTER

We have indicated that voluntary financing is not completely a matter of private philanthropy. Similarly, public (or government) financing of social welfare services is not quite as public a business as it may initially appear. In the broadest sense, taxation is a central instrument regulating the interaction between government and the private economy. The core ideological debate between redistribution and social justice, on the one hand, and the need for profit and economic efficiency, on the other, clearly comes into play here. In a narrower sense, tax policy directly affects the private, non-statutory realms of social welfare. Tax exemptions for charitable contributions illustrate one way in which government uses its taxing powers to subsidize private welfare—the exemption provides a substantial public incentive for private generosity.[52] Other tax incentives include federal income tax deductions for catastrophic medical expenses, home mortgage interest, and child and dependent care expenses. All of these represent private "welfare" elements in the public finance systems.

Tax exemptions and credits used by government to achieve social welfare purposes provide a high degree of freedom of choice to individuals in the consumption of social welfare benefits. In addition, when compared to provisions offered through subsidies, vouchers, and financial grants, they have some important organizational and technical advantages. Chiefly, they require a relatively simple administrative apparatus to implement beyond the existing structure for tax collection. Subsidies, vouchers, and grants usually require the development of extensive bureaucratic machinery.

Types of Taxation

Taxes affect the distribution of resources in our society just as much as social allocation. Redistribution is therefore a double-edged sword, achieved by measures both of finance and expenditure. We have discussed the allocative ends of redistribution in the chapters dealing with the basis of allocation and the nature of provisions. Now we want to look in some detail at some of these choices from the fund-raising viewpoint, specifically choices concerning the types of taxes levied and the unit of government levying them.

In the United States—as in most other industrial countries—taxes are imposed in a variety of ways. Most important, taxes are levied on income, both on individuals, through personal income taxes, and on corporations, through corporate income taxes. In the United States, individual income taxes are the largest single source of federal income, providing 45 percent of total federal revenue, with corporate income taxes providing an additional 11 percent. Taxes are also levied on the costs of things people buy (sales taxes), on earnings and payrolls (Social Security taxes), on the value of things people own (property taxes), and on estates and gifts.

One way to distinguish among types of taxes is to consider their redistributive effects in terms of a regressive-progressive continuum. At the *progressive* end of the continuum are levies like the individual income taxes, which are proportionally higher for the wealthy than for the poor. The federal graduated income tax, traditionally the most progressive tax in the United States, is an example, being levied in accordance with the ability to pay. As income rises, in other words, so does the tax rate.

TABLE 6–3   Progressivity/Regressivity: Tax Burden of Major Federal Taxes by Income Group, 1990

INCOME GROUP	PERSONAL INCOME TAX	PAYROLL TAXES	EXCISE TAXES	TOTAL FEDERAL TAXES
Bottom fifth	−1.5%	7.6%	2.4%	9.7%
Lower middle	3.5	10.1	1.4	16.7
Middle	6.7	10.7	1.0	20.3
Upper middle	9.0	10.6	0.9	22.5
Top fifth	15.6	6.8	0.5	25.8
All	11.3%	8.6%	0.8%	23.1%

Source: Congressional Budget Office, *The Economic & Budget Outlook: 1991–1995,* (Washington, DC: U.S. Government Printing Office, 1990), pp. 86–87.

Note: Total federal taxes include corporation income taxes and assume that half the corporate burden is borne by the top-income group, whereas the other half is shared equally by all other taxpayers.

Currently most poor families are exempt from federal income tax. Many, in fact, receive a tax credit (the Earned Income Tax Credit), which offsets a good part of their Social Security payroll taxes as well. When families cross over the tax threshold, above $13,000 for a family of four, the initial rate is 15 percent. As income increases, so does the rate, from 15 percent to 28 percent to 31 percent. This top rate, it should be noted, has dropped considerably in recent years. It stood at 91 percent in 1960 and 70 percent in 1980. As late as 1986 the top rate for individuals was 50 percent.

Although the federal income tax imposes heavier burdens on heftier incomes, the relationship between total income and taxes paid is neither simple nor direct. A variety of complicating factors makes total income, in and of itself, only a rough indicator of tax obligation. In addition to total income, for example, type of income, family size, and taxpayer spending patterns all strongly influence the amount of taxes owed.

Nevertheless, the federal income tax is modestly progressive. As Table 6–3 indicates, the top fifth of all taxpayers paid 16 percent in taxes, and the bottom quantile received a rebate (i.e., a negative tax) because of the Earned Income Tax Credit. Although the rate progression may not be as graduated or as steep as many would desire, higher-income groups do pay higher rates. When social welfare programs are financed by the income tax, then, the source of funding is progressive. Provisions so financed are therefore potentially redistributive, depending on the economic status of the major beneficiaries.[53]

A primary example of a *regressive tax* is the sales tax, under which everyone is taxed at the same rate regardless of income. Most states have sales taxes ranging between 2 and 7 percent. The result is that the poor pay proportionately higher percentages of their incomes than the wealthy. As Table 6–3 indicates, poor taxpayers, those in the lowest income group, paid 2.4 percent of their total income for federal excise taxes in 1990, compared to just 0.5 percent for the top-income group. Estimates of the impact of states and local sales taxes indicate a similarly disproportionate burden on the poor.

If social welfare programs are financed by sales taxes, then, the source of funding is regressive. Hence, the program is not likely to have a strong redistributive effect, although there may be a degree of redistribution introduced at its allocative end. The programs that are most redistributive are those that are financed through progressive taxes and that allocate greater benefits to lower-income groups.

Most taxes fall somewhere between the extremes of progressivity and regressivity. The payroll tax that finances Social Security is a good example. The tax rate is regressive in that (in 1992) all workers paid the same 7.65 percent on the first $55,500 of their earnings. Thus workers who earned $55,500 a year paid the same annual Social Security tax ($4,246) as those earning $200,000 a year. Nevertheless, Social Security is generally perceived as redistributive on its allocative dimension. That is, the benefits provided to those who contributed the smallest amounts are proportionately more generous than to those who contributed at higher levels. Some people, indeed, receive Social Security benefits without having made any contributions to the system. (All people over 72 are entitled to a minimum benefit whether they paid into the system or not.) The Social Security system is also redistributive between generations because payments to the presently retired come from the Social Security fund, which is supported by the current generation of workers.

Nonetheless, the regressive features of Social Security make it considerably less effective than the income tax as a means of redistribution. Unlike the income tax, the Social Security tax does not apply to total income, it is not graduated, and it does not take into account family size or extraordinary family expenses such as medical care and child care. Tax experts point out, in addition, that the employer's contributions to Social Security taxes are substantially passed on to consumers (through higher prices) and employees (through lower wages), further aggravating the regressive aspect of the program. For these reasons, many liberals support the idea of at least partially financing Social Security benefits through income taxes.[54]

In addition to the progressive-regressive characteristics of taxes, the unit of government imposing taxes has an important bearing on the design of redistributive programs. Generally speaking, redistributive programs must be financed by progressive taxes that are levied by large government units. Only the federal government can levy taxes in all jurisdictions at once, although states can levy almost all of the same kinds of taxes as the federal government. (In 1989, 46 states and the District of Columbia had an income tax.)[55] But the tax-levying powers of all subnational units of government are restrained by competition from other units of government and the possible loss of taxpayers who may choose to escape from excessive taxes in one area by locating elsewhere. That is, smaller units of government are in constant competition to attract revenue-producing residents and enterprises to their jurisdictions, putting high-tax units at a distinct disadvantage.[56] Only the federal government has the taxing power to implement revenue programs that can effectively bring about a large-scale redistribution of wealth.

What is the impact of the tax system on the distribution of income? Although economists have long debated this question—and the methodologies appropriate to answering it—the general consensus is that the tax system as a whole is, at best, only slightly progressive. In assessing the period since 1950, for example, Joseph Pechman concluded that the overall progressivity of the U.S. tax system—federal, state, and local—has been declining because of major reductions in the tax burden of the rich.

> While the tax burdens of the bottom 90 percent of the income distribution did not change very much . . . tax burdens of the highest income recipients fell because top federal income tax rates were reduced, the federal corporation income tax dwindled, [and] personal deductions, tax-exempt bonds, and tax shelters proliferated.[57]

In 1981, for example, President Reagan's "supply side" tax cuts reduced the top federal income rates drastically, from 70 percent to 50 percent. In 1986, the top rate dropped further, to 28 percent. Cuts in the tax rate for the rich at the federal level have been accompanied by major increases in state, local, and Social Security taxes and user fees, which burden the poor disproportionately.

The Congressional Budget Office (CBO), in a series of studies examining the impact of federal taxes during the 1980s, indicated the strongly pro-rich tilt of Reaganomics. The CBO figures show that by the end of the 1980s the poorest group of Americans were paying roughly 20 percent more of their earnings in taxes, and the richest group were paying about 20 percent less. This policy created the widest disparity between the family incomes of the rich and the poor since World War II. The CBO, indeed, reported that all but the richest American families paid a higher tax share in 1990 than before the "tax cuts" of 1981 and 1986.[58]

Social Earmarking

A broad body of policy analysis has examined social welfare financing in terms of "fairness," that is, issues of equity, redistribution, and antipoverty. More recently, the role of tax policy in influencing other aspects of social welfare has drawn considerable interest. Tax laws have been examined as a form of social intervention that can influence welfare problems and welfare responses in a variety of ways. The way taxes affect individual as well as organizational behavior, for example, has been increasingly recognized. So, too, has the way tax systems can be structured to focus revenues on special social needs.

Tax revenues can be designated for either general or specific purposes. General revenues, such as those provided by federal and state income taxes, finance the broad range of government operations. Special-purpose taxes, often called earmarked or dedicated taxes, are restricted to legislatively specified activities. The Social Security payroll tax is the best-known example, although in recent years policymakers at all government levels have enacted numerous programs that provide for their own revenues.

Pairing new taxes with new spending has been popular because it permits programs to be adopted or broadened without increasing budget deficits (at the federal level) or threatening spending limits (in the states). Earmarking, in addition, makes clear the connection between dollars raised and services provided. Taxpayers can see where their money is going, something that is not possible with general taxes. Experience with Social Security—as well as excise taxes such as gas taxes, which are linked to road improvements—indicate that such designation, especially in times of fiscal austerity, may be one of the few ways available to expand government activities.

An increasing number of designated taxes have been earmarked for social welfare. Many states utilize alcohol beverage taxes for social programs, especially education; some have financed programs for the blind with amusement taxes; and in several states alcohol and tobacco taxes support prevention and treatment efforts. Similarly, gambling taxes, lotteries, and other quasi-tax measures focus revenues on particular social ends. Since 1980, for example, a majority of the states have raised fees on marriage licenses, birth certificates, and divorce decrees to create children's trust funds to support programs to prevent abuse, neglect, and family violence.[59]

At the local level, cities like San Francisco and Boston have required commercial developers to put money into low-income housing and child-care trust funds on the principle that new office buildings create social needs. Other communities have added surcharges to property and sales taxes to support libraries and programs to serve the homeless, or they have created special taxing districts expressly to finance programs for children. Although not dissimilar in their legal structure from school districts—and other special-purpose districts—these taxing entities generate revenues expressly for health and social services. Palm Beach County voters, for example, created an independent taxing district in 1986, establishing a Children's Services Council as its policy-making body to plan, coordinate, fund, and evaluate programs for children. Among the priorities defined by the council in its first year of operations were substance abuse prevention, child care, and teen pregnancy programs.[60]

Earmarking places the burden of program support on a clearly identifiable source of payment. We have noted some of the general implications of this arrangement for contributory programs, in which the taxpayer is also the recipient of benefits, as in Social Security. In programs in which taxpayers do not benefit directly, earmarking may elicit less popular support, although creatively linking taxes and programs can substantially allay taxpayers' resistance.

Attaching revenues to programs, however, can be hazardous if it undermines the ability of policymakers to utilize revenues flexibly for priority needs. Linking programs to special taxes makes an overall, integrated planning and budgeting process difficult to maintain. Earmarking, in addition, is not likely to help disadvantaged groups with poor reputations or unpopular causes; voters are hardly likely, for example, to target taxes for higher welfare payments or affirmative action. Finally, the automatic nature of earmarking means that the magnitude and character of program spending may be driven by the amount of money generated rather than by changing needs.

Taxes and Behavior

Traditionally, public policy attention has focused on the ways taxes influence economic (particularly saving and investment) behaviors. But taxes also affect important social behaviors—such as when people retire, how much they save for it, whether they have children or care for dependent relatives, their philanthropic activity, and so forth. In contrast to regulatory legislation (like Prohibition) that directly outlaws certain kinds of behavior, taxes influence how people act through economic incentives. Certain kinds of activities are discouraged by making them costly; others are encouraged by making them inexpensive.[61] Activities that are socially detrimental can be reduced by heavy taxes; desirable behaviors can be promoted by light taxes or no taxes at all.

Taxation, for example, has been used internationally as a means of population policy. Along with children's allowances, tax policies can reward larger families. In France and the Netherlands, most notably, tax rates at all levels of income are negatively correlated with family size.[62] Even in the United States, the federal income tax provides a modest reward for extra children through the personal exemption. Of course, taxes can equally promote "reproductive nonproliferation." In 1979, for example, China enacted its first "baby tax" on couples having three or more children, imposing wage reductions up to 10 percent for the birth of a third child and as much as 20 percent for a fifth child. Small families, conversely, were rewarded with low taxes and preferential treatment with respect to pensions, housing, jobs, and schooling.[63]

Income tax deductions can be used to encourage families to care for ill or dependent relatives. Long-term care is an overriding need of many older people. Although programs like Social Security, Title XX, and Medicare and Medicaid provide important public support, many families caring for their parents or other relatives still face enormous financial and emotional burdens. In recent years, the magnitude of these costs and the belief that home care is better than institutional care have resulted in many tax proposals. But only a few have been enacted. Most notably, Congress changed the child-care credit in 1971 into the dependent-care tax credit to encourage at-home care. Presently, about 10 percent of all claims are for adult (mainly elderly) dependents.[64] Several states also give tax relief to families caring for elderly relatives.

Tax policy can also encourage other salutary behaviors. California, for example, permits taxpayers to deduct child adoption expenses that exceed 3 percent of their adjusted gross income; this limitation is waived for families adopting hard-to-place (disabled or older) children. Work behavior is frequently encouraged by making different kinds of work-related expenses deductible. And several states have devised tax schemes to help parents save for their children's college educations.

Just as tax policies encourage some activities, they discourage others. Excise taxes, in particular, are widely used to control behaviors that are viewed as harmful. In the United States, for example, excise taxes on cigarettes and alcohol are levied at federal, state, and local levels. Although such taxes are often simply a way of raising additional revenue or "punishing" people for bad conduct (thus the phrase "sin tax"), they also serve as a behavioral disincentive, rewarding those who eschew an undesirable, socially damaging product.

Most countries levy excise taxes on alcohol, tobacco, and gambling. Beverage taxes are used worldwide to control alcohol consumption, and Finland, Czechoslovakia, France, Norway, Sweden, and Switzerland all explicitly utilize excise taxes to reduce drinking. In these countries and others, furthermore, beverages are taxed differentially; those with the highest alcohol content are subject to the heaviest levies in an effort to shift consumption from hard liquor to beer and wine.[65]

In the United States, the federal government has levied alcohol excise taxes since the 1790s. Prior to the imposition of the federal income tax in 1913, alcohol taxes constituted the federal government's main revenue source, supplying nearly two-thirds of all treasury receipts. Despite periodic increases in these taxes in the years since, the overall trend, until quite recently, was steeply downward. Thus, in 1984, these taxes made up less than 1 percent of all federal revenues. Since then, however, the low rates have received considerable criticism, largely as a result of increasingly clear evidence of the positive correlation between social costs and drinking behavior. Although drinking habits are not easily changed, recent data suggest that alcohol taxes not only reduce alcohol sales and consumption but also affect alcohol-related problems, such as auto fatalities and cirrhosis mortality. The effects are modest but real.[66] Although critics argue that alcohol demand is relatively "inelastic"—that is, not responsive to price, especially for heavy users—support for tax increases has been growing. In 1984, for example, the federal tax on hard spirits was raised substantially, from $10.50 to $12.50 per proof gallon, and in 1991, it rose to its present value of $13.50 per gallon. States impose their own alcohol taxes on top of this.

Other detrimental behaviors can also be restrained. Cigarette taxes have increased as the association between tobacco and disease has become known. In 1982, the federal excise tax on a pack of cigarettes doubled, from 8 cents to 16 cents; in 1991 it became 20 cents, and in 1993 it will reach 24 cents. Moreover, all 50 states tax cigarettes, the rates per pack ranging from a low of 2 cents (North Carolina) to a high of 40 cents (Connecticut). In addition, nearly 400 local governments levy cigarette taxes, ranging up to 10 cents per pack.[67] In Norway, taxation is near draconian, with 85 percent of the price of a pack of cigarettes going for taxes and fees. In Canada, the price per pack is approaching $7 in some provinces.[68]

Much of the impetus for increased tobacco taxes has come from public health organizations, such as the American Medical Association, the American Heart Association, the American Lung Association, and the American Cancer Society. According to the Coalition on Smoking and Health, every 10 percent increase in the price of cigarettes decreases cigarette consumption among young people by about 4 percent. And the General Accounting Office, in a 1989 report that reviewed the impact of taxes on smoking, concluded that raising the federal cigarette excise tax by 20 cents would result in half a million fewer smokers—and 125,000 fewer "premature deaths."[69]

Taxes on beer, cigarettes, and gambling are often attacked for their regressive nature, and it is undeniable that they do impose a far greater burden on people with lower incomes. It is estimated, for example, that alcohol taxes absorb five times as much of the income of households with incomes under $15,000 than they do of those over $50,000. Nevertheless, it is shortsighted to dismiss the social value of excise taxes. First, excise taxes can be enacted as part of broader tax packages that include balancing progressive measures. Second, excise taxes can themselves be progressively structured; alcohol taxes, for example, can be linked to the price of the beverage so that drinkers of an expensive scotch like Chivas Regal pay higher rates than those imbibing Bud Lite. Finally, although sin taxes may fall disproportionately on poor and middle-income Americans, these groups make up most of the victims of cigarettes and liquor. Increased taxes may be burdensome; more important, however, they save suffering and lives.

Additional Considerations: Taxes and the Economy

In considering choices among the alternative sources and amounts of financing that are both possible and desirable, public officials must take into account other policy concerns in addition to redistributional objectives and the social and psychological impact on the taxpayer. The choices in public financing of social welfare programs cannot be realistically stated in such simple terms as "What are its differential costs and benefits to various economic groups, and will the voters buy it?"

One important concern of policymakers involves the *stabilization goals* of government: those that join monetary policy, human resources policy, fiscal policy, social welfare policy, and other policies to manipulate the level of aggregate demand for goods and services and thus avoid extremes of inflation, unemployment, and a detrimental balance of payments.[70] The consideration of stabilization means that designs for financing social welfare programs must be analyzed for their effects on the larger social system, specifically the functioning of the economic market.

Thus, schemes for financing social welfare must be evaluated against such questions as these:[71]

1. Should income tax rates be increased during economic upswings and decreased during downswings to enhance their countercyclical effects?
2. What effects will an increase in Social Security benefits have on withdrawal rates of the elderly from the work force?
3. What are the economic implications of distributing the costs of a program over longer periods by basing payments on the accumulation of a reserve fund (which withdraws monies from consumers) as compared to pay-as-you-go financing?
4. To what extent does financing unemployment compensation through employer contributions that vary according to a firm's employment records (taxes based on experience rating) encourage employers to stabilize employment in their firm?

Although there are limits on the extent to which the economic effects of different financing arrangements can be predicted, policymakers are attentive to these considerations. This will be true especially in the 1990s as the country faces huge deficits and inflationary pressures and as the issue of tax rates, and their impact on productivity and investment, continues to polarize the domestic policy debates of Democrats and Republicans. Although students of social welfare policy tend to emphasize the redistributional characteristics of alternative modes of public financing, it is important that they remain aware of these broad economic considerations.

Indirect Financing: Tax Expenditures

In Chapter Two we introduced the tax expenditure concept to denote the great variety of special features in the tax law that are designed both to encourage certain kinds of behavior and to help people facing special circumstances. Variously called tax credits, deductions, and exclusions, these provisions constitute a system of welfare that parallels regular social welfare spending. Although they are analogous to regular expenditures in that they represent a decision by government to direct resources to particular objectives, they are relatively invisible in that they are not identified and reviewed regularly as part of the regular (expenditure) budget.

The purpose of tax expenditures is not to finance government but rather to direct benefits to particular groups. But whereas regular benefits—like Social Security, AFDC, or farm subsidies—are cash outlays, allocated through the annual budget process, tax expenditures occur when the government does not tax at the level it normally would. To subsidize child care for working families, for example, Congress authorizes direct spending in the form of cash payments to eligible families and also provides program funding for day-care providers. In addition, it utilizes the tax system to help families with child-care expenses.

The use of the tax code as a system of special benefits has long been derided as welfare for the rich. And tax loopholes *have* long been used to advance a variety of complicated arrangements protecting and advancing the interests of people with high incomes. In the federal system, nevertheless, two of the most significant tax expenditures—the tax-free status of income-transfer payments and employee fringe benefits—serve distinct welfare objectives. The exclusion from income taxes granted for public assistance and Social Security payments derives from the simple logic of protecting the limited income of the poor. It hardly makes sense, after all, to provide income support with one hand and tax it back with the other. The exclusion, however, is not absolute. Since Social Security beneficiaries are often reasonably well-to-do, federal policy does tax a limited portion of the Social Security payments of the better-off elderly—currently 50 percent of any income over $32,000 for a couple and over $25,000 for an individual.

Since 1942, employee fringe benefits—compensation received in the form of health and pension plans; special housing allowances; and employee assistance services such as counseling, day care, and the like—have been doubly protected under the federal tax code. First, the cost to employers of all such benefits constitutes a deductible business expense. They can therefore be deducted from taxable income, appreciably lowering taxes owed. Second, employees benefit since all compensation in the form of wages and salaries is taxed but compensation in the form of fringe benefits

TABLE 6-4   Major Social Welfare Tax Expenditures
in the Federal Personal Income Tax, FY 1991
(in Billions of Dollars)

TAX EXPENDITURE	REVENUE LOSS
Social Security (OASI) exclusion	$17.0
Employer pension plans	48.0
Exclusion of employer contributions for medical insurance and care	29.6
Child and dependent care credit	4.2
Charitable contributions	
For education	1.3
For health	1.3
For other purposes	11.6
Earned Income Credit	2.1

Source: Office of Management and Budget, *Budget of the United States Government, FY 1992*, Part 3 (Washington, DC: U.S. Government Printing Office, 1991), pp. 34–36.

is not. Thus, a valuable and costly form of remuneration is given to employees on a tax-free basis.

These provisions have been enormously successful in broadening our system of private welfare. Clearly, tax expenditures have promoted pension plans by making them less costly for employers to sponsor. The pension deduction—the largest of the 109 items listed in the fiscal year (FY) 1991 federal tax expenditure budget (some of which are enumerated in Table 6–4)—totaled $48 billion, providing a huge tax savings for businesses, important benefits for employees, and of course corresponding losses in federal revenues.

Similarly, private health plans have been encouraged. Today, employers provide health insurance for over 60 million employees, deducting over $80 billion for these benefits and reaping nearly $30 billion in tax savings. Once again, in addition to providing a major business deduction, fringe benefits provide an enormous break for employees. Since health benefits are tax free, they constitute a favorable alternative to regular, taxable wages. Workers who are given $2,000 in medical coverage, for example, receive the full benefit value. If the $2,000 were given in the form of salary, that would buy only $1,440 worth of insurance for a worker in the 28 percent income tax bracket.

The overall cost to the government of tax expenditures is considerable—some $361 billion in FY 1988. In some areas, as Table 6–5 indicates, the magnitude of tax expenditures approaches that of direct spending. In the federal budget category "education, training, employment, and social services," for example, direct outlays in FY 1988 were $33 billion, just barely ahead of the $27 billion in tax expenditures. Thus, the amount lost

TABLE 6–5   Federal Tax Expenditures and Outlays Compared in Selected Budget Areas, FY 1988 (in Billions of Dollars)

	OUTLAYS	TAX EXPENDITURES	TAX EXPENDITURES AS PERCENT OF OUTLAYS
Commerce and housing	$ 8	$147	1,834%
Education, training, employment, and social services	33	27	81
Health	128	42	33
Income security	352	97	28
Veterans benefits and services	27	2	7
Other	521	46	9
Total	$1,069	$361	34%

Source: Joseph Pechman, *Federal Tax Policy*, (Washington, DC: The Brookings Institution, 1987) p. 363.

to the treasury in this category of tax expenditures was 81 percent of actual outlays. In the health field, outlays were $128 billion, tax expenditures $42 billion (33 percent of outlays); in income security, the corresponding figures were outlays $352 billion, tax expenditures $97 billion (28 percent of outlays). In the housing field, tax expenditures, chiefly the deductibility of mortgage interest and local property taxes, far exceed outlays, chiefly rent subsidy and related programs.

Public objectives, it is clear, can be advanced by both tax expenditures and regular outlays. As noted, day care is a major area of federal and local activity under spending programs such as Title XX, the Elementary and Secondary Education Act, the AFDC/JOBS Program, and Head Start, as well as under tax programs such as the dependent care credit. Spending programs generally provide revenues directly to program and agency providers, whereas tax credits and deductions give consumers additional purchasing power for use in the marketplace. In this way, they act like vouchers.

Are tax expenditures a good thing? Do they, on balance, help the poor? The answer to these questions is complex. Some tax expenditures clearly are not redistributive. For one thing, you have to pay taxes to benefit from them. If you do not, you get no special help. Even socially oriented tax expenditures—like those for day care, charitable contributions, and health plans—often wind up providing the most to those with the fewest needs. The dependent-care credit, for example, is tilted upward, with much of its benefits going to middle- and upper-income families.[72] Health plan tax expenditures also vary considerably in their impact since younger workers, women, minorities, and unorganized workers are, as a group, less likely to be covered than older workers, men, Caucasians, and union members. In addition, the benefits of those who *are* covered are likely to be far broader for the second group.

Overall, most economists agree that the system of tax expenditures is regressive. One recent calculation estimated that at least half of their total benefit goes to the richest fifth of the population.[73] According to Isabel Sawhill, moreover, few tax subsidies are targeted to help those who need them most. They "neglect the housing, health care, and income security needs of low-income families while simultaneously providing billions to assist the affluent and the middle class."[74] This kind of "welfare for the rich" clearly diminishes the overall progressivity of the income tax. It accounts, in addition, for the fact that although income taxes remain the most redistributive form of taxation, their real rates vary only moderately among income groups. (Real, or "effective," rates refer to actual taxes paid measured as a proportion of a person's overall income.) Despite the official 33 percent federal tax bite on the marginal income of the rich, even the top 1 percent of taxpayers pay only one-fifth of their aggregate income to Uncle Sam.[75]

Tax expenditures have other weaknesses. First, they are a relatively hidden form of public support, which means that they generally avoid the review and scrutiny given to direct spending. Many states and localities, for example, fail to identify tax expenditures in their annual budget documents, and most exert little fiscal control over them in their committee deliberations. For the most part, tax expenditures are a form of entitlement, continuing unexamined from year to year to subsidize qualifying taxpayers.

A second problem is their impact on the tax base. By their very definition, tax expenditures remove funds from the public coffers. At last count, indeed, federal tax loopholes reduced almost by half the amount of income subject to taxation.[76] Thus taxes that in many instances would have been paid by the better-off are foregone. And with less income taxed, less revenue is provided, meaning that tax-supported programs—social programs in particular—may be placed in jeopardy. A substantial portion of the present deficit problem, for example, is clearly the result of fewer dollars available for public support. In recent years there has been an enormous increase in the number and size of tax expenditures, resulting in a substantial gap between forfeited receipts and taxes actually collected, and an ever greater abandonment of the principle of the Sixteenth Amendment, which requires that federal taxes be paid on "incomes, from whatever source derived."

The erosion of the tax base, in addition to reducing government revenues, also impacts differently on different groups. The charity deduction, for example, not only results in the federal government giving up over $1 billion a year in revenue but also draws resources to the particular charities favored by the biggest givers—culture and research in particular. Without attempting to judge the relative value of differing nonprofit endeavors, it is clear that when J. P. Getty willed his fortune to a museum of classical art in Malibu, everybody paid for the project indirectly because of the taxes foregone. It is not the case, though, that everybody will benefit equally from what Getty's gift produced. In quite the same way, all citizens make up the taxes lost through the billions of dollars deducted for donations to religious institutions.

Like all tax expenditures, religious or cultural subsidies that accrue to some are paid for by others. Fundamentally, tax erosion assists those whose income, wealth, and spending are untaxed, shifting the burden of public support to others. If property belonging to elderly veterans is excluded from the rolls, the uncollected funds must be made up by higher rates on taxable property. If income from capital gains is taxed at a fraction of the regular rate, ordinary wage and salary income must cover the losses.

Tax erosion, in other words, results in two forms of tax shifts. First, the private economy—including nonprofit organizations—gains at the expense of the public sector. What philanthropic organizations, successful investors, or day-care users save on taxes is lost to public programs. Second, lower taxes for some mean higher taxes for others. These shifts illustrate a basic rule about the revenue trade-off between tax rates (the percent levy) and the tax base (the amount of income or resources subject to taxes): A given amount of money can be raised at a low rate only if the tax base is broad. When the base is eroded by major tax expenditures, the remaining portion must be taxed at a higher rate to produce the same amount of revenue.

SUMMARY

The public, voluntary, and for-profit funding systems constitute a three-tiered mixed economy of welfare that provides a high degree of choice in meeting the social welfare needs of the American public. The ways in which these financing arrangements operate have major impacts on issues of equity and accountability.

Professional social service workers must be equipped with an understanding of these different funding arrangements because they constitute the critical foundation of the resources available to meet human needs. Knowledge of funding arrangements is especially important in the developing professional specializations of social work in health and medical institutions and in corporate settings. For example, a growing number of social work professionals are working in employee assistance programs in the workplace. In addition to the kinds of knowledge they must have about human behavior and psycho-social development, they must be able to understand how to enable workers and management to make use of the wide range of alternative arrangements available for funding welfare services.

NOTES

1. Michael O'Neill, *The Third America* (San Francisco: Jossey-Bass, 1989), p. 9.
2. "NPT 100, America's Biggest Charities," *The Non Profit Times*, 1991, pp. 5–6.
3. *Giving USA, 1990* (New York: American Association of Fund-Raising Counsel, 1990), pp. 79–84.
4. U.S. Bureau of the Census, *Statistical Abstract of the U.S., 1990* (Washington, DC: U.S. Government Printing Office, 1990), p. 373.
5. Ralph M. Kramer, *Voluntary Agencies in the Welfare State* (Berkeley: University of California Press, 1981), pp. 5–6.
6. Roland L. Warren, *The Community in America*, 3rd ed. (Chicago: Rand-McNally, 1978), pp. 163–169.
7. Neil Gilbert, "The Transformation of the Social Services," *Social Service Review*, Vol. 51, no. 4 (December 1977), 628.
8. For an analysis of public views toward OASDHI and unemployment insurance, see Michael E. Schlitz, *Public Attitudes Toward Social Security 1935–1965* (Washington, DC: U.S. Government Printing Office, 1970).
9. Martin Wolins, "The Societal Function of Social Welfare," *New Perspectives*, Vol. 1, no. 1 (Spring 1967), 12.
10. Daniel Cherkin, "The Effect of Office Visit Co-Payments on Utilization in a Health Maintenance Organization," *Medical Care*, July 1989.
11. Eveline M. Burns, *Social Security and Public Policy* (New York: McGraw-Hill, 1956), p. 157.
12. For a more detailed discussion of tax-deductible philanthropic contributions, see Charles T. Clotfelter, *Federal Tax Policy and Charitable Giving* (1985).
13. Gordon Manser, "The Voluntary Agency—Contribution or Survival?" *Washington Bulletin*, Vol. 22, no. 20 (October 1971), 107; *Voluntary Giving and Tax Policy* (New York: National Assembly for Social Policy and Development, 1972).
14. One interesting note on tax-exempt contributions in this context is that the majority of taxpayers contribute only a small proportion of the funds that could be given tax free. In studies of patterns of philanthropic giving it has been found that most taxpayers, including those reporting exceedingly high annual incomes, do not contribute anywhere near the percentages of the resources for charitable purposes that would be allowable under the exemption system. C. Harry Kahn, *Personal Deductions in the Federal Income Tax* (Princeton: Princeton Univ. Press, 1960) and William S. Vickrey, "One Economist's View of Philanthropy," in *Philanthropy and Public Policy*, ed. Frank G. Dickinson (New York: Columbia Univ. Press 1962).
15. Kramer, *Voluntary Agencies in the Welfare State*, pp. 9, 193–211.
16. For example, see Oscar Handlin, *The Uprooted* (New York: Oxford University Press, 1964).
17. For example, see C. Wendell King, *Social Movements in the United States* (New York: Free Press, 1957).
18. Charles Richard Henderson, "The Place and Functions of Voluntary Associations," *American Journal of Sociology*, Vol. 1 (November 1895), 334–39.
19. Kramer, *Voluntary Agencies in the Welfare State*.
20. Peter Marris and Martin Rein, *Dilemmas of Social Reform: Poverty and Community Action in the United States* (New York: Atherton, 1967). For a dramatic account of how founda-

tions undertake projects that the government may abjure because of political considerations, see Thomas C. Reeves, *Freedom and the Foundation: The Fund for the Republic in the
Era of McCarthyism* (New York: Knopf, 1969).

21. Alvin L. Schorr, "The Task for Voluntarism in the Next Decade," presented at the
Centenary Conference on Voluntary Organization in the 1970s, sponsored by the
Family Welfare Association, University of Sussex, Brighton, England, June 1969.
Schorr cites five pioneering ventures of the 1960s, which he notes were largely inspired
and set in motion by government: juvenile delinquency programs, community action,
amendments to the Social Security Act, community care of the mentally ill, and the
Model Cities Program.

22. Kramer, *Voluntary Agencies in the Welfare State.*

23. This example is based on the article by Herman Levin, "The Future of Voluntary
Family and Children's Social Work: An Historical View," *Social Service Review,* Vol. 38,
no. 2 (June 1964), 164–173.

24. Salvatore Ambrosino, "Family Service Agencies," *Encyclopedia of Social Work,* 17th Edition (New York: National Association of Social Workers, 1977), 429.

25. Herman Levin, "Voluntary Agencies in Social Welfare," *Encyclopedia of Social Work,* 17th
Edition (New York: National Association of Social Workers, 1977), p. 1574.

26. "Social Work Unit Changing Tactics," *New York Times,* January 29, 1971, p. 1.

27. Arlien Johnson, "Public Funds for Voluntary Agencies," in *Social Welfare Forum, 1959*
(New York: Columbia University Press, 1959).

28. Lester Salamon and Alan Abramson, *The Federal Budget and the Non-Profit Sector* (Washington, DC: The Urban Institute, 1982).

29. Ibid., p. 28.

30. Ralph M. Kramer, "Voluntary Agencies and the Personal Social Services," in *The Handbook of Non-Profit Organizations,* ed. Walter W. Powell (New Haven, CT: Yale University
Press, 1985).

31. Elizabeth Wickenden, "Purchase of Care and Services: Effect on Voluntary Agencies,"
in *Proceedings of the First Milwaukee Institute on a Social Welfare Issue of the Day* (Milwaukee:
School of Social Welfare, July 1970).

32. Ira Glasser, "Prisoners of Benevolence: Power vs. Liberty in the Welfare State," in *Doing
Good: The Benefits of Benevolence,* David I. Rothman, ed. (New York: Pantheon Books,
1978), p. 110.

33. Marris and Rein, *Dilemmas of Social Reform,* 130.

34. Austin W. Scott "Charitable Trusts," in *Encyclopedia of the Social Sciences,* Vol. III, eds.
Edwin R. A. Seligman et al. (New York: Macmillan, 1937), pp. 338–340.

35. The Tax Reform Act of 1969 made the prohibition on social and political action even
more stringent for organizations classified as private foundations by removing the
qualifying word, "substantial."

36. See *General Explanation of the Tax Reform Act,* 9162, H.R. 13270, Public Law 91–1972
(Washington, DC: U.S. Government Printing Office, 1970), pp. 48–49.

37. For a detailed discussion of the concept of charitable immunity, see George W. Keeton,
The Modern Law of Charities (London: Pitman and Sons, 1962).

38. *Giving USA, 1990,* p. 42.

39. Ibid.

40. Warren Weaver, *U.S. Philanthropic Foundations* (New York: Harper & Row, 1967), pp. 11,
23; see also Julius Rosenwald, "Principles of Giving," *The Atlantic Monthly,* May 1929;
and Wilmer Shields Rich, "Community Foundations in the U.S. and Canada" (New
York: National Council on Foundations, 1961).

41. For a detailed history of the Girard College case, see Milton M. Gordon, "The Girard
College Case: Desegregation and a Municipal Trust," *The Annals of the American Academy
of Political and Social Science,* March 1956, pp. 53–62.

42. For further discussion of *cy pres* see Keeton, *Modern Law of Charities*; and Edith L. Fisch,

The Cy Pres Doctrine in the United States (New York: Matthew Bender, 1950), pp. 141–142. On the general controlling legal principle as applied to Girard College, see "Validity and Effect of Gifts for Charitable Purposes Which Exclude Otherwise Qualified Beneficiaries Because of Race or Religion," in 25 ALR 3d 736 (1969).

43. For a discussion of varying conceptions of social need, see Jonathan Bradshaw, "The Concept of Social Need," in *Planning for Social Welfare: Issues, Models, and Tasks,* eds. Neil Gilbert and Harry Specht (Englewood Cliffs, NJ: Prentice Hall, 1977), pp. 290–296.

44. Waldemar A. Nielsen, *The Big Foundations* (New York: Columbia University Press, 1972), p. 32.

45. Ray H. Elling and Sandor Halebsky, "Support for Public and Private Services," in *Social Welfare Institutions,* ed. Mayer N. Zald (New York: Wiley, 1965), p. 329.

46. For example, see the following: *New Directions Report* (San Francisco: United Bay Area Crusade, June 1971); *Reexamination Project* (Toronto: United Community Fund of Greater Toronto, May 1971); *Priorities Study* (Detroit: United Foundation, April 1971); *UCS Implementation Program* (San Diego: United Community Services of San Diego County, November 1971); and Bertram M. Beck, "The Voluntary Social Welfare Agency: A Reassessment," *Social Service Review,* Vol. 44, no. 2 (June 1970), 147–54.

47. Stanley Wenocur, Richard V. Cook, and Nancy L. Stekelee, "Fund-Raising at the Workplace," *Social Policy,* Vol. 14, no. 4 (Spring 1984), 55.

48. John Pierson, "I Gave at the Office," *Foundation News,* September 1986.

49. Lester Salamon, "Nonprofit Organizations—The Lost Opportunity," in *The Reagan Record,* eds. John Palmer and Isabel Sawhill (Cambridge, Mass.: Ballinger Publishing Co., 1984), pp. 261–85.

50. Salamon and Abramson, *Federal Budget and the Non-Profit Sector.*

51. *New York Times,* August 16, 1984, p. 9. Somewhat similar findings are reported in Harold W. Demone, Jr., and Margaret Gibleman, "Reaganomics: Its Impact on the Voluntary Not for-Profit Sector," *Social Work,* Vol. 29, no. 15 (September–October 1984), 421–427.

52. Charitable contributions are allowed as an itemized deduction, with few limits. Since lower-income taxpayers generally select the standard deduction, rather than itemizing, the deduction is substantially restricted to better off individuals and families.

53. For an assessment of the redistributive effects of tax and spending programs, see Joseph Pechman, *The Rich, the Poor, and the Taxes They Pay* (Boulder, Colo.: Westview Press 1986), pp. 19–30.

54. Joseph A. Pechman, et al., *Social Security: Perspectives for Reform* (Washington D.C.: Brookings Institution, 1968), 175–78; Eveline M. Burns, *Social Security and Public Policy* (New York: McGraw-Hill, 1956); and Richard Titmuss, *Essays on 'The Welfare State'* (London: Unwin University Books, 1963).

55. Tax Foundations, *Facts and Figures on Government Finance* (Baltimore: The Johns Hopkins University Press, 1990), p. 199.

56. Walter Heller, "Reflections on Public Expenditure Theory," in *Private Wants and Public Needs,* ed. Edmund S. Phelps (New York: W. W. Norton, 1965).

57. Joseph Pechman, "The Future of the Income Tax," *The American Economic Review,* Vol. 80, no. 1 (March 1990), 3.

58. Congressional Budget Office, "The Changing Distribution of Federal Taxes, 1977–1990," U.S. House of Representatives, Ways & Means Committee, March 26, 1990. See also Citizens for Tax Justice, *Inequality & the Federal Budget Deficit,* Washington, D.C. March 1990.

59. Thomas Birch, *Children's Trust Funds: An Update* (Chicago, Il.: National Committee for Preventing Child Abuse, 1984). See also Ronald K. Snells, "Earmarking State Tax Revenues," *Intergovernmental Perspective,* Vol. 16, no. 4 (Fall 1990), 12–16.

60. Healthy Children Report, *Special Taxing Districts for Children* (Cambridge, MA: Harvard University Division of Health Policy, 1988).

61. Charles Lindblom refers to "tax inducements" and "tax punishments." See his "The Market as Prison," *Journal of Politics*, Vol. 44, no. 2 (May 1982).

62. Harvey E. Brazer, "Income Tax Treatment of the Family," in *The Economics of Taxation*, eds. Henry J. Aaron and Michael J. Boskin (Washington, DC: Brookings Institution, 1980) p. 223.

63. *International Family Planning Perspectives*, November 1979

64. General Accounting Office, *Assessment of the Use of Tax Credits for Families Who Provide Health Care to Disabled Elderly Relatives*, August 27, 1982, p. 3.

65. Mavis M. Brown, Margo F. Dewar, Paul Wallace, *International Survey of Alcohol Beverage Taxation and Control Policies*, 5th ed. (Brewers Association of Canada, November 1982), p. 378.

66. Philip J. Cook, "The Effect of Liquor Taxes on Drinking, Cirrhosis, and Auto Fatalities," in *Alcohol and Public Policy: Beyond the Shadow of Prohibition*, eds. M. H. Moore and D. Gerstein (Washington, DC: National Academy of Sciences, 1981), p. 256.

67. *The Taxation of Cigarettes, Alcoholic Beverages and Parimutuel Wagering Activity in California* (Sacramento: State of California Legislative Analyst, October 1981), pp. 7, 9.

68. See, for example, "Canadians Fired Up Over Cigarette Tax," *San Francisco Chronicle*, May 16, 1991; and "A Clamor in Norway to Ban All Smoking," *New York Times*, May 4, 1991.

69. General Accounting Office, *Teenage Smoking*, GAO/HRD-89-111, June 1989.

70. Heller, "Reflections on Public Expenditure Theory."

71. For a detailed analysis of these and other issues concerning the relationship between public finance arrangements and stabilization goals, see Margaret A. Gordon, *The Economics of Welfare Policies* (New York: Columbia University Press, 1963).

72. Douglas Besharov, "Fixing the Child Care Credit," *Harvard Journal on Legislation*, Vol. 26, no. 2 (Summer 1981), 509.

73. Daniel Weinberg, "The Distributional Implications of Tax Expenditures," *National Tax Journal*, Vol. 40, no. 2 (June 1987), *237–254*.

74. Isabel Sawhill, quoted in Urban Institute, *Policy & Research Report*, Winter/Spring 1990, p. 28.

75. Pechman, "Future of the Income Tax," p. 16.

76. Taxable income constitutes about 55 percent of total personal income. See Advisory Commission on Intergovernmental Relations, *Facts & Figures on Government Finance* Washington D.C. 1990), Table C41, p. 130.

Chapter Seven
MODE OF FINANCE: SYSTEMS OF TRANSFER

Where the money flows, the client goes.

Current aphorism

We have left an era when the trend was to assign to the Federal government an ever-increasing responsibility for identifying the needs for social services and for designing programs to meet those needs. Current public policy dictates that decisions are best made at the level of government closest to the target populations served.

Policy Statement, U.S. Office of Human Development Services, 1989

The political system of the United States divides power in two major ways—horizontally, among the executive, legislative, and judicial branches, and vertically, among the different levels of government. These divisions create a complex set of checks and balances in policy-making, administration, and finance among a vast number—nearly 84,000—of local, county, state, and federal units of government.

Jurisdiction over programs and services to meet this country's social welfare needs is distributed among the three basic levels of government in various ways. A particular program (e.g., public assistance) may be under the exclusive administrative authority of a state or it may be under combined state and county authority. The powers of a particular government, moreover, vary from program to program. States, for example, share authority with the federal government in AFDC and Medicaid, have almost complete authority for unemployment insurance, and have almost no authority in Social Security.

Within this complexity, a limitless number of arrangements can be made for transferring funds from their source of origin to the point of service delivery. Choices regarding the system of transfer are affected by, and affect, the other dimensions of choice. These influences can be illustrated in the case of public assistance. When the federal government adopted the policy of separating the delivery of social services from income assistance, several innovations in the system of transfer were introduced. The federal government provided financial incentives for states to reorganize the delivery of service and cash provisions. In addition, it reorganized its own operations so that states would report financial grants to one office and services to another. This change made it not only economically unrewarding but also operationally cumbersome for the states to maintain a unified system. Specifically, in 1967, the federal Department of Health, Education, and Welfare (the predecessor to the Department of Health and Human Services, (HHS)) was reorganized, a new Social and Rehabilitation Service Administration (SRSA) assuming responsibility (and holding state and local agencies accountable) for services, and an Assistance Payments Administration (APA) assuming responsibility for money payments. In 1974, the Title XX program became the major vehicle by which the federal government supported state efforts in planning and providing social services. Title XX is administered at the federal level by the Office of Human Development Services (OHDS), a freestanding agency in HHS. The creation of OHDS completed the separation of income supports from social services. In 1977 the SRSA and APA were abolished and a new Office of Family Assistance became responsible for AFDC payments.

For a different example, we can compare the legislative origins of the Office of Economic Opportunity (OEO), the Model Cities Program, and Title XX. The War on Poverty was based in a new and independent agency (OEO), whereas Model Cities was placed in an established cabinet-level agency, the Department of Housing and Urban Development (HUD). As part of HUD, the organizational resources available for Model Cities were greater than those for OEO, but the commitments of HUD to its numerous constituencies were also greater in comparison to the uncommitted OEO. Thus, Model Cities could bring significant resources to bear but was confined by competing HUD obligations; OEO could be more freewheeling but had fewer organizational means to back up its policy goals; Title XX, an amendment to the Social Security Act, was placed in HHS. Because it was part of the Social Security legislation and was administered by a freestanding federal agency, one with powerful parallel bureaucracies in all the states (i.e., state departments of social welfare), Title XX has the most resilient organizational arrangement of all three programs.

The Office of Economic Opportunity was able to respond to a wide variety of arrangements for transferring money to the local level because the Community Action Programs (CAPs), the local vehicles for implementation, could be constituted by different kinds of public or private groups. The Model Cities Program did not have this freedom because its enabling legislation required City Demonstration Agencies (CDA), the local service delivery vehicles, to be established by city and county governments. While Community Action and Model Cities were overwhelmingly federally funded, Title XX operated until 1981 on a cost-sharing basis, the federal government paying 75 percent of the costs of most services and the states paying 25 percent. However, states were given wide latitude in determining what programs to support. As noted earlier, the Omnibus Budget Reconciliation Act of 1981 removed the 25 percent state contribution as well as other planning and reporting requirements.

The effect of these differences was that OEO often bypassed established governments, developing its own constituencies in the cities. In contrast, HUD could not implement Model Cities without the cooperation of local governments, and Title XX explicitly gave the states the most latitude in program administration. The details of the costs and benefits of these different systems of transfer are complex, of course, but even this minimal description makes it clear that the choice of the hands through which program funding passes affects other aspects of policy. These choices are, to a large extent, based on both the objectives of government and the political constraints that are perceived to exist in attaining the objectives.

These examples point up two major features of the system of transfer: first, how money flows and, second, how its transfer is conditioned. Readers should bear in mind that these features apply equally to publicly and voluntarily financed programs, although the political nature of these arrangements is not as obvious in voluntary programs.

HOW THE MONEY FLOWS

All countries face the question of dividing political, administrative, and fiscal powers and responsibilities among governments at different geographical levels. Should policy be heavily centralized, reliant on substantial national decision making, or should it be heavily decentralized, relying substantially on regional and local control? Can a system somehow effectively combine the best features of both arrangements?

In establishing its own system of differentiation, the United States devised a unique answer to the question of structure and balance—American federalism. The federal division of powers between the national capital and the states, formulated in the Constitution in 1789, has remained the fundamental legal framework of local-national relations. The concept, of course, has evolved considerably over the years. At first it referred to an arrangement of "dual sovereignty," in which the different levels of government operated more or less separately, each with a large amount of autonomy. Today, federalism is characterized by a substantial measure of cooperative activity. Indeed, when we speak of federalism nowadays we are really speaking of *intergovernmental relations,* of different levels of government jointly formulating, operating, and financing domestic policies. The foremost instrument of modern federal relations is the intergovernmental grant-in-aid, commonly known as federal aid.[1]

Federal grant programs express the common interest of localities, states, and the national government in addressing common purposes in a cooperative fashion. The federal government, often taking leadership, provides money to states and localities for the conduct of particular types of programs. In this fashion, federal aid is both a fiscal and a policy device for collective decision making. The purpose of aid programs is defined by Congress, often in very broad terms, whereas actual program implementation is the responsibility of states and localities. And since states and localities run the programs and often share in their financing, they have a great deal of influence over their character. State and local participation, it is important to note, is fully voluntary. The core of the federal relationship, in other words, is built on cooperation, not coercion, on preserving local diversity within a framework of nationally shared values.

Although federal cash grants to states date back to 1879, their importance as a basic organizing instrument for social welfare did not emerge until the New Deal. When the Social Security Act became law in 1935, for example, all but two of its dozen or so programs were organized and financed through grants-in-aid. Aid to Dependent Children, Aid to the Blind, and Old Age Assistance, the three programs that established America's basic public assistance system, were all formulated as grants-in-aid. Other titles of the act provided aid to states for maternal and child welfare services, crippled children, and vocational rehabilitation.

In the 1960s, the second major era in the development of the American welfare state, Congress again relied on the grant-in-aid principle. Except for Medicare, all the principal social programs enacted as part of the Great Society followed the federal format—financial aid from Washington in exchange for program commitments by states and localities. Lyndon Johnson, like Roosevelt before him, used federal money to promote national purposes by enlarging and diversifying the scope of state and local programs. During the 1960s, however, greater stress than ever before was focused on antipoverty and urban programs, and more and more federal dollars went directly to cities rather than (as in the past) almost exclusively to states. In some instances, indeed, like the community action programs

TABLE 7–1   Federal Grants-in-Aid, Selected Years

	AMOUNT (IN BILLIONS OF DOLLARS)	AS % OF FEDERAL DOMESTIC OUTLAYS	AS % OF STATE-LOCAL OUTLAYS	# OF GRANT PROGRAMS
1950	$ 2.3	11.6%	10.4%	60
1960	7.0	20.6%	14.6%	130
1970	24.1	25.3%	19.2%	400
1980	91.5	23.3%	25.8%	540
1990	123.6	18.7%	17.0%	450

Source: Richard Nathan and John R. Lago, "Intergovernmental Fiscal Roles & Relations," *The Annals*, Vol. 509 (May 1990), 63.

(CAPs) of the War on Poverty, aid was funneled directly to private, non-governmental community organizations at the neighborhood level.

Today, the vast majority of America's social programs are multilevel partnerships. Only in a few areas of social welfare policy (mainly social insurance, American Indian programs, and veterans' affairs) does the national government have sole responsibility. States, for example, are the responsible program partner in mental health, AFDC, social services, and Medicaid. Local governments take principal responsibility for operating aid programs in elementary and secondary education, community development, urban mass transit, and employment and training. State programs are generally administered at the federal level by HHS, whereas city and county programs are generally administered by HUD.

As Table 7–1 indicates, grant policy has evolved somewhat fitfully over the past 40 years. During the years of the Great Society, the number, size, and relative importance of federal grants grew rapidly. Indeed, in 1964, 1965, and 1966 a total of 198 new federal grants were authorized. During the decade of the 1960s, grant outlays more than tripled, from $7 billion to $24 billion annually, making state and local governments increasingly dependent on federal aid as a source of revenue. The federal aid budget, measured in constant dollars, peaked in 1978 and then declined. Grant outlays in some program areas dropped quite dramatically. Between 1980 and 1985, for example, social services were reduced by 25 percent, urban renewal by 67 percent, and training and employment by 69 percent. By the end of the Reagan years, the overall level of federal aid as a portion of the federal domestic budget had fallen to that of the early 1960s.

But although the level of support has fallen, the principle of federal-state-local partnerships has never been stronger. Given the fundamentally centralizing trends that characterize modern society, this is surprising. The endurance of the states is particularly surprising, given the many predictions over the course of this century that their days as viable units of government were numbered. In 1933, for example, Luther Gulick, an eminent scholar of government, wrote, "Is the state the appropriate instrumentality for the discharge of . . . important functions? The answer is not a matter of conjecture or delicate appraisal. It is a matter of brutal record. I do not predict that the states will go. I affirm that they have already gone."[2]

Gulick's view represents a dominant theme of the Great Depression years, one that considered the states unprepared to deal with the enormous economic and social problems facing the nation. The states, primarily rurally oriented, did not seem to have the financial, administrative, or leadership powers required to deal with the effects of the Depression, which fell most heavily on urban areas. And the centralization of power that occurred under Roosevelt and, later, Johnson, did significantly change American politics, making "the White House, not the State House . . . the fountainhead of ideas, the initiator of action, the representative of the national interest."[3] However, through it all, the federal principle has endured, and with it the importance of the states. Federal aid, indeed, helped modernize state and local governments, transforming them into primary instruments for meeting domestic policy needs.

Finance and Politics

Power to implement and administer programs carries with it some degree of control over the nature of provisions, the bases of allocations, and the systems of service delivery. However, the devolution of power also has implications beyond choices for designing programs. The transfer of program funds confers the ability to dispense benefits to a constituency, to hire and appoint staff, and to award contracts. Apart from programmatic choices, therefore, the transfer of funds among government units represents the exchange of important political resources.

Social welfare agencies and programs are established by a combination of law, tradition, and experience and come to be supported by an organizational and institutional apparatus. Hence, they do not change as quickly as political coalitions. The arrangements for transferring funds that are made in the formulation of policy are likely to reflect current political coalitions.

Model Cities, OEO, and Title XX all illustrate how political coalitions are a consideration in transfers. Both OEO and Model Cities were directed at urban areas, whereas authority for the allocation of Title XX funds is clearly lodged with state governments. In OEO, the system of transfer reflected the desires of the incumbent Democratic administration to link itself with newly developing voting blocs in the cities, particularly with minority groups. Model Cities represented a variation on this theme because the federal administration pushed the development of new coalitions between low-income and minority residents and city hall. We point out in the next chapter how developments in Model Cities reflected the interest of the federal government in increasing the power of executive-centered government in cities. Under general revenue sharing and block grants such as Title XX, state governments were strengthened by federal resources.

The term *general revenue sharing* refers to arrangements whereby the federal government makes grants to lower units of government with virtually no strings attached. Block grants are federal aid programs that place only limited conditions on recipient units. The development of both kinds of programs during the Nixon administration of the early 1970s offers a final example of how the system of transfer reflects political coalitions.

The thrust toward general revenue sharing, especially with the states, was clearly in the political interest of a Republican national administration. The Republicans inherited a vast conglomeration of categorical programs from their Democratic Great Society predecessors. Because these programs were established in law, tradition, and experience and were supported by an elaborate organizational and institutional apparatus, the Republicans had to live with them temporarily while attempting to contain and modify them with an eye to their reduction and, at least in some cases, their ultimate elimination. Low-income and minority groups in urban areas did not represent a major segment of the Republican constituency. State governments were more likely to reflect Republican interests and to represent important parts of the Republican constituency. Therefore, revenue sharing with the states was of greater interest to Republicans than to Democrats.

We have described the flow of money as though it is a simple exchange between two parties, but this is not always the case. Several actors may be involved, and the benefits to each may vary. For example, OEO legislation required funds to local CAPS to have the approval of the state's governor. (However, the 1967 amendments to the act gave the national director of OEO authority to override a governor's veto.) Thus, governors could exercise some control over the transfer. Similarly, in Model Cities, funds for the CDA had to "pass through" the city, giving the mayors some control over expenditures. In both programs, guidelines (that is, the rules set down on the basis of administrative discretion) required "sign-offs" from various local, state, and federal agencies, meaning that funding required their general approval.

Although political considerations may influence choices concerning the units to which funds will be given, some degree of scientific analysis also enters into these decisions. That is, technically, some identifiable characteristics of units can be utilized in selecting the one most appropriate to receive funds: the degree of expertise and resources required to administer a program, the appropriate government size given the substantive nature of the program, and the nature of the problem for which a programmatic solution is being sought. However, application of these technical considerations requires the utmost care and scrutiny. Often, for each logical reason given to vest a program in one unit ("They will be more efficient," is one example) another equally compelling reason can be found to vest it in another unit ("They are more committed to the policy goals" or "They are closer to the problem").

Moynihan's observations on a report by the Task Force on Jurisdiction and Structure of the State Study Commission for New York City illustrate how technical considerations apply to the allocation of program responsibility. The task force suggested that rat control services should be a central function, whereas service centers to provide information on poison control should be a local responsibility. In both cases Moynihan argued that the reverse arrangements were technically superior. As for rat control services he notes,

> Given stable food and harborage, the model urban rat lives and dies in an area extending at most a few hundred feet . . . the urban rat is preeminently a neighborhood type, preferring, when possible, never even to cross the street. As for rodent control, opinion is universal (as best I know) that the fundamental issue is how humanoids maintain their immediate surroundings. I cannot conceive a municipal service more suited to local control, nor one which more immediately calls on those qualities of citizenship which the Task Force describes as constituting in some degree a "quasi-governmental responsibility" toward the community. It comes down, alas, to the question of keeping lids on garbage cans. What better issue for Neighborhood Service Representatives to take up?[4]

In contrast, poison control centers provide services that require great knowledge about the chemical nature of different substances that people might ingest as well as possible antidotes if the chemicals are poisonous. Quick access by day or night to a tremendous bank of information is required. In light of these requirements, Moynihan suggests,

> At the very least it should be a city function although a good case could be made for making it regional, or perhaps national: one telephone number anywhere in the nation, putting the doctor through to a laboratory/computer facility that would provide the information fastest. The idea that such a function could be broken down into thirty to thirty-five separate centers, in New York City alone, each to be manned day and night is . . . not persuasive.[5]

Finally, a major consideration in the flow of funds is whether lesser units should operate programs for which they have no financial responsibility. Here, the issue is how careful a unit will be in spending funds that it does not have to raise and whether it will act in the financial interests of the granting authority. For example, one general critique of public assistance financing is that the federal government gives almost a blank check to the states by paying the major costs of a program in which the basic determinants of costs—the number of recipients and level of benefits—are left to the control of the states.[6]

THE IDEOLOGY OF TRANSFERS

In addition to preferring voluntary methods of financing social welfare activities, conservatives favor localism in the allocation of government funds. This is the heart of the New Federalism strategy, which has dominated federal domestic policy in this generation. For conservatives, the states and localities should have primary responsibility for directing and administering social welfare programs, not big government in Washington.

The Nixon-Reagan New Federalism countered a centralizing trend of nearly 50 years of grant-in-aid policy. Beginning in the 1930s, the focus of federal aid moved increasingly toward establishing national standards in the provision of income support and social services. In the 1960s, the Great Society established a nationally directed, urban-focused system of social welfare provisions that utilized grant funds as primary instruments for national direction. Great Society programs not only expanded the total sum of grant aid available but also ushered in new goals and procedures that significantly altered the character and balance of intergovernment relations.

In terms of ultimate purpose, the programs of the 1960s sought to guarantee minimum levels of opportunity and well-being throughout the nation. Comprehensive (if not precise) statements of national welfare goals were incorporated into a framework of grant-funded services for the disadvantaged—especially the urban disadvantaged. Although Great Society programs recognized the importance of utilizing community organizations as partners in the planning and delivery of services, these new programs incorporated extensive and detailed federal regulations and substantial program monitoring and oversight.

The ideology underpinning the aid transfer programs of the Great Society generation was decidedly centralist. Program direction as well as program finance shifted to Washington. The nation's obligation to eliminate poverty was asserted, and administrative procedures were formulated to ensure that national purposes were properly carried out. Presidents Kennedy and Johnson both knew how very easily social programs could sway off target when carried out by states and localities that were not fully committed to social objectives. Memories of Jim Crow and antiurban biases in policy were still fresh in the minds of Washington policymakers. Grant policies were therefore formulated carefully to ensure that benefits, in fact, were effectively routed to the needy. Controls and guidelines were highly detailed.

By the mid- to late 1970s, the Great Society era had run its course. Although the programs it spawned were maintained, for the most part, their underlying spirit, along with the substantial reliance on federal leadership, faded away. Confronted with a series of major managerial problems and a new farther-to-the-right philosophical zeitgeist, federal policies acquired a different face. Federal control and program expansion was replaced by "devolution, disengagement, and decremental budgeting."[7] The Great Society was replaced by the New Federalism.

Reagan's New Federalism (the phrase was initially popularized by Richard Nixon) initiated a transfer system that was far more heavily reliant on states and localities. Whereas Great Society programs expressly advanced specific national purposes, New Federalism grants were formulated as a means of helping state and local government accomplish their objectives. Federal interventionism was abdicated in favor of decentralized policy-making. Federal spending, federal control, and federal regulation were all sharply reduced.

The New Federalism and the Conditions of Transfer

The contrast between Great Society and New Federalism arrangements can be seen clearly in the basic components of the intergovernmental transfer of funds. Financial transfers, whatever their philosophical rationale, always impose a set of reciprocal relationships; aid is never provided without conditions. The conditions that are required—often called strings or controls—govern how the aid can and cannot be used.

There are four fundamental types of federal aid conditions: *program conditions,* which define the purpose of the grant; *financial conditions,* which govern the matching arrangements; *beneficiary conditions,* which determine who is eligible to be assisted; and *procedural conditions,* which specify planning, administrative, and reporting procedures. In each area, the character of grant policy has changed markedly over the past 30 years as the respective roles of federal, state, and local governments have been redefined.

Program conditions. Federal aid laws generally specify the kinds of activities they are intended to support. We therefore have grants for nutrition, mental health, runaway centers, drug and alcohol abuse, special education, foster care, medical care, cash support for the poor, and so on. Historically, the great majority of grant-in-aid programs have been defined rather narrowly, which is why they are often referred to as *categorical*; that is, they are targeted on specific categories of issues or population groups. According to one recent program inventory, over 95 percent of all federal aid programs remain categorically specific.[8]

Programs are categorical when their basic purposes are specified in detail (see Table 7–2). Categorical grants specify who is to be served, what benefits they are to receive, and how the delivery system is to be organized. For this reason, AFDC public assistance is often described as the prototype categorical program, although the term applies to many others. Categorical programs may specify any number of conditions, including requirements regarding certification and licensing of personnel, how recipients are to be

TABLE 7-2 Mode of Finance: Systems of Transfer

FUNDING ARRANGEMENTS	SPECIFICATION OF PURPOSE	ROLE OF STATES/LOCALITIES
Categorical grants	Specified narrowly	Strictly implementing federal policies and procedures
Block grants	Specified broadly	Establishing and implementing policy within a given functional area
General revenue sharing	Unspecified	Independent policymakers

interviewed, and appeals machinery to handle clients' complaints. Categorical funding, very clearly, ensures that the unit of government providing revenue has substantial control over its expenditure.

Since the Great Society, the federal aid system has become considerably less categorical. This shift is in keeping with the New Federalism's conservative critique of the welfare state, which supports a reduction in the scope of big government. For conservatives, big government, especially centralized government, threatens democracy and efficiency because basic decisions are made in Washington rather than in local communities, where, it is said, the problems "actually are." For the New Federalists, categorical aid is wasteful, supporting programs in which there is no compelling national interest and creating excessive red tape, paperwork, and regulation.

One major objection to the categorical system has been principally managerial: The great number of specific programs are often difficult to administer effectively at the local level. It has been said that although individual programs made individual sense, the aggregate of programs produced administrative overload. Each program was usually separately administered; coordination was absent. In many cases mayors or governors would not even be aware of all the programs serving their jurisdictions. When they were aware, they often found themselves powerless to make the system work as a whole.

To deal with these concerns, the New Federalism decategorized federal aid. When Ronald Reagan took office in 1981, a major plank in his domestic platform was to consolidate multiple, detailed, categorical grants into a limited number of broadly formulated block grants. Though many of Reagan's proposals were not accepted by the Congress, 77 categorical grants-in-aid were collapsed into 9 block grants under the Omnibus Budget Reconciliation Act of 1981. For example, 10 separate grants that provided state aid for addressing different aspects of alcohol, drug abuse, and mental health were combined into 1 new block grant, streamlining administration, reducing paperwork, and giving the states increased discretion to define programs as they chose. Thirty-seven categoricals in education were similarly consolidated, as were 27 in health.

These new block grants defined goals broadly, giving local officials significant discretion within functional areas such as community development, employment and training, and social services. Although the federal government continues to provide some general direction on spending, recipients have considerable leeway in specifying program priorities as well as administrative and service delivery arrangements. These features, of course, mark a significant retreat in federal intervention, with a commensurate increase in the role of states and localities.

Under Title XX, for example, close to $3 billion a year in federal money is currently available to the states for "social services." Title XX is a block grant because these services are not defined in programmatic terms. Instead of specifying money for family planning, homemaker services, marital counseling, day care, child-abuse prevention, or any other specific activity, Congress simply requires priorities to be set by the states. Similarly, the Job Partnership Training Act provides funds for "employment and training," however specified. The Community Development Block Grant program provides support for "community development," a term that can encompass anything from street repair to day-care services to low-interest facility loans for neighborhood nonprofit agencies.

A more radical, decentralist reform—one that did not prove to be as successful as block grants—was general revenue sharing (GRS). Initiated in 1972, GRS constituted a major break with the categorical tradition in that it provided, for the first time, federal aid without *any* specification of program priority. In other words, revenue sharing was unconditional with regard to function. Depending on their preferences, localities or states could develop new programs, use the money for tax relief, or build new facilities. If they decided to develop new programs or expand old ones, they could invest in health, recreation, police, sanitation, or code enforcement. For over a decade, GRS provided more than $6 billion a year—one-third to the states, two-thirds to local authorities—for their unhampered use.

The program, despite its appeal to conservatives, was abolished in 1987 as part of the effort to trim the federal deficit. This is rather ironic, given the Reagan administration's commitment to "returning power to the people," but it indicates the political vulnerability of grants that lack a clear program and client focus. General revenue sharing was extremely popular among states and local elected officials. It was, after all, money for nothing, grant aid for free. But GRS was never terribly appealing in Washington, DC.

Financial conditions.   The second major type of federal control relates to financing. In general, aid recipients must be willing to put up what is called a "local match." That is, states and localities must be willing to pay a share of program costs if they want federal aid.

Matching serves a variety of purposes. For one thing, it reduces the cost burden on the providing unit. Just as important, matching helps to ensure cooperation and efficient program management. A state or locality putting up its own resources is more likely to take its administrative responsibilities seriously than when simply using somebody else's funds.

Matching is also used to influence policy-making. Federal funds provide incentives for state and local involvement to participate in particular programs. Because states and localities, through long periods of American history, were reluctant to take on social responsibilities, federal aid was one of the major tools available to Washington to promote social welfare initiatives. States and localities are less likely to move into new areas of activity if they must pay the entire cost for such programs. But federal aid in the form of 50 percent, 75 percent, or even 100 percent grants may be difficult to turn down. The offer of ten federal dollars for just one raised locally is very enticing.

Different cost-sharing formulas apply to federal aid programs. In most cases, especially in the older categorical programs, the state and/or local share ranges from 10 to 50 percent. California, for example, splits AFDC costs 50–50 with the federal government. Under the Maternal and Child Health Act, states must contribute three dollars for every four dollars received from the federal government.

Over time, however, state and local contributions have been diminishing. In the 1960s, to ensure state and local participation in new social efforts, the federal government "sweetened the pot," offering higher and higher payment shares. The War on Poverty, for example, was 90 percent federal, 10 percent local. Public housing and Elementary and Secondary Education Act Title I grants were 100 percent federal, with recipient governments required to pay only the administrative costs. Food stamps operated the same way. Had Congress demanded more, full national coverage could not have been achieved, given the reluctance of many jurisdictions to contribute even small amounts to social programs.

The trend to minimize the local share continued under the New Federalism. General revenue sharing required no local share; it was "free" money. Block grants, for the most part, are the same. Title XX initially required a 25 percent state match, but that was eliminated in 1981. Nine of the 12 block grants currently operating require no state or local funds.

Beneficiary conditions.   A third area of federal control concerns the definition of the beneficiary. Federal aid is often conditioned on both the units of government that are eligible for assistance and the types of individuals who can receive benefits. Both conditions are often described in terms of targeting.

One way to distribute federal aid is proportionally, strictly by population. Title XX social services operate in this way. California has about 12 percent of the national population, so it gets 12 percent of the available funds. Every other state also gets funds proportional to its population.

Clearly there is no targeting in this procedure, no special effort to focus help on those states with the greatest needs for services.

When the federal government wants to target aid to the neediest, it utilizes allocation formulas based on need. For example, HUD housing grants frequently focus aid on communities with the worst housing stock. Education aid, such as the Elementary and Secondary Education Act, provides support to "districts serving areas with substantial concentrations of children from low-income families." Other programs concentrate funds on jurisdictions with high AFDC rates, high unemployment rates, or low per capita incomes.

Targeting focuses aid not only on particular jurisdictions but also within recipient jurisdictions on particular population groups. Many federal aid programs, for example, require means tests to determine clients' eligibility. All the public assistance programs are targeted on the poor. Other federal aid programs, such as food stamps, are assistance-linked, meaning that eligibility is restricted to people eligible for AFDC, SSI, or some other welfare program.

Title XX, the social services block grant, was targeted on low-income people until the Reagan changes of 1981. Previously, states had to use at least 50 percent of all expenditures to assist welfare clients. Similarly, the mandate that 75 percent of Community Development Block Grant funds be targeted to low- and moderate-income citizens has been repealed.

Prodecural conditions.   In addition to financial, program, and beneficiary conditions, aid legislation frequently contains a variety of procedural conditions relating to planning, audits, personnel, reporting, clients' rights, and the like. Some of these standards are cross-cutting, meaning that they apply to all aid programs. All programs, for example, prohibit discrimination in hiring personnel and allocating benefits to clients. These civil rights requirements were expanded in the 1970s and 1980s to prohibit discrimination against racial and ethnic minorities, women, the handicapped, and the aged. Other cross-cutting requirements exist for environmental protection, labor standards, merit personnel systems, and disclosure of information to the public.

Many conditions, however, apply only to specific programs. Some require citizen participation; for example, Community Action mandated "maximum feasible participation" of the poor in formulating and running antipoverty programs. Others require advisory committees and public hearings. Under Model Cities, each city had to undertake a "comprehensive" planning process that involved community residents and public officials in producing detailed analyses of community needs and one- and five-year plans of action. The 1987 McKinney Homeless Assistance legislation requires jurisdictions to submit comprehensive homeless assistance plans that include statements of need; inventories of existing services and facilities; and remediation strategies that take into account the homeless mentally ill, families with children, the elderly, and veterans.[9]

Some grants require procedures to ensure that funded activities are coordinated with related programs. Others call for appeal procedures for applicants who are denied benefits, for strict confidentiality standards, or for hiring employees with particular kinds of education. For many years, community mental health legislation required that only psychiatrists head clinical programs; early social welfare programs promoted the use of social work professionals, especially in child welfare.

There is a large and varied body of regulation governing record keeping and program reporting. The federal government generally specifies report standards concerning expenditures and clientele. These demands may be relaxed or they may be rigorous. Probably no other grant condition excites more outrage and resentment than reporting requirements. Detailed report forms submitted in octuplicate on a monthly basis may often be a fact of bureaucratic life, but that hardly makes it palatable to action-oriented practitioners. At the same time, reporting requirements can also be frustrating to funders, who depend on timely and appropriate information to determine the extent to which program goals are achieved.

Generally speaking, there are limits to the utility of reporting requirements as a mechanism to maintain control over expenditures, especially in large programs with ambitious objectives. In the Model Cities Program, for example, local Community Development Agencies were able to report their financial expenditures, but it turned out to be impossible to develop a system that could inform HUD of what they were actually accomplishing. Attempts to develop such an information system became bogged down in the uncertainty inherent in a complex, multifaceted program in which broad latitude was given to local administrators. What information should be used to measure program progress? How much weight should be given to the number of people and agencies participating in planning, the quality of the process, or its outcome? What criteria indicate the quality or relevance of programs planned? All these factors relate to the goals of the Model Cities Program, but the goals as stated in the legislation were so vague, global, and comprehensive that in many respects they defied measurement.

In general, the New Federalism reduced the number of procedural strings attached to grant-in-aid programs. Title XX, for example, no longer required states to have an annual planning process or to maintain formal procedures for the involvement of the public. Federal standards imposing fees to better-off clients were eliminated. All told, the federal regulations governing Title XX were reduced from 50 to 8 pages.

The overall impact of the New Federalism on the system of transfer, and on the welfare state in general, is difficult to assess. Most commentators point to the continuing vitality of intergovernmental policy-making and policy management and the continuity of aid programs themselves. A Brookings Institution study found that there was a "singular failure [of the New Federalism] to dislodge in any fundamental way the basic post-New Deal safety-net function of the federal government. Despite Ronald Reagan's intentions," the study continued, "the welfare state remains alive and well—not only in Washington but subnationally."[10]

Privatization

Public finance for public purposes does not always occur strictly within the confines of federal, state, and local government operations. As noted in previous chapters, public policymakers frequently rely on private institutions for carrying out major social welfare responsibilities. One of the major themes of the Republican administrations of the 1980s, paralleling the emphasis on decentralization, was privatization—offering government-funded services through nongovernmental, especially profit-making, mechanisms.

The basic idea behind privatization is that competition combined with the profit motive will provide services that are efficient and effective. Public agencies, conservatives believe, become slothful and wasteful because they have a virtual monopoly over services. Supported by public funds—largely guaranteed funds—they need not compete for either resources or clients. This process undermines their incentive to strive for low costs, quality services, and satisfied customers.

Although privatization is not a new idea, it has become a worldwide slogan of welfare state critics who argue that government is inherently unable to do a good job of service delivery.[11] And worldwide, there has been great growth in private operations in fields of service such as residential care of the frail aged and care of released mental patients. In the United States, for example, close to 80 percent of nursing home facilities are operated on a private for-profit basis, absorbing approximately two out of every three Medicaid dollars. Profit-making agencies have also become the dominant contractors in providing government-supported residential treatment, day care, and group homes in the field of child welfare.[12] A recent survey of American cities found that almost all of them contract at least one service to local contractors. These services range from towing and storing vehicles to garbage collection to operating day-care centers, emergency shelters and drug treatment programs.[13]

We mentioned earlier some of the various procedures supporting market-oriented mechanisms, such as voucher systems (in which recipients are given coupons or certificates that allow them to purchase a service from a provider), capitation systems (whereby providers are paid a fixed fee per client for a range of services), and fee-for-service schemes (whereby providers are paid varying fees for ensuring provision of a range of services).

These entrepreneurial schemes may be implemented by individual professionals in private practice or group practice or by business organizations and insurance companies. Currently in the United States, approximately 25 percent of professional social workers are in private practice for some part of their time.[14] It is estimated, in addition, that approximately 50 to 65 percent of the $2.7 billion Title XX social services funds are spent on services purchased from both private nonprofit and for-profit organizations.

The influence of privatization on social work is significant enough to warrant a brief digression. As noted, approximately one-quarter of all professional social workers are in private practice for some part of their time, double the proportion 20 years ago. As an organizational matter, privatization has an enormous impact on public accountability and responsiveness to social need. Its impact on social work as a profession is equally if not more significant. It undercuts in a major way the very quality that makes the profession "social." That is, social work is the community's response to social needs. It is the social sponsorship of the charitable impulse that has given the social work profession its mission in modern industrial society. Social sponsorship may occur through various agencies and levels of government and through a variety of voluntary and charitable organizations. Until recently, social work has not been perceived as merely the interaction between a professional and a client. Rather, its special character as a helping profession has been its particular concern with enabling persons to make use of social resources to solve their problems. These resources include friends, family, and public and voluntary organizations in the community.

The drift toward privatization in social work practice may provide new career opportunities, but these careers are more like those of psychiatrists, clinical psychologists, and marriage and family counselors. They may be good careers for those who follow them, but they are not the kinds of careers that will strengthen social work as a service profession for the contemporary welfare state.

CENTRALIZATION VERSUS DECENTRALIZATION OF AUTHORITY

Given the size and diversity of our federal system, the balance between centralization and decentralization is a perennial issue. In the design of social welfare policy, values and assumptions related to centralization and decentralization are expressed in choices concerning pluralism versus uniformity, public versus private, the flow of money between governments, and the conditions placed on financial transfers. In the past 20 years, the ideals of decentralization and limited public control have been ascendant.

Particularly during the Reagan era, service responsibilities were returned to the level of the states and localities. Although these units were generally eager to increase their program authority, they have been less prepared to cope with fiscal retrenchment and federal aid cutbacks, and their record in social investment has been mixed. The consequences for the poor of reduced federal control are far from uniform, but the combination of decentralization and funding reductions that characterized the 1980s clearly harmed those dependent on public assistance and social services.

This is not to deny the values of decentralization. Local governments are often more knowledgeable than large centralized units about problems in their areas and more responsive to the special needs of their constituencies. In addition, small units can more easily experiment, and if they fail, all is not lost. Indeed, losses suffered through the failure of one unit's experiment may be compensated for by the lessons of successful alternatives. Finally, there is an existential quality about small decentralized units that is appealing. They lend themselves more readily to visions of the gemeinschaft, marked by warm, meaningful relationships and a sense of belonging to a community, in contrast to the bureaucratic alienation of big government.[15]

Yet localism can also be parochial and oppressive. Privacy and freedom may shelter more securely in the cold impersonality of large centralized units. As McConnell argues,

> Impersonality is the guarantee of individual freedom characteristic of the large unit. Impersonality means an avoidance of arbitrary official action, the following of prescribed procedure, conformance to established rules, and escape from bias whether for or against any individual. Impersonality, and the privacy and freedom it confers, may be despised, and the human warmth and community concern for the personal affairs of individuals characteristic of the small community preferred. Nevertheless, the values involved are different, and are to a considerable degree antagonistic.[16]

The defense of minority interests in small units is often more difficult to achieve than in larger units. In small units it is easier to weld a cohesive majority that may disregard the interests of others or may bring great pressure for conformity. Historically, large centralized units have been more progressive and have attracted and supported administrative expertise more than smaller units. Moreover, national units command greater resources; some problems are clearly beyond the scope of local initiative.

From the perspective of most social welfare advocates, states and localities have major weaknesses. Their revenue systems are often deficient. Constrained by regressive tax systems, the fear of losing businesses to rival jurisdictions, and an increasing proliferation of spending limits, they lack the wherewithal to address pressing needs. Their technical and administrative capacity, despite vast improvements since the 1960s, are often inadequate, with poorly trained and badly paid personnel more the rule than the exception.

The decentralization of authority also results in a troubling degree of variation in local social welfare efforts. Having significant diversity in state and local activities may reflect a salutary degree of pluralism, but it also blocks a national approach to problems and can result in substantial discrepancies in benefit arrangements from place to place. Perhaps the most dramatic example is the variation in AFDC payments. In 1990, for example, maximum benefits for a family of four in California were five times as high as in Alabama. Although the federal government modifies this discrepancy a bit through the food stamp program—which has uniform nationwide eligibility and benefit standards—the gap between high-payment and low-payment states in this and in other program areas remains dramatic.[17]

The more general critique of decentralization, of course, is that it tends to reduce the emphasis on helping the poor. Historically speaking, in this country and in others, it has been national leadership that has evidenced the greatest degree of concern with society's misfits, disadvantaged, and vulnerable. Although it is difficult to characterize the multitude of state and local policies with glib generalizations, it is certainly clear that for the most part they have often been less than willing, and perhaps financially less than able, to undertake an effective social agenda.

Several nations have, nevertheless, sought to invest local government with primary social responsibilities, especially in the social services. In 1982, a British group appointed under the authority of Margaret Thatcher reviewed the British social care system and recommended that the United Kingdom adopt a system of community social work, which in essence would be extremely decentralized and locally based. Professor Robert Pinker of the London School of Economics wrote a sharp critique of the proposal, which can be paraphrased as follows:[18]

> A stubbornly persistent notion of social policy is that the concept "community" can be used to resolve our policy dilemmas. However, it is an erroneous idea that this concept can provide a basis for shared values in a complex society.
>
> The capacity of local communities, especially poor ones, to support sustained patterns of informal care may be exaggerated. It should be borne in mind that formal provision of social services developed because the family and other local community groups were often incapable of meeting needs for mutual support.[19]
>
> The potential threat to privacy and civil liberties that inheres in some of the Working Party's proposals for state intrusion into the private world of individuals under the guise of prevention and community work is not insignificant. It constitutes an invitation "to endorse the creation of a proliferation of local databanks based on hearsay, gossip, and well-meaning but uninvited prying" by "secular evangelicals, who wish to advertise their services in every pub, pulpit, and private residence in the country."

Pinker concludes his attack on community social work in a colorful metaphor:

> It conjures up the vision of a captainless crew under a patchwork ensign stitched together from remnants of the Red Flag and the Jolly Roger—all with a license and some with a disposition to mutiny—heading into the gusty winds of populist rhetoric, with presumption as their figurehead and inexperience as their compass, straight for the reefs of public incredulity.

Thus, the sovereignty of local units is not without potential limitations and abuses, as the centralization of authority is not without some virtues. Further arguments can be made in the abstract to support one or the other of these options, but it is clear that in practical matters most groups support different degrees of centralization or decentralization in regard to specific social welfare policies. The political left traditionally supports centralization of income-maintenance programs and substantial community involvement. The political right, although strongly decentralist by inclination ("the best government is the least government") often supports a strong unified national standard on social issues such as abortion and prayer in school.

Finally, it is possible to find parties supporting centralization and decentralization at the same time because different system levels are involved in either choice. For example, it is possible to support decentralization of programs at the federal level and centralization at the state or municipal level. We illustrate some of these possibilities in the next chapter.

NOTES

1. A brief historical review of American federalism can be found in Daniel J. Elazar, "Opening the Third Century of American Federalism: Issues and Prospects," in *American Federalism: The Third Century, The Annals of the American Academy of Political & Social Science,* ed. John Kincaid, Vol. 509, Philadelphia, May 1990, 11–21.

2. Luther H. Gulick, "Reorganization of the State," *Civil Engineering,* August 1933, p. 420; as quoted in *The Book of the States, 1976–77,* Vol. 21 (Lexington, KY: Council of State Governments, 1976), p. 21.

3. William E. Leuchtenburg, *Franklin D. Roosevelt and the New Deal* (New York: Harper & Row, 1962); as quoted in *Book of the States,* p. 24.

4. Daniel P. Moynihan, "Comments on 'Re-structuring the Government of New York City,'" in *The Neighborhoods, the City, and the Region: Working Papers in Jurisdiction and Structures* (New York: State Study Commission for New York City, 1973), p. 15.

5. Ibid., p. 16.

6. Eveline M. Burns, *Social Security and Public Policy* (New York: McGraw-Hill, 1958), p. 230.

7. Robert Reischaur, "Fiscal Federalism in the 1980s: Dismantling or Rationalizing the Great Society," in *The Great Society and Its Legacy,* eds. M. Kaplan and P. Cuciti. (Durham, N.C.: Duke University Press 1986), p. 179.

8. Advisory Commission on Intergovernmental Relations, *A Catalog of Federal Grant-in-Aid Programs: Grants Funded FY 1989,* M167, Washington, D.C. October 1989.

9. General Accounting Office, *Homelessness: McKinney Act Reports Could Improve Federal*

Assistance Efforts, GAO/RCED-90-121, U.S. General Accounting Office, Washington D.C. June 1990.

10. Timothy Conlan, *New Federalism: Intergovernmental Reform from Nixon to Reagan* (Washington, DC.: Brookings Institution, 1988), p. 229.

11. Peter Drucker, "The Sickness of Government," *The Public Interest*, Vol. 14 (Winter 1969).

12. See, for example, Catherine E. Born, "Proprietary Firms and Child Welfare Services: Patterns and Implications," *Child Welfare*, Vol. 62, no. 2 (1983), 109–118.

13. John Herbert, "Cities Turn to Private Groups to Administer Local Services," *New York Times*, May 23, 1983, p. 1.

14. Harry Specht, "Social Work and the Popular Psychotherapies," *Social Service Review*, September 1990, p. 345.

15. For a creative explication of the decentralist position, see Paul Goodman, *People or Personnel* (New York: Vintage Books, 1968).

16. Grant McConnell, *Private Power and American Democracy* (New York: Knopf, 1966), p. 107.

17. Ford Foundation Project on Social Welfare and the American Future, *The Common Good: Social Welfare & the American Future*, New York: May 1989, p. 63.

18. The National Institute for Social Work, *Social Workers: Their Roles and Tasks* (London: Bedford Square Press, 1981), pp. 214–250.

19. Ken Judge and Jillian Smith, "Who Volunteers?" Personnel Social Services Research Unit, Discussion Paper #267, University of Kent at Canterbury, February 1983 (mimeographed).

Chapter Eight
WHO PLANS? CHOICES IN THE PROCESS OF POLICY FORMULATION

The dispute between the modern planners and their opponents is not a dispute on whether we ought to choose intelligently between the various possible organizations of society; it is not a dispute on whether we ought to employ foresight and systematic thinking in planning our common affairs. The question is whether for this purpose it is better that the holder of coercive powers should confine himself in general to creating conditions under which the knowledge and initiative of individuals are given the best scope so that they can plan most successfully; or whether a rational utilization of our resources requires central direction and organization of all our activities according to some consciously constructed "blueprint."

Friedrich A. Hayek
The Road to Serfdom

In preceding chapters we examined a series of choices affecting the design of social welfare policies. Generally speaking, these choices address questions of what is to be done, what alternative courses of action can fulfill social welfare objectives, and what their implications might be. In this chapter our attention shifts to a dimension of choice that is found, not in the product, but in the *process* of policy formulation. Although we have emphasized policy issues that relate to the product, it is important to recognize that the arrangements governing how decisions are made involve as significant a policy choice as questions pertaining to their substantive content.

Hayek, writing in 1944, claimed that the dispute between "modern planners and their opponents" is not over the desirability of planning per se, but over the merits of alternative planning arrangements and the degree to which they allow for the expression of individual interests as opposed to the collective will. This issue may be expressed in the question "Who plans?" Specifically, the question is whether smaller units of society— individuals and groups—are directly involved in planning in their own interests or whether plans in the public interest are centrally determined. It was the latter course—centrally planned change—that Hayek perceived to be the "road to serfdom."[1]

In recent years this dispute has lost a good deal of its edge. Certainly, the collapse of the planned "command economies" of eastern Europe and the Soviet Union has eroded most of the world's faith in socialist arrangements that rely on centralized, long-range plans for economic and social development. Few modern planners anywhere in the globe still advocate unitary, nationally determined plans. But even before the great upheavals of 1989 and 1990 changed the face of Europe, skepticism had been growing concerning the utility of the planning model for directing activity at regional and local levels, particularly in the area of social policy. As Paul Davidoff, an influential advocacy planner of the 1960s and 1970s put it,

> A practice that has discouraged full participation by citizens in plan making in the past has been based on what might be called the *"unitary plan."* This is the idea that only one agency in a community should prepare a comprehensive plan; that agency is the city planning commission or department. Why is it that no other organization within a community prepares a plan? Why is only one agency concerned with establishing both general and specific goals for community development, and with proposing the strategies and costs required to effect goals? Why are there not plural plans?[2]

Pluralistic planning occupies a middle-range position somewhere between the laissez-faire, highly individualistic approach that Hayek advocates and the highly collectivist approach of the centralized unitary plan. The pluralistic approach conceives of planning as a contentious process involving the clash of different interests in the community but emphasizes the group (or microcollective) rather than the individualistic nature of these competing interests.

There is considerable distance on the spectrum of political thought between the nineteenth-century laissez-faire liberalism of Hayek and the twentieth-century liberalism of Davidoff; and to be sure, their positions contain disparate views on various aspects of the social planning enterprise. Yet their convergence of thought on two fundamental points is interesting. First, both favor diversity in place of the centrally produced unitary plan. On this point Hayek's views are more extreme in favoring a laissez-faire approach that permits a diversity of individual choices. Davidoff's position favors pluralistic planning and the diversity of group choices. Second, they both have similar conceptions of the public interest. That is, both Hayek and Davidoff believe that the common good derives from contending individual and group interests.[3]

THE PLANNER'S ROLE

Other conceptions of the public interest call for different answers to the question "Who plans?" Before examining these conceptions, however, we would like to clarify the planner's role in the planning enterprise. The policy issue might be put to rest simply by saying that planners plan. But in so doing they are influenced and directed by their own values, knowledge, and inclinations as well as by the values, knowledge, and inclinations of other parties in the planning environment. The issue turns on the degree to which planning decisions are more or less influenced by the planner in comparison to the influence exerted by others. Thus, "Who plans?" is a relative matter that depends on the organizational arrangements among planners, political and bureaucratic leaders, and consumer publics. To whom is the planner primarily accountable? Whose values and interests guide the planning choices that are made? Efforts to answer these questions constitute the major policy choices that govern the planning process and the development of organizational arrangements to decide what is to be done.

Role refers to the ways in which responsibilities, expectations, and commitments are structured in regard to the planner's job. There is a body of knowledge, skill, and expertise that all planners who claim professional status are supposed to have mastered. But in any given professional position there are specific tasks the worker must do, there are expected ways in which the professional must behave, and there are people to whom the professional is accountable. These components vary from job to job. Thus, in addition to a guiding set of professional ethics, there is some sponsor, usually an agency and/or clients or constituents to whom the planner is accountable. The competing and often contradictory claims of profession, sponsor, and client frequently constitute a great source of strain (and sometimes conflict) for the planner.

The profession, placing importance on "professional standards" of practice, awards recognition and status to practitioners who observe and defend these standards (e.g., seeing that only properly credentialed people perform professional tasks). The sponsor, having a greater interest in economy and efficiency than in standards, may constrain the planner to find the least expensive way of doing things. Clients and constituents, evaluating the planner in terms of what is produced for them, are not likely to have as great an interest in the maintenance of professional standards or in economy. (This is not to say, of course, that professional standards, economy, and effectiveness are necessarily contradictory.)

The social context of the planner's role, then, is one of the factors that determines the nature of the process to be followed. The planner's relationships with other actors (sponsors and clients) play an important part in determining the values and interests that will predominate in the planning process. To a large extent the planner is both committed and limited to working in certain ways by the nature of these relationships. Professionals involved in policy planning must be cognizant of the features of the social context that bear on their work.

The planner's role requires the integration of knowledge and skill to deal with both interactional and analytic functions. As noted in Chapter One, the planning process is frequently discussed and analyzed according to both sociopolitical and technical perspectives. These perspectives are different sides of the planning coin, and each is important in bringing the process to fruition. Technical (analytic) tasks involve data collection, quantification of problems and analysis in light of the data, ranking priorities, specification of objectives, program design, and the like. Sociopolitical (interactional) tasks involve the development of an organizational network, which requires building up the structure of a planning system within which communication and exchange of information among relevant actors take place and planning decisions are made.[4] The ways in which these interactional tasks are completed are the means of resolving the question "Who plans?" The distinction between the technical and sociopolitical aspects of the planning process may be illustrated by examining the planning requirements of the Model Cities Program. We use this example from the late 1960s because it was the last of the Great Society programs based on the belief that the federal government should support and encourage local communities to undertake systematic and comprehensive social planning.

AN EXAMPLE: PLANNING IN THE MODEL CITIES PROGRAM

Under Model Cities, all cities were invited by the Department of Housing and Urban Development (HUD) to submit applications for planning grants. In these applications, cities described their characteristics, social problems, and "plan for planning." During the first application period in 1967, 193 cities submitted proposals. After a careful and complex scrutiny of the applications and the applicants, 75 cities were selected to receive planning grants.[5] A similar process was used the following year to select another 73 cities, bringing to 148 the total number of cities given grants.[6] The Model Cities experience for any given city was expected to last approximately six years (the first for planning and the next five for implementation).

The HUD guidelines for Model Cities participants were clear and firm on technical planning but vague and loose on sociopolitical planning.

Technical Approaches

The HUD planning model stipulated that cities follow a predefined, rational, analytic process in developing their Comprehensive Demonstration Plans (CDPs). Initially, this entailed a three-part CDP framework:

> Part I was to describe and analyze problems and their causes; to rank problems in order of local priorities; and to indicate objectives, strategies, and program approaches to solving these problems. This document was to be submitted to HUD two-thirds of the way through the planning year. Based on these documents, HUD was to provide appropriate feedback to the City Demonstration Agencies (CDAs) that would be useful for the completion of Parts II and III.
> Part II was to be a statement of projected five-year objectives and cost estimates. This document was to be submitted at the end of the planning year, along with Part III.
> Part III was to be a detailed statement of program plans for the first action year, the costs involved, and administrative arrangements for implementation. This document was to be a logical extension of the analysis, strategies, and priorities outlined in Part I.[7]

Toward the end of 1969 this framework was simplified by eliminating Part II and changing Part I to a Mid-Term Planning Statement (limited to 75 pages), which was to be submitted halfway in the planning year and then revised and merged with what was previously designated as the Part III document for the final submission—the CDP.

The extent to which cities were able to satisfy the requirements of the planning process has been detailed in a number of studies.[8] In general, the cities made considerable effort to follow the guidelines, but few were able to approximate the ideal process prescribed by HUD, in part because the demands were strenuous even for those cities that commanded the required technical expertise. Their causal analyses of problems had a tendency toward infinite regress, and the problem-analysis approach often proved to be frustrating and unilluminating. Given the limited planning resources that were available, five-year projections could hardly secure the investment of time, effort, and commitment that planning for the following year's programs received; in fact, Part II CDP submissions were often superficial. Moreover, many cities simply did not have the staff expertise to perform comprehensive planning according to HUD's model. Sixty-four percent, indeed, used private consulting firms to provide technical assistance during the planning period.[9]

Sociopolitical Approaches

Whereas the technical requirements of the Model Cities planning process were spelled out in detail, the sociopolitical aspects were left largely to local determination. The major prescription HUD offered was that ultimate administrative and fiscal responsibilities were to be vested in the local chief executive. Beyond this, the guidelines left considerable latitude for the types of linkages and relationships among groups that might develop to imbue CDP decision making with an element of social choice as well as technical procedure. The first Program Guide stated,

> [The CDA] should be closely related to the governmental decision-making process in a way that permits the exercise of leadership by responsible elected officials in the establishment of policies. . . . It should have sufficient powers, authority, and structure to achieve the coordinated administration of all aspects of the program. . . . It should provide a meaningful role in policy making to area residents and to the major agencies expected to contribute to the program.[10]

Although "a meaningful role in policy making to area residents" is an innocuous enough statement, the HUD administrative staff responsible for Model Cities vigorously promoted citizen involvement in decision making. (Model Cities staff came largely from outside of HUD; many were former Office of Economic Opportunity personnel.) First-round planning awards, for example, were often accompanied by stipulations that the cities strengthen their provisions for residents' participation.[11] A study of the Planning Grant Review Project, the means used by HUD to select the cities that were to be funded for first-round planning grants, showed, further, that project staff gave highest ratings to those cities that later proved to be most successful at achieving high degrees of citizen participation.[12]

Although citizen influence in the planning process was emphasized, the guidelines for its achievement and the structure of relationships among professional planners, political leadership, and citizen groups were relatively vague. Overall, a number of planning arrangements emerged in which planners were accountable, in varying degrees, to different parties.[13] In general terms, these different patterns of relationships are associated with the ways in which the "public interest" is defined.

CONCEPTIONS OF THE PUBLIC INTEREST

One justification for any form of social planning is that the decisions arrived at and the choices made will serve the common good, whether planners are primarily accountable to themselves, to political or bureaucratic leaders, or to the consumer public. It is true whether planning is done under public auspices or by private agencies. Consider, for instance, the United Way of America. This private organization explicitly disclaims that its community planning reflects the special interests of particular groups and agencies. United Way literature states,

> The process by which community resources . . . are marshalled and focused to bring remedies to problems . . . is essential to problem-solving. The pro-

cess may be manifested in a variety of ways such as convening, facilitating, mediating, and conciliating. It usually requires that significant segments of the community agree that action is needed; and also on the nature of the action.[14] This is done to assure donors that their contributions are being used . . . not to solve one problem or support one group, but *to meet priority human care needs.*[15] [Emphasis added.]

The problem with the claim that planning activities serve the public interest is that there are different conceptions of what the common good is and the means by which it is served. It is a matter of opinion whether, for practical planning purposes, "a total community point of view" is attainable or even desirable as a means of defining the public interest. Depending on how the idiom is interpreted, planning pro bono publico may be expressed through several sociopolitical processes, each of which involves different relationships among planners and other relevant parties in the planning environment. To illustrate, let us examine three conventional meanings of the term *public interest.* As described by Meyerson and Banfield, these are the organismic, communalistic, and individualistic conceptions.[16]

The organismic view.   According to the organismic view, there is an ideal public interest that transcends the specific preferences and interests of the individuals making up the public body. The public body is viewed as a unitary organism whose interests are greater or different than the sum of its parts. For example, in community planning the community is believed to have certain anthropomorphic needs and interests that are essential to its health: Its arteries must be able to sustain a sufficient flow of goods and services; its tax base must be sufficient to nourish growth and provide maintenance; and police are needed to protect, social services to mend, and sanitation agencies to cleanse its parts. To stretch the analogy a bit further, the planner's relationship to the community is akin to that of doctor to patient. In diagnosing the community's interests the planner is guided primarily by professional values and technical expertise. Although planners may be working for a public or private agency, their primary accountability is to the profession. In essence this conception of the public interest, in its purest form, gives rise to *technocracy.* This approach is often used by city and regional planning officials in developing long-term "master plans" governing physical development.

The communalistic view.   In the communalistic view, one envisions a unitary public interest made of the interests that all members of the public share in common. This single set of common ends is viewed as more valuable in calculating the public interest than are the unshared objectives of individuals and groups. The public's common ends are embodied in political leaders and community institutions. This view of the public interest is associated with a planning process that includes, as Rothman notes, "legislators or administrators who are presumed to know the ends of the body politic as a whole and to strive in some central decision-making locus to assert the unitary interests of the whole over competing lesser interests."[17] In this context the planner is accountable primarily to political or *bureaucratic* leadership. Planning choices are guided by the values and interests these leaders express. (The United Way of America, as noted, operates primarily with this kind of planning perspective.)

The individualistic view. In the individualistic view, there is no single public interest. Rather, there are different publics with different interests. The unshared ends that are held by individuals and groups are seen as more consequential than shared ends in determining the common good. In this view the public interest is a momentary compromise arising out of the interplay among competing interests; it is constantly shifting as new groups make their interests known and respected. Individualistic conceptions of the public interest are associated with *advocacy planning,* an arrangement in which the planner is accountable to a particular group whose values and interests guide planning choices. The objective is to increase this group's participation and influence in the competitive process through which one or another particular point of view wins public support.

Three Planning Models

Each of these conceptions of the public interest implies sociopolitical processes that involve different planning roles and different relationships among planners, political and administrative leaders, and consumer publics. Along the continuum of possibilities, three planning models emerge:

1. Organismic: The planner is a *technocrat*, accountable primarily to the profession and operating with a view of the public interest derived from special skills and professional knowledge.
2. Communalistic: The planner is a *bureaucrat*, accountable primarily to the political and administrative hierarchy and operating with a view of the public interest derived from institutional leadership.
3. Individualistic: The planner is an *advocate*, accountable primarily to those that purchase his or her services and operating with a view of the public interest derived from group preferences.

These models represent planning arrangements corresponding to organismic, communalistic, and individualistic conceptions of the public interest. We indicate that they range along a continuum because reality sometimes intrudes on conceptual distinctions such as these in a disconcerting manner.[18] Students of social planning will find that inconsistencies are incorporated in the operations of individuals and organizations engaged in the social planning enterprise. As Banfield explains,

An institution may function as a mechanism which asserts at the same time different, and perhaps logically opposed, conceptions of the structure of the public interest. The members of a citizen board, for example, may endeavor to explicate the meaning of some very general ends which pertain to the body politic or *ethos* while at the same time—and perhaps inconsistently—seeking to find that compromise among the ends of individuals which will represent the greatest "total" satisfaction.[19]

Alternative views of the public interest are sometimes held simultaneously because of the dynamic interplay of competing social values that are associated with these views.

THREE COMPETING VALUES: PARTICIPATION, LEADERSHIP, AND EXPERTISE

There is a continuing cycle of competition among three values that govern the management of community affairs and that affect the degree to which different conceptions of the public interest are emphasized. These are the values of participation, leadership, and expertise. All three are prized values, which compete for ascendancy in community life. These values and their significance for social planning are noted and described in the literature.[20] Our interest is to point out the dialectical relationship among them and how this relationship affects community planning. Each value, when maximized, contains the seeds of its own undoing. Each generates conditions that will, in turn, encourage another of the values to emerge. Although policy planners have relatively little control over these dynamics, there is benefit to understanding the process.

Participation

Participation is a value that extols the virtue of each and every person joining meaningfully and directly in decisions that affect their welfare. In the extreme it supports a vision of a participatory democracy, championing schemes for community control and decentralization. In the 1960s and 1970s it was celebrated in the slogan "power to the people." Theoretically, this value is supported by findings from small-group experiments and industrial psychology that indicate that people who participate directly in the decisions that impinge on their lives are more likely to feel a part of their community. Decisions arrived at with a high degree of participation are more likely to be binding, and alienation and apathy are reduced.[21]

Countervailing theory contends that an urban industrialized society is too large and complex to allow the value of participation to operate in the extreme. Rather, participation must be organized and expressed through a system of representation. The New England town meeting might have been an appropriate decision-making device for nineteenth-century small-town America, but modern society needs electoral machinery for selecting representative leaders.

The value of participation in the management of community affairs always exists, although at some times and places it is more prominent. For example, the Jacksonian era, which followed the Revolutionary War; the Populist period of the late 1880s; and the period of social upheaval in the 1960s and 1970s were times when issues of participation were paramount.

Participation becomes the primary value in community governance when leadership or expertise is perceived to be unresponsive. Then decentralization, localism, and constituency satisfaction are likely to be the major programmatic goals of planning. Major evaluative concerns about programs will derive from this central question: "Do the people like it?"

Leadership

Leadership as a value is the antithesis of participation because complex decisions must continuously be made and executed, and to do so, leadership is required. In a heterogeneous society like ours, with a swarm of competing claims to the public interest, community decision making is bound to generate a hopeless drone of discussion and debate unless citizens can find leaders they trust, whom they can hold responsible, and who have the ability to mitigate conflict and regulate competition with equity and dispatch. Unless the executive committee, the board of directors, the officers—in short, leadership—undertake these tasks for the community, chaos will reign. The extreme example of local leadership in government is the boss system and the political machine. Historically, both the nineteenth-century movement against the "long ballot" and the twentieth-century political reform movement were aimed at strengthening the power of governors and mayors.

When leadership emerges as the prime value in community life, centralization and growth become major programmatic goals of planning. The major evaluative question is "Does it work?" But the capacity to rule and lead does not ensure the capacity to plan and implement. Leaders searching for ideas, concerned and constrained to rule with economy and efficiency, eventually turn to the repository of another set of values—the experts—for assistance.

Expertise

Expertise is a value that makes rationality the supreme criterion for decision making. Theoretically, experts choose among programmatic alternatives on the basis of merit rather than politics. Expertise is an antidote to corruption, waste, and inefficiency in government. Historically, expertise in government, whether in the form of civil service, the merit system, or the nonpartisan city manager, has evolved as an antidote to unrestrained leadership. Presumably insulated from the vagaries of politics, experts are free to bring knowledge and skill to bear on the problem-solving process, enabling leaders to make the most sensible decisions for the community.

As the expert gains primacy, the planning enterprise moves to the touchstone of professionalism—technique. Refinement of professional skill, experimentation, coordination, and the attainment of improved methods of executive intervention become the major planning interests. Evaluative concerns deriving from this perspective focus on information about how and with what consequences different programs operate.

However, experts and leaders often succumb to their own ambitions. They may be inclined to preserve the status quo and to protect their privileged positions, whether as *eminences grises* to the ruling coalition, as the vanguard of an emergent technocracy, or as entrenched administrators of planning "empires." In time, experts may come to suffer from "hardening of the categories," leaders may become despots, and both may become major obstacles to innovation and change. The synthesis is then transformed to a new thesis in the dialectic process. Technocracy and leadership may be challenged and community renewal brought about by new efforts to mobilize the disaffected, organize the disadvantaged, and from their ranks draw fresh leadership. Sooner or later, these leaders will call on the experts for advice—and the cycle recurs.

The Cycle of Values

The political scientist, Robert Michels, saw this dialectic in the evolution of European socialist political parties earlier in this century. His "iron law of oligarchy" was based on the doctrine that history is a record of a continuous series of struggles over values, all of which culminate in the creation of new oligarchies that eventually fuse with the old, "representing an uninterrupted series of oppositions . . . attaining one after another to power and passing from the sphere of envy to the sphere of avarice."[22] His insights into this process are timely:

> The democratic currents of history resemble successive waves. They break ever on the same shoal. They are ever renewed. This enduring spectacle is simultaneously encouraging and depressing. . . . Now new accusers arise to denounce the traitors; after an era of glorious combats and inglorious power, they end by fusing with the old dominant class; whereupon once more they are in their turn attacked by fresh opponents who appeal to the name of democracy. It is probable that this cruel game will continue without end.[23]

Contemporary experience suggests the ways in which the dialectic of social planning operates. In the years following World War II, the technician emerged as the central figure in community welfare planning. The notion of a professionally developed community master plan achieved broad support, but in the 1950s, dissatisfaction grew with this process of planning and its effects. Citizen participation, as a check on the professional planners, was a significant ingredient in the seven-point Workable Program for urban renewal contained in the Housing Act of 1954. Initially, participation involved the appointment of a citywide advisory committee, generally made up of civic leaders, to work with planners; representation of the poor, the people who were usually most affected by renewal activities, was neither mandatory nor commonplace. But as experience with resident opposition to renewal increased, agencies began to give greater consideration to the involvement of neighborhood residents, although overall citizen participation remained modest.[24]

Other efforts in the late 1950s and early 1960s gave citizens an increasingly active role. These included the Ford Foundation Grey Area Projects, the planning programs spawned by the President's Committee on Juvenile Delinquency, the War on Poverty, and the Model Cities Program. All gave emphasis to the value of participation vis-à-vis leadership and expertise. (It is interesting to note that at their inception, all community planning programs seem to invoke all three values, although this kind of *tout ensemble* never comes off very well. One of the values is sooner or later elevated above the rest.) By the mid-1960s, the value of participation reigned; the expertise of professionals was rejected in favor of the direct experiences of neighborhood residents.[25] Meanwhile, leadership fretted, floundered, and failed to achieve consensus. By the end of the 1970s there had developed a disenchantment with social planning of any variety. And although participation as a formal element of the planning process has not been revived, de facto arrangements in most large American communities in the 1990s reflect significant social and economic diversity; well-organized and competing interest groups; and decision-making systems that substantially incorporate a plurality of concerns, including, to a degree unrivaled in the past, participation by neighborhoods (rich and poor), ethnic and racial and sexual minorities, and women.

SHIFTING POWER TO CITY HALL

As federal interest in citizen participation has subsided, the national government has increasingly emphasized policy and planning processes that engage state and local elected leadership. Despite the continued existence of a great number of detailed categorical aid programs, and a not inconsequential number of guidelines and mandates, the intergovernmental system, as described in Chapter 7, has moved significantly toward decentralization. The most dramatic expression of this change—general revenue sharing—has been noted. When revenue sharing was created in 1972, it marked a vital shift in power over the use of federal funds. Eschewing the tradition of categorical centralization, revenue sharing gave city and state officials—particularly mayors and governors—virtually unlimited flexibility in spending federal funds.

The shift toward decentralization has also been marked in the HUD-administered programs. In 1970, under the Planned Variations experiment, HUD gave up much of its review and oversight responsibility in favor of mayoral decision making. Mayors, for example, were given the responsibility to review, comment, and sign off on all HUD programs serving their cities. This change was not unimportant because the growth of federal aid in the 1960s had resulted in mayors often being bypassed. Before the New Federalism, for example, local public agencies and private nonprofit organizations frequently received federal assistance over which local elected chief executives had little if any influence. Given the hundreds of centralized, limited-focus programs in existence, mayors often found it a formidable task simply to keep abreast of their amounts, purposes, and locations.

A further departure from the old model came with the passage of the Housing and Community Development Act of 1974. Like other New Federalism block grants, this consolidated a number of categorical grants (urban renewal, neighborhood and public facilities, and economic development, along with Model Cities) into a single decentralized program. Although local officials had to direct programs to one of three national objectives (assisting low- and moderate-income people, reducing blight, and meeting urgent community needs), their discretion was quite broad. The balance of spending among housing development, social services, and economic development, for example, became largely a municipal decision. Especially since 1981, when Congress approved the Reagan-backed Community Development Bloc Grant (CDBG) amendments, which eliminated detailed grant applications and citizen participation requirements, the program has operated with maximum local discretion.

Although officials in some cities have kept the CDBG planning process open to a broad spectrum of local interests, including residents of poverty neighborhoods, mayors and elected council members have a degree of freedom and flexibility in setting local priorities that provides at least a promise of overall, integrated planning. In this sense, intergovernmental decentralization has resulted in local centralization (see Figure 8–1). The workloads of mayors' offices, for example, have increased substantially. Special staffs have been hired to develop, review, and assess projects and to create the mechanisms and procedures to organize planning and program activities in conjunction with local agencies, nonprofit organizations, development and rehabilitation entrepreneurs, and target area residents.

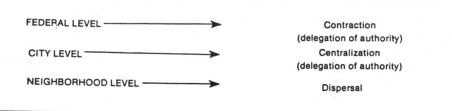

FIGURE 8-1   Impact of decentralization on allocative decision-making.

Figure 8–1 indicates the shifting locus of allocative decision making along two dimensions of the federal aid system. On the horizontal plane, the changes occur within the levels; on the vertical plane they occur between the levels. At the federal level, reduced oversight and program review responsibilities have substantially limited the national leadership role. Instead of a complicated system of federal grant reviews and an extensive number of precise guidelines, the New Federalism has relegated basic decision-making authority to governors and mayors, enhancing their planning, coordinating, and service delivery powers. Without strong federal emphasis on neighborhood involvement, in addition, the intensity of citizen participation has diminished. On the neighborhood level, CDBG and other New Federalism programs have resulted in greater power for traditional political leadership and less focus on indigenous leadership. From a focus on poverty and designated target neighborhoods (e.g., the Model Cities demonstration area), urban development has evolved into citywide programs with substantial involvement by chambers of commerce, banks, downtown developers, and a variety of housing and community development activists.[26]

As noted in the preceding chapter, the HUD experience is not unique. The Omnibus Reconciliation Act of 1981 transferred broad decision-making authority over federal aid programs to states while eliminating almost any system of accountability for how the monies are used. There are, of course, certain obstacles to the realization of federal decentralization goals. As Banfield points out, organized beneficiaries of the categorical grant system are not enthusiastic about changes that deprive them of their special status, dissolving their identities in a mass of supplicants through grant consolidation.[27] Members of Congress, too, have a special affinity for categorical grants that can be tailored to suit particular groups of constituents. Moreover, the rhetoric of local control notwithstanding, it is unclear how anxious mayors and governors are to assume responsibilities that may prove politically awkward when the foil of federal control is removed.

Nevertheless, as a result of these alterations in the system of authority, two major changes have occurred in the nature of local social planning. First, mayors and governors are being held increasingly more accountable by their constituencies for their plans and programs. In the past, these officials could claim that they had little authority over the local agencies receiving federal funds and that they were hamstrung by federally designed program guidelines. With decentralization, the accountability that was impaired by the exigencies of the categorical grant system has been considerably enlarged.

Second, citizen participation characterized by grass-roots organizations, created in Community Action and Model Cities neighborhoods and later on by citizen participation requirements in such programs as Title XX and the Older Americans Act, has been deemphasized. As federal programs came to be designed for broader urban constituencies and whole states, the influence of neighborhood groups diminished. Instead, the focus of political activity shifted to the formal citywide and statewide political apparatuses, injecting a new vitality into urban politics. Although detailed federal participation requirements were largely deleted from grant legislation during the Reagan years, the tradition of citizen involvement continued in more conventional political forms through interest group activity, neighborhood meetings, direct contact with policymakers, electoral advocacy, and the like. Yesterday's poverty workers have become today's mayors and council members; yesterday's radicals have become today's establishment. In some ways, indeed, citizen action has moved from the fringes of social institutions to the center of things, and this shift has had a profound effect on social planning and community organization.[28]

SOCIAL WELFARE PLANNING: DRIFT OR DESIGN?

Where does the policy planner fit into all this? Does the planner gravitate toward executive leadership when leadership is in the saddle and "back to the people" when the impulse for participation arises? Is there any meaning for professional planners in what we describe as the dialectical relationship among the values of participation, leadership, and expertise beyond, perhaps, the recognition that planning is an awfully complex business?

Rein suggests that the conflicting values of participation, leadership, and expertise invest the planning enterprise with insoluble dilemmas.[29] From the dialectical perspective, however, the competition among values is not a dilemma but a dynamic, necessary, and continuously unfolding process that sustains democratic vigor in the planning endeavor. Policy planners should encourage rather than avoid the dialectical relationship among these values; no single value should become the professional's polestar. The contradiction among these values is a healthy stimulant to the profession; each value can become salient as emphases in the community change.

CONCLUSION

To conclude, we should like to emphasize our own view about the values described in this discussion. Shifts in the values that guide social planning bear careful scrutiny. In the short run, the change from participation to leadership was welcomed by many members of the planning profession who experienced some of the turbulence and frustration of the citizen participation era. They were inclined to embrace the value of leadership warmly. Leadership perpetually looks to expertise, and planners can expect to be well received.

Nevertheless, as local executives extend their spheres of authority and as the number of planners on their staffs increase, the executive's ability to control planners is reduced, laying the ground for technocracy. Instead of being advocacy planners for the poor, as they were in the 1960s, the planner-technocrats of the 1990s could become remote from the would-be beneficiaries of their enterprise. Only by continuing to work with representatives of different groups, including consumer publics, can this estrangement be avoided.

If one fact has been made clear in the evolution of social policy over the past half century, it is that excessive faith in planning can be as damaging to the community's interest as an unquestioned belief in "the people." Professionals do not know everything; there are problems they cannot solve; they are as much creatures of their values, their culture, and their generation as anyone else.

NOTES

1. Friedrich A. Hayek, *The Road to Serfdom* (Chicago: University of Chicago Press, 1944), pp. 32–42.
2. Paul Davidoff, "Advocacy and Pluralism in Planning," in *Community Organization Practice,* eds. Ralph M. Kramer and Harry Specht, (Englewood Cliffs, NJ: Prentice Hall, 1969), p. 440.
3. Hayek, *The Road to Serfdom,* pp. 56–65; and ibid., pp. 438–450.
4. Robert Perlman and Arnold Gurin, *Community Organization and Social Planning* (New York: Wiley, 1971), pp. 52–75; and Ralph M. Kramer and Harry Specht, *Readings in Community Organization Practice* (Englewood Cliffs, NJ: Prentice Hall, 1969), pp. 8–9.
5. For a detailed description of this process, see Neil Gilbert and Harry Specht, *Planning for Model Cities: Process, Product, Performance, and Predictions* (Washington, DC: U.S. Department of Housing and Urban Development, U.S. Government Printing Office, 1970).
6. For further details on the Model Cities Program legislation, guidelines, and operational procedures, see the following: ibid.; Neil Gilbert and Harry Specht, *Dynamics of Com-*

munity Planning (Cambridge, MA: Ballinger, 1977); *Improving the Quality of Urban Life: A Program Guide to Model Neighborhoods in Demonstration Cities,* U.S. Department of Housing and Urban Development, HUD PG–47, December 1966, and HUD PG–47, December 1967 (Washington, DC: U.S. Government Printing Office); Marshall Kaplan, *Model Cities and National Urban Policy* (Chicago: American Society of Planning Officials, 1971); Marshall Kaplan, Gans, and Kahn, *The Model Cities Program: A Comparative Analysis of the Planning Process in Eleven Cities* (Washington, DC: U.S. Department of Housing and Urban Development, U.S. Government Printing Office, 1970); and Roland L. Warren, "Model Cities' First Round: Politics, Planning, and Participation," *Journal of the American Institute of Planners,* Vol. 35, no. 4 (July 1969), 245–252.

7. Summarized from *Improving the Quality of Urban Life.*

8. See note 6.

9. Gilbert and Specht, *Planning for Model Cities.*

10. *Improving the Quality of Urban Life,* p. 11.

11. See, for example, Kaplan, Gans, and Kahn, *Model Cities Program*; and Warren, "Model Cities' First Round."

12. Gilbert and Specht, *Dynamics of Community Planning.*

13. For example, in the Kaplan, Gans, and Kahn study, *Model Cities Program,* five types of planning systems are identified: staff dominant, staff influence, parity, resident influence, and resident dominant. Each of these systems is characterized by different sets of relationships among planners, political leadership, and citizen groups, which are analyzed in Gilbert and Specht, *Dynamics of Community Planning.*

14. United Way of America, "Report of Special Study Committee on the Role of United Way in Community Problem-Solving" (Alexandria, VA: United Way of America, October 19–20, 1983), p. 8.

15. *Giving U.S.A.* (New York: American Association of Fund Raising Counsel, 1984), p. 82.

16. Martin Meyerson and Edward Banfield, *Politics, Planning and the Public Interest* (New York: Free Press, 1955), pp. 322–329. These conceptions are similar, respectively, to the idealist view, the rationalist view, and the realist view of the public interest as analyzed by Glendon A. Schubert, *The Public Interest* (New York: Free Press, 1960).

17. Jack Rothman, "Three Models of Community Organization Practice," in *Social Work Practice 1968* (New York: Columbia University Press, 1968), p. 38.

18. For an excellent analysis of the complexities and variations in these planning relationships, see Francine F. Rabinovitz, *City Politics and Planning* (New York: Atherton, 1969), pp. 79–117.

19. Meyerson and Banfield, *Politics, Planning and the Public Interest,* p. 329.

20. For example, see Herbert Kaufman, *Politics and Policies in State and Local Government* (Englewood Cliffs, NJ: Prentice Hall, 1964); Martin Rein, "Social Planning: The Search for Legitimacy," *Journal of the American Institute of Planners,* Vol. 35, no. 4 (July 1967), 233–244; and George A. Brager and Harry Specht, *Community Organizing* (New York: Columbia University Press, 1973).

21. For example, see Eric Fromm, *The Sane Society* (New York: Holt, Rinehart & Winston, 1955); Ralph White and Ronald Lippitt, "Leader Behavior and Member Reaction in Three Social Climates," in *Group Dynamics,* eds. Dorwin Cartwright et al. (Evanston, IL: Row, Peterson, 1953); Jacob Levine and John Butler, "Lecture vs. Group Decision in Changing Behavior," *Journal of Applied Psychology,* Vol. 36 (February 1952), 29–33.

22. Robert Michels, *Political Parties* (New York: Dover Publications, 1915), p. 319

23. Ibid., p. 408.

24. Peter Rossi and Robert Dentler, *The Politics of Urban Renewal* (New York: Free Press, 1961); James Q. Wilson, "Planning and Politics: Citizen Participation in Urban Renewal," in *Urban Renewal: People, Politics, and Planning,* eds. Jewel Bellush et al. (New York: Anchor Books, 1967); and Scott Greer, *Urban Renewal and American Cities* (Indianapolis: Bobbs-Merrill, 1965).

25. Neil Gilbert and Joseph Eaton, "Research Report: Who Speaks for the Poor?" *Journal of the American Institute of Planners,* Vol. 36 (November 1970), 411–416.

26. William Frej and Harry Specht, "The Housing and Community Development Act of 1974: Implications for Policy and Planning," *Social Service Review,* June 1976, pp. 275–292. See also Richard E. Klosterman, "A Public Interest Criterion," *Journal of American Planning Association,* Vol. 46, no. 3 (July 1980), 323–333.

27. Edward Banfield, "Revenue Sharing in Theory and Practice," *Public Interest,* Vol. 23, no. 2 (Spring 1971), 33–45.

28. Harry Specht, "The Grass Roots and Government in Social Planning and Community Organization," *Administration in Social Work,* Vol. 1, no. 3 (Fall 1978), 319–334. See also Thomas R. Dye, *Politics in States and Communities* (Englewood Cliffs, NJ: Prentice Hall, 1988).

29. Rein, "Social Planning."

SUBJECT INDEX

NAME INDEX